# THE CAR AND THE CITY

# THE CAR AND THE CITY

## THE AUTOMOBILE,
## THE BUILT ENVIRONMENT,
## AND DAILY URBAN LIFE

Edited by Martin Wachs and Margaret Crawford
*With the Assistance of*
Susan Marie Wirka
*and* Taina Marjatta Rikala

THE UNIVERSITY OF MICHIGAN PRESS

ANN ARBOR

**Library of Congress Cataloging-in-Publication Data**
The Car and the city : the automobile, the built environment, and
daily urban life / edited by Martin Wachs and Margaret Crawford ;
with the assistance of Susan Marie Wirka and Taina Marjatta Rikala.
      p.  cm.
   Includes bibliographical references.
   ISBN 0-472-09459-9 (alk. paper)
   1. Automobiles—Social aspects—United States—History.   2. Urban
ecology—United States—History.   3. City and town life—United
States—History.   4. Automobiles—Social aspects—California—Los
Angeles Region—History.   5. Urban ecology—California—Los Angeles
Region—History.   6. City and town life—California—Los Angeles
Region—History.   I. Wachs, Martin.   II. Crawford, Margaret, 1948–   .
HE5623.C33  1992
303.48′32—dc20                                                    91-42411
                                                                          CIP

Book and jacket designed by Lorraine Wild

*Dedicated to the memory of*
**REYNER BANHAM,**
*a pioneer in the study of the relationship*
*between the car and the city*

## ACKNOWLEDGMENTS

The Car and the City Symposium was held April 9–10, 1988, at the University of California, Los Angeles (UCLA). In addition to the authors, many people and organizations contributed to the success of the symposium and to the production of these proceedings. In particular, we are grateful to the Graham Foundation for Advanced Studies in the Fine Arts which funded the symposium, and provided additional funding for the publication. The Institute of Transportation Studies at the University of California, the University of California Transportation Center, and the administration of the University of California, Los Angeles, provided additional funding necessary to cover the costs of the symposium and the production of this volume. While these organizations provided support necessary to produce these proceedings, opinions and positions stated in this book are those of the authors and do not represent those of any supporting organization or its officers.

Dean Richard S. Weinstein, of the Graduate School of Architecture and Urban Planning at UCLA, and former Executive Vice Chancellor William D. Schaefer encouraged us to proceed with the symposium, and were instrumental in obtaining financial support from the university. Professor Gordon J. Fielding, statewide director of the university's Institute of Transportation Studies also provided enthusiastic support and advice. Harriett Gold, of UCLA's Graduate School of Architecture and Urban Planning, helped organize the symposium and offered many helpful comments on the program. As director and curator of the school's gallery, she also played the leading role in organizing the art exhibition which accompanied the symposium. Lyn Long, of the Institute of Transportation Studies made many helpful suggestions regarding speakers, organization of the program, and references. Professor Rebecca Morales, of the Graduate School of Architecture and Urban Planning, participated in the early planning and organization of the symposium. Diane Mills provided financial management of the several grants which supported the project.

The UCLA Extension Program managed the symposium, and we are especially grateful to LeRoy Graymer and Elizabeth Brooks, whose advice and counsel made the event a success. The graphic design offices of John Coy were responsible for the poster and brochure which publicized the symposium.

The idea for the symposium originated and was proposed by Margaret Crawford, associate professor at the Southern California Institute of Architecture, who approached Professor Martin Wachs, of the Graduate School of Architecture and Urban Planning, for intellectual support. Together they identified speakers and, with the assistance of Susan Wirka, spent many months beforehand organizing and preparing for the symposium.

Subsequent to the symposium, the papers that had been presented were reviewed and assessed, and we invited many of the authors to revise and finalize their manuscripts for publication. We are grateful for their cheerful cooperation. The substantive and technical editing of the papers was completed by Taina Marjatta Rikala and Susan Marie Wirka, respectively. Ms. Wirka was also responsible for keeping the editorial team in contact with the authors on a regular basis. John Chase was a consulting editor who provided valuable assistance. After our team edited the manuscripts, we returned them to the authors for final approval, and several of the authors refined their papers once again.

Mary Erwin, of the University of Michigan Press, was a thoughtful advocate and advisor throughout our long process of negotiation with the press.

Ken Cabaong, Erika Roos, and Marsha Brown provided word processing, secretarial, and administrative support throughout the project. Lakshmi Srinivas proofread the page proofs.

To all those who contributed and participated, and especially to the authors of the essays included in this volume, we express our appreciation and gratitude.

# CONTENTS

*x*

*Contents*

**PART 5**

**REFLECTIONS, INTERPRETATIONS, ANTICIPATIONS**

# TABLES

# FIGURES

Martin Wachs and
Margaret Crawford

**INTRODUCTION**

A recent television documentary asked half a dozen centenarians what they remembered as the most exciting moments of their lives. Without hesitating, each of them mentioned their first automobile ride among two or three of their most prominent memories. When asked what development had changed daily life the most in the century through which they had lived, all six mentioned the automobile. The modern American city is home to nearly as many cars and trucks as it is to people, and surely the automobile has molded daily life as profoundly as any other object of technology created by humankind.

The automobile is a critical part of American economic life, with one out of six of us earning a living by building, selling, advertising, servicing, insuring, or driving cars and trucks. It is similarly an important part of our cultural life, with car clubs, competitions, car fashions, auto designs, commercial messages, and auto shows commanding ever-increasing attention, along with images of autos in film, television, music, and literature.

Automobiles strongly influence the design of our neighborhoods and individual buildings, and we spend increasing amounts of time in cars on a variety of types of streets and highways. From the trip to the hospital to give birth to the ride to the cemetery to be buried, the automobile is as central an aspect of our lives as any object can be. It is party to family activities, careers, and leisure activities.

Despite its importance, the car is the subject of surprisingly little intellectual inquiry. Some historians have examined the evolution of the automobile industry and the "great men" whose companies have risen and fallen during the course of its history. A few architects have debated whether the car must destroy urban ambiance, or whether it can give life and variety to the modern city. Transportation planners and policymakers have debated alternative city forms and have evaluated the merits of investments in public transit as an alternative to highways. Environmentalists have decried the pollution and resource depletion brought on by dependence on the automobile. Artists and social critics have portrayed the American's love affair with the automobile. In unflattering terms, it is fashionable for intellectuals to present us as increasingly governed by our technology rather than by our minds and hearts. Rarely, however, have these different specialists talked with one another in efforts to understand how the automobile, the city, and modern life interact in a holistic and integrative way.

Few cities have become as associated with the automobile in popular imagery as Los Angeles. While the car was perfected in Detroit, the mild climate and relative affluence of Los Angeles made it one of the earliest and most active markets for automobiles. Los Angeles grew to prominence as a world city after the widespread adoption of the automobile, whereas the city's major competitors matured much earlier during the streetcar era. Thus, while all major world cities are influenced by automobile traffic and highway patterns, Los Angeles is more widely understood to be the product of its cars and freeways, and the automobile here is considered the premier object of conspicuous consumption and style consciousness. Although Los Angeles may have been one of the world's first largest cities to be considered a product of the automobile, all modern cities in every corner of

the globe are facing the realization that the automobile is influential in determining urban form and in patterning daily life. For this reason, we regard this book as being about the automobile and the city more than we consider it specific to Los Angeles. Many authors have taken Los Angeles as a case study or a point of departure, but the intent has been to generalize from the experience and the analysis of this one metropolis, and most of the authors reject the notion that Los Angeles is in some way different from other cities because of its relationship to cars.

"The Car and the City," a symposium held at the University of California at Los Angeles (UCLA) in April of 1988, brought together one hundred sixty participants committed to developing an understanding of the automobile, the city, and daily life that went beyond disciplinary specializations and popular stereotypes. Los Angeles seemed the natural focus for many of the speakers. While a number of case studies and analyses dealt specifically with Los Angeles, most saw this city as a prototype or example, and the discussion was usually generalizable to other urban settings. But not all the speakers were from Los Angeles, and neither were they of similar disciplinary backgrounds. Architects were consciously paired with economists, urban planners shared panels with historians, and social scientists debated artists in efforts to understand automobiles and their influences on the city and daily living. The speakers included some who were internationally prominent because of their prior work on the motor car, the city, or the relationship between the two. It also included distinguished social commentators, who were asked to turn their attention to this topic for the first time, and some junior scholars taking fresh and exciting looks at the subject matter of the symposium. The papers led to lively interchanges, after which the authors each had the opportunity to expand and rewrite their papers. The twenty chapters in this volume are the products of this process.

The book has been organized into five parts to focus attention on some common themes that ran through the symposium. Within each part, there are chapters dealing with historical development of current patterns and analyses of current patterns and problems. While we hope that the grouping of chapters makes the subject matter digestible, we recognize that the approaches and styles of the authors remain quite diverse. The authors all had strong personalities and unique perspectives, and that is what made the symposium interesting. To a great extent their work resisted easy classification, and the reader may note strong links between chapters that have been placed in different sections.

Part 1 consists of three chapters that address the automobile's linkage to the daily economy—the work done by urban residents and the commutes between home and work. It is through working and navigating the city that most people experience the automobile, and we believe that an interdisciplinary examination of the car and the city should begin with that experience. Part 2 includes four chapters that have in common an emphasis on family life, gender differences and roles, and the automobile as an object of status in daily life. Part 3 focuses on the ways in which the automobile has affected and been affected by ideas about design. It contains analyses of individual buildings, communities, commercial strips and downtowns, with an eye toward understanding the interaction between cars, traffic, people, and buildings. It also looks at the automobile as an object to be designed and the ways in which the design of cars affected and has been affected by the design of buildings in the automobile era. Part 4 consists of five chapters that examine the special character of Los Angeles *in relationship to the automobile. Spanning nearly a hundred years, the chapters look at its early days, and carry the analysis to the present. These chapters consider the special place of Los Angeles in the evolution of the automobile industry and the special place of the automobile in the evolution of the "idea" of Los Angeles. Part 5 includes three authors' speculations about what makes the car so special a part of American life and what is in store for us in the future. While many want to control or tame the auto and others want to accommodate to it, the authors of these final chapters try to explain why the auto has been as influential as it has and what its past implies for future policies and programs.*

*While no collection of essays on disparate subjects can be complete or definitive, we believe this anthology is unique. It is surely one of the most integrative scholarly treatments of the automobile and its impacts that has yet been assembled. It contains some original historical analysis, a variety of perspectives on the social meaning of the auto and its use, strong personal statements about the relationship of the car to urban design, and some speculations on how these themes are woven together into the fabric of the modern and future metropolis. It is offered as a contribution to a small but growing body of thought on one of the most important objects of everyday life.*

# PART 1
## THE CAR, THE CITY, AND DAILY WORK

*Three authors address the relationship between the car and the city in terms of the urban economy. They all argue, in one way or another, that a proper understanding of the mutual influences of the car and the city on each other requires study of the world of work—the spatial separations between home and work and the use of the automobile and truck at work and to travel between home and work. The contention is not new, but the approach taken by several of the authors is indeed novel.*

*Historian Sam Bass Warner, Jr., examines the evolution of American city form, focusing on Los Angeles. Warner looks for the roots of today's travel patterns in earlier concepts of community and neighborhood. He finds that Los Angeles was a deliberately planned response to earlier notions of work and community and that in earlier years public transportation was depended upon to provide contact between racial and ethnic groups who worked together in commercial centers but lived in more segregated residential communities. Today's lower density living and working*

*communities, connected by freeways and autos, provide greater class segregation in both workplaces and living places than he deems desirable. Warner examines the emerging urban economy and concludes that there is a need for conscious policies to promote affordable multiclass housing and community-based services including transportation.*

*J. B. Jackson, an astute, individualistic observer of the American landscape, points out that, as the American community evolved, the motor truck played a very critical role. He argues, however, that the role of the automobile has been far better understood and enumerated than the role of the motor truck, which he sees as playing an equally critical part in structuring the metropolis. The automobile as a "work vehicle" is the subject of his chapter, which includes some interesting statistics and anecdotes about the evolution of the truck and such mobile workplaces as ambulances, cement mixers, and other specialized vehicles. As interesting as the trucks are the working landscapes with which they are associated—the space-consuming, nondescript, sometimes grimy industrial districts filled with transfer points, warehousing sheds, and terminals. These districts occupy an important and large part of the urban scene, but they seem to have been mostly ignored by urban designers and commentators on urban form and function.*

*Joseph Corn, an historian of technology, comments on the chapters by both Warner and Jackson,* *and takes their perspectives a step further. He writes about another contribution of the automobile to the world of work: the automobile repairing and servicing industry, which has itself become a major employment sector. Corn discusses its evolution from humble beginnings in the blacksmith trade. He traces the service industry from a necessary support for new car sales to a profitable independent business enterprise.*

**1.** Sam Bass Warner, Jr.

## *LEARNING FROM THE PAST:*
### SERVICES TO FAMILIES

The work of the past defines both problems and opportunities for the metropolis. The inheritance is clear enough. As a twentieth-century city, Los Angeles grew up with a population that knew and liked single-family houses and thought family, home, and garden could serve as the basis for a good community life. Even before the domination of the automobile Los Angeles spread out as a city of houses and gardens.[1]

The automobile reinforced these values and facilitated their realization by the means of working husbands and homemaking wives and mothers. As Scott Bottles has shown in his recent book, *Los Angeles and the Automobile*, in Los Angeles as throughout the United States, public transportation ceased to be an innovative industry after World War I.[2] At the same time public and private organizations, highway engineers, auto clubs, and manufacturers banded together to build today's network of streets, arterial roads, and freeways. This system of facilities enabled the manufacturers to elaborate the car itself into a mass luxury. It is not that Los Angeles had public transportation and lost it. Instead, from 1920 through the 1960s the city built itself a new public transportation system. It is a special kind of public transportation: the public provides the road, and, to use it, you must bring the car.

In these two respects, housing and transportation, Los Angeles is not different from other twentieth-century American cities such as Detroit, Dallas, or Atlanta. Yet there is an inheritance of Los Angeles that is often overlooked. To an extraordinary degree the metropolis embodies the conventional good practices of twentieth-century city planning. The high proportion of planned subdivisions seems to have come from many sources—in part because open land was held in large ranch and orchard parcels and in part because families gathered up oil leases and later developed their land in large blocks.[3] Years ago I made a tour through the region and, as far as I could tell, there were neighborhood unit plans for subdivisions from Panorama City to West Covina. Everywhere I saw uniform set-backs, orderly side yards, and land-use uniformities.

It is a useful inheritance to build upon. Like the single-family house itself, this sort of planning, especially the neighborhood unit with its park and school, rests upon a central value and an unspoken coordination of private and public activities. The core value is the residential environment of families. They are to be protected from heavy traffic by restricting it to exterior arterial streets, and all commerce is pushed to the outside edges. The unspoken coordination between the home and the community assumes that housewives will be mothers. The mothers, in turn, will supervise public spaces through their child care and errand rounds and will supplement the school and maintain the neighborhood by informal socializing and volunteer activities.

If we compare Los Angeles to its preceding wonder city, Chicago, we can see in simple outline how the inheritance of this twentieth-century metropolis differs from the inheritance of a nineteenth-century one. The residents of the two cities reflect recent social geography more than they reflect past history. Los Angeles is an Anglo, Afro-American, Hispanic, and Asian city, an urban mix (18.5 percent foreign-born) that the world never before attempted. Chicago used to be the gathering place of all the peoples of Europe, but now its immigrant grandchildren are Anglos and the city is predominantly a Anglo and Afro-American mix (9.9 percent foreign-born). The residents of both metropolises gather into households as all Americans do these days. The households with retired people, the households of people living alone, and the female-headed households are major social units in today's metropolitan regions. These categories add up to 61 percent of Los Angeles's own households, 61.9 percent of Chicago's.

The big differences between the two cities are automobile-related. During its period of most active growth, from 1850 to World War I, Chicago was a city of pedestrians and streetcar riders. Accordingly, it is a city of apartment buildings, six-flats, two-families, and singles all jammed onto small lots. Despite a very far-reaching automobile suburbanization since 1920, the metropolis has a gross density of 1,420 inhabitants per square mile. Los Angeles, with its ranches of detached single-family homes, has a density of 364 persons per square mile. The transportation pattern follows from these historic differences. When Los Angeles goes to work, 70.2 percent of its inhabitants drive alone; only 58 percent of Chicagoans do. In Los Angeles 5.1 percent rely on public transportation; in Chicago 16.5 percent do.[4]

The surprise lies among the two cities' vanpool and carpool statistics: 17 percent of the commuters are in car pools. Why should the proportion of commuters who double up be the same in both regions? Why should both regions so resemble the national average of 19 percent? The answer must be that carpooling is not related to the presence or absence of early twentieth-century public rail-based transit systems. People carpool because their origins and destinations lie beyond the reach of the old transit. They carpool because they are living or working (or both living and working) in the private-auto part of the metropolis, and they cannot afford to operate a private car alone. These carpoolers are a very important group of people. They are the heroes of our current traffic problems and one clue in the answer to freeway lockup.

The dispersed Los Angeles–style metropolis has been the best living arrangement ordinary Americans ever enjoyed. Yet it functions well only so long as a series of special conditions prevail: the freeways and streets must be generous in capacity and continue to grow with the region as a whole; open land must be cheap and abundant; new construction must be active and propel a vigorous housing filter; jobs have to be plentiful and wages sufficient to support a family, its children, a house, and a car on one person's earnings. For many residents of this region these conditions are slipping away.

I do not want to assume the grandiose position of the outsider who confidently reads the minds of twelve million people. I do, however, detect some emanations from the city that suggests that people here in Los Angeles are thinking about change. I assume that, as elsewhere in the United States, most people are either comfortably situated or they are fatalists. But when reports of ferment from Orange County reach Boston, I think something is starting to move.

Mark Baldassare of the University of California, Irvine, recently published his analysis of a poll that was designed to understand the current politics of growth control. He reported finding, beneath conflicting attitudes toward growth, a revival of the old class politics of America. This time the conflict is not between penny-pinching farmers and free-spending city slickers, but it is between working-class and lower-middle-class homeowners and the well-to-do. With great effort, the former have moved out of the inner metropolis in the hope of finding clean, safe neighborhoods. They are worried about their investments and their payments, so, like the farmers before them, they are reluctant to vote for more taxes. The city slickers now are the well-to-do suburbanites who want high-amenity, high-service suburbs, and they are willing to pay taxes if they get the services. But they are often frustrated and in conflict with their tax-reduction neighbors. On the other hand, the two opponents can, and often do, unite against apartment houses and newcomers of all kinds. Both groups also doubt that the local government they know can summon either the skill or the resources to make things better. The privatism and pessimism of the two groups make a discouraging report against hopes for improved living in the metropolis.[5]

I think we can make good progress toward fresh and useful ideas if we rephrase Baldassare's growth and local government questions. He is reporting worry, turmoil, and frustration in what Dolores Hayden more usefully calls the "public realm of families."[6] The people of Orange County are saying that the supports they depend upon and the sorts of services they need they can neither afford nor get. I agree. I have the same problems myself in Boston. Therefore, let me restate the legacy of Los Angeles in family terms and concerning three interrelated needs for improved service delivery: freeway problems, housing problems, and the packaging of commercial space.

*Freeway Problems.* There are several ways in which the freeway system is no longer giving adequate service to the families of the metropolitan region. Because the region has grown so large and the freeways so crowded, the economic safety that freeways offered to families in the 1960s is now disappearing. It used to be that an hour's drive would give a wage earner a wide selection of employers; that selection is shrinking as driving times lengthen. Moreover, the costs of purchasing and maintaining a car are rising faster than wages and salaries, and they will continue to rise. In fact, real incomes have declined for most families since 1973.[7] Two–wage earner families are thus becoming more and more common, and the burden of two cars and two separate commuting paths precludes a decent amount of time for either child care or leisure.

*Housing Problems.* Land costs in Los Angeles, and other American metropolises, have skyrocketed because of federal and local fiscal and tax policies and because of sheer metropolitan growth. Building costs have leapt forward too. Consequently, many young families are now priced out of the new housing market, and many more are having to spend well beyond the traditional one-quarter of their incomes on housing. In some areas of the metropolis, housing costs are so high that the employees of local firms, public employees like policemen and teachers, and private employees like salespeople, carpenters, clerks, and secretaries cannot afford to live near their work.

There is a kind of nasty class politics of housing, jobs, and transportation that is now becoming common. The executives and high-paid staff live near their jobs, the low-income people have long commutes either by public transportation to old center-city neighborhoods or a long drive to distant fringe areas. I understand that Pasadena exhibits this pattern these days.[8]

*Commercial Packaging.* It is the genius of modern real estate development and modern retailing to segment the market for products and services. Market analysts study the metropolis and its existing residential segregation with an eye to the location of large developments. The shopping mall, the industrial park, the suburban office park, and the new housing development are all targeted toward specific tenants and buyers. As a result, there are upscale malls and discount malls, one-story industrial and warehouse parks, and fancy suburban downtowns like Santa Monica and Irvine in California. And, of course, there are the housing developments to match.

Class segregation is dangerous, and many have commented on its multiple effects upon the contemporary metropolis. There are additional impacts on the delivery of services to families. Planning for these large projects requires a large staff and a lot of investment, and, if ecological and growth controls multiply in the future, the size of the firms that engage in development will continue to grow. Because the developers must fill their new spaces with the best-rent tenants, they must seek out the best-known tenants, franchises, and chains. Small-scale neighborhood retailing and services are disappearing, or they are being transformed into uniform packages themselves. Compare your favorite mall to your favorite mile or two of strip. Which offers the most variety of stores and services?

The inherited form of the Los Angeles metropolis is not now adapting to serve the majority of the families in the region. The wives and mothers who occupy traditional roles are having their errand, child care, and socialization routes stretched way out in time and distance because of the absence of the development of subcenters and the absence of reliable and quick public transportation for their children and neighborhoods. In addition, wages in many industries, offices, and services are not keeping up so that women who would like to be at home full-time cannot afford to do so. Thousands of two-earner families are overstretched in time and expanse for lack of decent public transportation. And in such families the women are most likely to be double-day workers since they must shop and do most of the cooking, housework, and after-school child care.[9] Such families need help with child care, and, even more desperately than at-home wives, these women need a manageable errand path.

Finally, two of the groups who now hang around the malls—the old and the adolescent—can be regarded as wasted human resources. They need to be put to work in family assistance, child care, local health services, recreation, and other community-based programs. The absence of physical places for these two age groups to be in our current metropolitan developments manifests their lack of useful social roles. If you think about it, with many mothers working, we have few other human resources for vital social services save the retired and the junior high and high school youth.

The set of family needs for public transportation, affordable multi-class housing, and the availability of nearby services suggests to me that clustering will help a lot. Los Angeles' low density makes the incremental process of increasing density relatively easy to do. Strips can be reformed, and neighborhood unit–plan subdivisions can have a dense edge or corner. High-density, low-rise structures will fit nicely with established styles here. I hope we will talk more of future ideas for improvement.

Whatever the architecture might be, clustering is essential because there is no other way to maintain good short-haul neighborhood transport systems. Neither can long-distance reliable express bus service be instituted unless it be from cluster to cluster. Designated lanes, new busways, bus-activated traffic signals, and other measures can be undertaken to make the existing streets, roads, and freeways work better. But such reforms will be more easily achieved and more effective if they rest upon cluster plans for the metropolis.

Let me conclude by reminding the reader that, to make clusters work, two sorts of public institutions must be expanded. We can discuss later whether these need be new institutions or whether they can just be added functions of existing local governments.

In either case, public transport will not be reliable and will not grow efficiently unless it has active interest groups to drive it forward. First, each cluster must form a Traffic Management Committee of its merchants, public officials, and commuters. These committees can supervise the local management of parking, traffic, and short-haul public transportation, and they can lobby effectively for decent intercluster service.

Second, each cluster must have a local Community Development Corporation that buys and develops land in the cluster. If no such corporation exists, then the effect of the improved public transportation will be to drive up rents in the cluster, and soon there will be a rental envelope as exclusive as a shopping mall. The plumbers, carpenters, small-appliance repair people, Boy Scouts, dance studio, vegetable stand, home-cooked food restaurant, child care center and nursery school, tax accountant, and hardware store will disappear to a distant strip. The Community Development Corporation must use its resources to maintain cheap space in its cluster so that the many small retailers and service providers come together in a way that is convenient for their clients. I have in my mind some architectural forms, and I look forward to discussing such matters with experts.

In sum, I see the answer to the inherited problems of Los Angeles and other American cities lies in the coordination of local life and the improvement of services to the public realm of families. As Dolores Hayden wrote a few years ago in *Redesigning the American Dream*, "domesticating public space is also essential to new forms of private and public life."[10]

# TRUCK CITY

Today there are more than 176 million cars in the United States. Eighty years ago there were less than 200,000. Two years later, in 1910, there were close to half a million. Each year thereafter the number increased by more than a third.

Americans have always been fascinated by the automobile. Initially, few families could afford to buy one. When the average worker earned only a dollar a day and a medium-priced automobile cost more than a thousand dollars, automobiles were clearly for the rich. But the thought of how the automobile was going to transform and enrich American life was endlessly exciting for all. We followed every step in its evolution. We discussed speed records and endurance records; we applauded improvements in the motor, and the daredevil feats of drivers and racers were recalled. What we were especially interested in was elegance in design; what caught our attention was the passenger car, also known as the touring car or pleasure car. The rich and sporting element in American society took to the automobile because of the adventurous and mobile way of life it fostered. The social pages of newspapers gave details of the groups of fans and the meets and rallies of exclusive automobile clubs and told of who had attended the concours d'elegance. Conversely, academics and admirers of the traditional rural culture tried to turn us away from the automobile. In 1906 President Wilson told us that the automobile might represent an ostentatious display of wealth that would incite envy and class feeling, but quite the opposite proved true; we fell in love with the passenger car and dreamt of the day when we too could own one.

So much favorable publicity had the effect of rousing widespread interest in the manufacture and sale of automobiles. Investors, manufacturers, and engineers began to take the new invention seriously and promoted research and experimentation. Yet the greatest appeal lay in the kind of lifestyle it promised; the newly dawned century was to see a new culture, emancipated, healthy, infinitely mobile, and full of hitherto unknown pleasures and experiences—all due entirely to the automobile. But the commercial automobile, the bus, the taxi, and especially the truck were all excluded from this cordial welcome. In 1910 there were only eight thousand trucks in the country, and most of them were so uncouth in appearance, so disappointing in performance that they belonged in a special category.

In the early years before World War I it was the custom among the drivers of passenger cars to show their solidarity by tipping their hats to one another. The same custom prevailed until recently among motorcyclists. But the drivers of trucks and vans were not included in the exchange of high signs. Given the stylish implications of the passenger car, it is not hard to understand the discrimination. The passenger car stood for a leisurely suburban or rural existence based on family togetherness, love of nature, and a good income. The truck, on the other hand, stood for work, and work of a menial kind.

Dating back to colonial times, the word *truck* was used to describe a heavy wagon capable of carrying a load. It was a uniquely American usage. With the coming of the automobile we redefined the word to describe an *automotive* vehicle designed to carry a load—still the accepted definition, but nevertheless a poor one, for it is used to include the pickup, the van, the mini-van, and the jeep. We could do better than that. In everyday parlance, we almost always use *truck* to mean a large vehicle that can haul heavy loads for some distance, and does so *for pay*. Vernacular usage often defines an object—whether a house, car, or piece of furniture—not by how it is made but by how it is used, and most trucks are used to make money. To be sure there are marginal cases; the pickup, like the jeep, is undergoing a process of suburban gentrification, and both are much used in leisure activities and in certain offbeat sports. At one time the station wagon was a modest passenger car equipped with extra seats and was called a depot van. It was a money-making vehicle—but look at it now.

Many of those eight thousand trucks in 1910 were probably small electric delivery trucks used by businesses such as laundries, bakeries, and dairies, and by the U.S. Post Office for making daily deliveries along established city routes. They were a great improvement over previously used horse-drawn wagons, surreys, or buggies. Electric trucks had several advantages: they made no noise, they did not smell, they were easy to drive, and they were durable. In appearance, they resembled the horse-drawn wagon, and, as passenger cars, the last feature appealed (so we are told) to that diehard element that was still prohorse and anti-automobile—the turn-of-the-century equivalent, perhaps, of the contemporary bicycle.

The electric van or truck, however, had a serious shortcoming; it ran on batteries, slung under the chassis, that were large and heavy and had to be frequently recharged. At best they could go eighty miles without the driver having to turn in at one of the infrequent stations, and the operation took time and cost fifteen dollars. Largely because of the weight of the batteries, the electric truck had trouble climbing hills. It was also expensive, and no working man could think of buying a truck and going into the delivery business on his own. Would he have wanted to? Driving an electric delivery van for pay, even if only a dollar a day, probably had its appeal. It was safe, relaxing, and without surprises. But Americans, even in those days, had the distinct impression that the automobile represented freedom and personal responsibility. A vehicle like the electric van, which had to stay in the city and abide by a fixed routine, was in a class with the railroad train or the streetcar, confined to a pair of rails and a timetable. In any case, as gas trucks and passenger cars became cheaper and more efficient the electric car dropped out of favor. It lingered until 1925 as a sedan, small and elegant and eminently suited to lady drivers. Then it too vanished.

There remained that other contingent out of the original eight thousand trucks. They were gasoline-powered, and in fact the gasoline truck had been around just as long as the gasoline passenger car, but it had failed so far to show promise. For one thing it had been given none of that encouragement lavished on the passenger car by social and financial leaders. No one attended the strenuous truck endurance runs, and the press had little to say about the experimental trucks being produced by amateurs: inventors, mechanics, retired bicycle makers, dedicated tinkerers working in stables and blacksmith shops or on the road. A few manufacturers of trucks turned out a dozen or more models, then either they went bankrupt or were bought out. There were no standard parts, only parts taken from carriages or pieces of machinery. The trucks often unhappily resembled in appearance the conventional wagon—wheels, dashboard, and all—and did not always perform much better. They were slow and heavy—far heavier than the load they carried. Steel-rimmed wheels gave little traction on smooth city streets, and motors deficient in power prevented them from traveling on rough and muddy country roads. It was generally concluded that all these hybrid vehicles could be used for was hauling freight from the railroad station to the factory or warehouse or making routine deliveries, like the electric van, within the city.

Trucks were usually owned by shipping or distributing firms or by such public agencies as the police and fire departments. They were too expensive and unreliable for the average small business, so they operated in fleets. Each morning would-be truck drivers went to the yard where the motley collection of trucks was parked, and they waited to be given a job for the day. In those times drivers knew nothing about maintaining or repairing trucks, especially those they had never driven before. As a result they often returned their trucks at the end of the day in bad condition. Strictly speaking, the truck driver was an unskilled day laborer, easily replaced. He was loaned a clumsy, unfamiliar tool to do a dull job that for him had no future, and his status was not much higher than that of the factory or field hand. His pay was two dollars for a twelve-hour day.

The trucking industry might well have continued in that vein—fleets of trucks operating like the old fleets of taxis—but two surprising developments overtook the truck. First, it became a versatile and adaptable piece of mechanical equipment, capable of doing much more than simply hauling heavy loads and coming back empty. Second, it broke away from centralized management and in time provided many men with small businesses of their own. It became an important part of an American vernacular way of life, and it remains so to this day.

In these transformations the manufacturers played a role, though a minor one at first; most of the work came from those persistent small-time mechanics and engineers. It was they who in effect created a whole new industry, not a cottage but a garage industry, and it was largely they who produced the modern truck. Many of them were farmers, and farmers were well acquainted with stationary engines long before they had seen automobiles. They were already mechanics, electricians, tinsmiths, and blacksmiths and had already automated much of their work. It was natural for them to experiment and find out how this new machine could be used for other purposes.

One of their problems was getting their vegetables and dairy products to the city markets on time. Railroad schedules were often inconvenient and involved several time-wasting transfers and delays. It was a master blacksmith in a small Wisconsin farm town who first produced the four-wheel drive, which enabled trucks not only to negotiate bad roads but also to cut across fields, pick up produce, and take it directly to the distributor. It was another small town mechanic who built the first auto trailer, something that often doubled the truck's capacity. Another now-forgotten innovator gave the truck headlights and enabled it to travel by night; someone else devised the dump truck and the truck with the low bed, easier for loading heavy loads and for dockside loading. None of these were technological breakthroughs, but they contributed to a redefinition of the truck and, eventually, to its being used for other than transportation purposes. Thus it sometimes became a snowplow, a digger of post holes, a temporary platform for derricks, and a source of emergency power. Its increasing versatility made it an essential element in heavy construction, road building, and the extraction of hitherto inaccessible natural resources like oil and timber located in rough terrain where the railroad could not go. All that it asked was accessibility and pay.

The Ford Model T, introduced in 1908, proved to be particularly useful in rural areas and on isolated farms. Strictly speaking, it was a passenger car, but it could be transformed easily into a pickup truck for carrying milk and other produce to market, and even loads of hay. When pulleys were attached to the crankshaft or the rear wheel, the Model T provided power for innumerable farm and household tasks: grinding grain, sawing wood, and pumping water. In the 1920s various farm equipment firms sold attachments that were supposed to transform the Ford into a tractor or cultivator, but they saw little success.

There is probably a law to the effect that, as an apparatus or machine becomes more and more reliable and competent as a tool, we begin to discover new jobs for it. This would account for the fact that, before it was more than twenty years old, the truck began to do more than *carry* a load; it undertook to *process* or modify the load, even as it traveled. The mobile cement mixer, familiar to us all, made its appearance in 1916. The refrigerator truck, a product of the 1920s, controlled the temperature of the products it carried, and the modern ambulance, a mobile hospital, was equipped to give temporary aid in transit. The new function brought with it a more complex, more job-specific type of vehicle, far different from the old generic truck. Depending on its job, it became part-time office, part-time workshop, part-time operations center, and part-time sleeping quarters. The introduction over the past decades of the two-way radio and car phone has given the truck and its operator a greater freedom of movement and decision making, so that it can be said that certain kinds of trucks have become small, semi-autonomous businesses or service enterprises.

But increasing competence and the concentration of expertise suddenly appearing down the road and then taking over to solve problems in a hurry had an unforeseen impact. Operating as it usually does on a schedule and charging by the hour, the truck imposed standards of promptness and efficiency on many customers and clients, not only on the farm but in construction and even in the factory. A well-known instance of this intervention is how the truck, the large carrier truck, influenced the location and layout of many inner-city industrial plants and ultimately helped persuade them to move.

The traditional American factory, located as it was near the railroad tracks in a multistoried building, was no longer practical. New methods of production and new roles for management were changing the organization of the workplace, and what was being tried in many industrial plants was a system of continuous material flow, off the assembly line. But for such a system to be effective, it required more horizontal space, a faster, more efficient flow of goods in and out of the plant, and a cutting down of storage facilities; the old idea of keeping a large inventory on hand was being abandoned.

Truck transportation in the 1920s had proven already that it was fast, flexible, and cheap, so one important reason for wanting a new layout for factories and warehouses was the provision of efficient loading and unloading facilities for the truck—facilities that integrated the doors and tailgate of the truck into the horizontal interior of the plant. The result of all these changes was a carefully designed loading dock with plenty of space for trucks to maneuver and park and the extensive use of fork lifts and other types of conveyors, and since this entailed much modification of the building, it was evident that constructing a brand new building emphasizing uninterrupted interior spaces on one floor with ample loading docks for the trucks was the only answer. Accordingly, factories and warehouses began deserting the crowded town area and moving out to where land was cheaper and closer to the highways used by larger trucks.

So the truck—or the increased use of the truck—contributed to the decay of the inner city and the growth of industries in the outlying districts. That accomplishment probably marked the truck's ultimate triumph; at the turn of the century it had been a humble, little regarded conveyor of heavy loads, slowly and noisily lumbering between station and warehouse. Twenty-five years later, it had not only acquired its own unique form and status, but it had acquired the power to alter the built environment, helping to determine the location, plan, and effectiveness of many commercial buildings.

The industry-oriented truck, the monster tractor-trailer unit with its load of thirty tons or more, is less identified with the city than with interstate and cross-country travel. It is now well integrated into the national transportation system and is discussed in terms of billions of ton-miles and dollar percentage of the gross national product carried per mile and per day. It has its own vernacular culture, its own folklore, and its own music—more Southern than metropolitan in tone. Occasionally, some semi-trailer, its aluminum body shining, creeps cautiously through the dense downtown traffic and unloads after work hours when the streets are comparatively empty. We never see it in a parking lot—it is far too large for that—and the best and most impressive view we get of this breed of truck is when we see rows of them parked at a truckstop near an interchange. Its earlier role of modifying the city and altering its morphology has been taken over by the smaller trucks, vans, and pickups which are better adjusted to shorter runs and smaller loads.

The truck terminal, usually located, like the truckstop, near some interchange, is where the larger intercity or interregional trucks discharge their loads that are then taken and distributed by the smaller, largely retail-oriented trucks. Here, as in the industrial plant, the emphasis is on a continuous flow of goods in and out. In the words of John Rae in *The Road and the Car in American Life*, the modern warehouse, unlike the earlier railroad warehouse, is no longer a storehouse but a 'transit shed' for continuous inventory replenishment. More space is devoted to processing orders, docks and aisles for self-propelled vehicles than to actual storage. As a building meant to house a highly disciplined enterprise, it has its own specifications. Almost invariably prefabricated, it features large, uninterrupted spaces, a minimum of single-function rooms, and a deliberate absence of individuality. Ideally, the transit shed can change ownership, and change business, without any structural alteration. Such is the contribution of the truck to contemporary architecture: generating a building without inherent characteristics, an enclosed space meant to serve the transient customer.

We have only to look around us to see that the transit shed or variations of it are not confined to the warehouse or truck terminal district of the city. It is beginning to appear in new developments, along commercial streets, and in brand new suburbs. Because it is ideally suited to retail business operating with small inventories and counting on a rapid turnover (probably counting on closing out in the near future), a transit shed type of structure is comparatively easy to dispose of. The small businesses are dependent on the truck (or van) to serve them and replenish their stocks. Fast-food establishments along the strip, supermarkets, and many gas stations are good examples, though they are in a sense doubly dependent on the automobile: first, to bring the consumer and, second, to provide for and service them. Businesses of this sort contribute little in the way of permanent quality to a neighborhood, but there is no denying the tendency for small businesses and services to operate in terms of a continuous flow. Restaurants, hotels, and department stores are conforming to it. Hospitals are often sheds with a formal facade entrance for visitors and a precisely designed loading dock and storage space in the back—and plenty of parking space for the indispensable ambulances and trucks. The day might not be far off when museums without endowment or a stockpile of works of art will operate with temporary traveling exhibitions that after a prescribed period will be trucked to another city.

Without presuming to pass judgment on the architectural or urban consequences of the omnipresence of the automobile—particularly the commercial automobile—we cannot ignore the fact that the traditional street, with its uninterrupted facades and walls of masonry, is being perforated by drive-in facilities, parking lots, underground garages, and service alleys. Auto accessibility, seen by many as the enemy of architectural permanence, and of seclusion in work and domestic life, is not far from winning the day.

What emerges in the newer and low-income sections of the city are certain ancient but long obscured vernacular traits. The dwelling, already reduced in size, loses its autonomy, its rich self-sufficiency, and its life spills over onto the sidewalk and the vacant lots. Bordered by one transit shed after another—supermarkets, used-car displays, gas stations, discount houses, and motels and fast-food outlets—the commercial street is itself an elongated transit shed devoted to steady flow automatically controlled by lights. Here is where the car sets the pace. Indifferent to the traditional spatial hierarchy of the city, social interaction takes the form of cruising or collecting in parking lots and around gas stations, and work is housed in vans and trucks. As of now, the proportion of trucks to passenger cars is approaching one in three. "Things fall apart, the center cannot hold." It becomes a pedestrian precinct for tourists, and traffic flows in all directions—through the financial section and the slums, in the silent residential district, and out among the factories and mobile homes.

What keeps those trucks and vans and pickups and jeeps forever on the move?

In all probability, their drivers are going about their day's work by driving their vehicles, truck or van or pickup or converted passenger car or jeep, to make their deliveries, to collect and distribute goods, to haul light loads, to repair and service, to install and remove and replace, and to reassure stores and households and people that they have not been forgotten or neglected and will always be taken care of—provided the bills are paid. They are weaving together the decentralized and fragmented city that an earlier and more powerful generation of vehicles tore apart, and they are even bringing back into the urban fabric elements that in the past had been neglected because they were too distant from the center, too poor, or too different to be counted as neighbors.

Both kinds of automobile, the passenger car and the commercial car, share responsibility for decentralization of the city, the decay of the downtown, and the spread of a suburban settlement pattern. But in a way each has mitigated the effect of the other. Whereas the passenger car has weakened communities and located many experiences and pleasures, previously identified with home and neighborhood, in the public realm, the truck has reintroduced small-scale services and skills into the private realm and newly created centers, and in a sense it has reasserted the fact that, in the satisfaction of workday needs and desires, we have to depend on others coming to us. Both responses make for a less structured, more fluid, and more vernacular type of city. When he has finished his rounds of servicing and selling, repairing and distributing, and has been paid, the owner-operator parks his van or truck in the driveway and starts to work on it. For the small garage industry has become an essential element in our new vernacular way of life.

# 3. Joseph J. Corn

## WORK AND VEHICLES:
### A COMMENT AND NOTE

The contributions to this volume by Sam Bass Warner, Jr., and J. B. Jackson suggest some lessons from the past that might be instructive for those of us concerned about the vehicle-related problems of the present. In his essay Warner asks how the arrangement and efficacy of transportation in cities has affected the provision of services to families. The question leads him to a somewhat anxious assessment of Los Angeles' future. He claims the dispersed, auto-dependent metropolis "has been the best living arrangement ordinary Americans ever enjoyed," but that the special conditions that historically brought it into being no longer apply. Without changes in population density, transportation patterns, and economic arrangements, he argues, the automobile's impact on daily life will continue to be negative rather than positive.

In his contribution to this volume, J. B. Jackson says we have talked too much about cars in our effort to understand automobility and not enough about trucks, or what he calls "commercial cars." It has been trucks, he asserts, particularly light, utility vehicles, that have supported the revolutionary decentralization we associate with cities like Los Angeles. Unlike Warner, Jackson views very positively this decentralization, or at least the dispersion of decision-making that enabled individuals to employ a vast variety of trucks for myriad business purposes. Below I shall explore briefly some of the historical questions posed by the authors' divergent perspectives on the dispersed metropolis, but first let me commend Jackson and Warner for their overall approaches to the relationship between cars and cities.

I applaud their utter disregard for the alleged American love affair with the automobile. In the past, much too much intellectual energy has been expended on elucidating this romance. It is a sign of the present maturity of scholarship on the automobile that these papers offer no psychologizing about the relationship between speed and sex, the meaning of Dagmar bumpers on fifties Caddies, or the impact of motoring on the early twentieth-century libido.[1] Nor do they seek the roots of American automobility in conditions peculiar to the American mind or character. Instead, Jackson and Warner know that this country's early and widespread adoption of automobiles, far from being a love affair, with all the connotations of frivolity, irresponsibility, and lack of necessity suggested by that phrase, instead has been a largely practical matter, driven in short by the compulsions of labor, not love.[2]

As early as 1910, and certainly from the 1920s, the automobile figured heavily in the daily life of millions of Americans, not least in southern California and Los Angeles. By daily life I mean the daily grind, working nine to five, not motoring out to the club, going for a ride in the country, or, as one character did in a 1920s novel, just spinning over to "San Berdoo" to pick up some pins to sew a dress.[3]

The emphasis Jackson and Warner put on the automobile and truck's relationship to jobs, business, and work is therefore important, but it is a subject about which we still know very little. In commenting on the authors' exploration of this theme, I take the liberty to point out some issues they do not address in the hope that others will pursue them in future research.

Among the questions Warner's essay poses is this: what has been the historical origin, development, and economic consequence of what we call carpooling, a mode of getting to work that, if not growing dramatically today, represents an obvious and easy way to reduce urban traffic congestion? I find his suggestion that people carpool because they cannot afford to operate a car themselves intriguing, but I am skeptical that economics explains all we want to know about carpooling. Obviously, the high costs of owning a car have compelled many to rely on alternate modes of getting to work, including carpooling. Yet sellers of transport (driver-owners) and buyers (riders) are seldom matched in a true marketplace; factors such as friendship or acquaintance no doubt have been (and remain) important determinants of who gets to ride to work with a car-owning driver. In addition to considerations of cost, calculations regarding time and convenience help determine who does and does not use car pools. Many professionals, for example, accustomed to controlling the pace and quantity of their work seem especially loath to give up the control over time that they associate with driving their own cars to work. Their reluctance probably stems from more than merely an understanding that, in the words of the old adage, time is money. It reflects in part the perception that wasted time is only that time they themselves do not schedule and control. To find out whether such considerations motivated carpoolers in the past may be difficult or even impossible, yet to my knowledge the questions have hardly been asked.

For many workers, however, cars or light trucks were not simply commuting vehicles. They were often essential to the job itself—hauling, collecting, distributing, transporting, and servicing, as Jackson noted in speaking of the commercial car or truck.[4] Sometimes the vehicle actually becomes the workplace, as with mobile vegetable vendors, knife sharpeners, meals-on-wheels, ambulances, and other rolling enterprises. While we know that many sales and service jobs took to the road with the first automobiles, we lack a coherent and connected account of their development over time. James Flink's pioneering 1970 study, *America Adopts the Automobile*, reveals that physicians were among the first occupational groups to dispense their services via automobiles.[5] But between his physician-motorists in the first decade of this century and Jackson's service, maintenance, repair, and delivery drivers of today, there have been two or three generations of workers dependent on automobility about whom we know virtually nothing.

Another question that demands further research is this: what have been the historical relationships between population dispersion and the quality of service delivered by industry? Or, to phrase it somewhat differently, what kinds of social and spatial configurations have generated an environment most conducive to servicing the modern family and its complex technical possessions? In his discussion, Jackson voted for the dispersed automobile city, seeing in the turbulent traffic snarls of mini-vans and light trucks evidence not only of a diverse, competent, and generally responsible service establishment but also a harbinger of a new interdependency that he deems healthy. By contrast, Warner seems to view the dispersed city as a place where service is hard to get and, when available at all, standardized at low levels of quality, thereby threatening family stability. Almost every reader can think of examples from personal experience that give plausibility to *both* Warner's and Jackson's perspectives. To help resolve the debate, perhaps some scholars could once again revisit Robert and Helen Lynds' *Middletown* and, comparing it with a more modern, dispersed city, focus on the relative success the two kinds of spatially arranged cities and their respective styles of automobility have had in delivering services to residents. We also need to learn more about the history of small-service businesses before we can fully assess the impact of automobility, for better or worse, on services to families.

I think we can all agree, however, that the vehicles themselves have played a crucial part in the delivery of goods and services in the dispersed metropolis, not to mention to the more densely populated and concentrated city. Jackson notes that much ingenious tinkering and experimenting underlay the creation of early commercial vehicles.[6] We need to know more about this work. But while small custom shops adapted a significant portion of motor vehicles to work roles by fashioning special bodies (and they still do), we must not neglect the more prosaic, mass-produced working vehicles. And I do not mean only trucks. Detroit itself manufactured hundreds of thousands of other vehicles commonly utilized in work roles beyond mere commuting. Two varieties come immediately to mind: the station wagon and the so-called business coupe.[7]

While the station wagon originated early on as a vehicle to carry afflu- ent suburbanites and their luggage to the train station, it did not become popular until the 1930s. And only in the late 1940s and 1950s did it become the carrier of choice for suburban housewives shuttling children and husbands to appointments around the decentralized city and its suburbs. As historian Ruth Schwartz Cowan argues in her book, *More Work for Mother*, the auto- mobile was just one of a number of technologies that, instead of saving labor for the homemaker, merely added to her responsibilities.[8] Running a family transport service and doing work formerly performed by retail deliverymen, postwar housewives in station wagons plied some of the least "manageable errand paths," to employ Warner's phrase, ever devised. While automobiles might have helped to create this crazy routine, station wagons provided some semblance of a solution, permitting housewives to carry large loads of Cub Scouts, dog food, or lawnseed and avoid double trips. But again, we have very little specific data about their deliveries, pickups, and other work at the wheel. Similarly, we know virtually nothing about what factors have prompted many independent contractors—house painters, gardeners, and carpenters—to use station wagons rather than pickup trucks or vans. One can speculate that some contractors chose station wagons because they were more comfortable and perhaps faster than trucks, or possibly cheaper, but few scholars have looked into the history of how people actually used such vehicles.

The other working vehicle Americans could purchase right off the show- room floor was the business coupe, a stripped-down, two-door coupe, with a minimal rear seat and an enlarged rear trunk. A number of automobile makers introduced this type of car in the 1930s or 1940s and built them through the 1950s. It would be interesting to know why such vehicles were built in this period, who purchased them, and in what kinds of businesses they were actually used. Perhaps business coupes merely represented a De- troit styling fad, but my guess is that they addressed some real shift in the folkways or practice of mobile commerce that social historians and business historians ought to know about.

Let me suggest one more aspect of the historical relationship between automobiles and work that has been studied little, though it is a subject on which I have recently been doing research. This is the work done *on* automobiles—in other words, their maintenance, adjustment, and repair. Generally, historians have ignored this subject, which is not surprising, given our culture's preoccupation with the new.[9] Scholars have focused mostly on the invention, design, and manufacture of new technologies, including cars.[10] Yet maintenance and repair have always been essential aspects of using new technologies. Without them, in fact, the widespread adoption and successful utilization of cars and trucks would have been impossible. In the remainder of this comment, I want to touch on some of the highlights of this history and identify some questions requiring further research.

The first point is that, regarding the early decades of motoring, the sources are virtually unanimous in suggesting that operators had to do at least some work on their own cars. Indeed, considerable skill, knowledge, and effort was required just to start, let alone to keep running, the user-unfriendly machines of that era.[11] I am not referring only to the muscle power employed for cranking the engine to start the car: If a story told to me recently is any guide, we probably exaggerate the strength needed for this procedure anyway. A seventy-year-old man I was interviewing recalled how, when he was a boy in 1930, every morning he and his family would entertain themselves by watching the couple next door try to start their old touring car. The couple would come out of their house, the man would get behind the wheel, and the wife would get out in front and begin furiously cranking. Much signaling and yelling would ensue between the couple, and many minutes would pass before the engine would finally come to life. At that point the wife would climb into the passenger seat and the couple would drive off.[12]

This story not only raises questions regarding much conventional wisdom concerning male and female roles vis-à-vis early automobile operation but it also points to some of the new work skills entailed in operating early cars. My informant reported that the reason why the wife cranked was that her husband believed the really difficult part of starting the car was controlling the throttle and the spark advance levers on the steering wheel. Such work obviously demanded delicate fingers and responsive intuition, not exactly male monopolies, according to traditional gender stereotypes. How many others emulated this couple's division of labor in starting that highly complex, unruly machine called the automobile we may never know. At the moment, however, perhaps because we take it so for granted, at least it is worth asking how men and women in the early years of the century approached the new and daunting work of operating cars.

Once started, the odds were considerable that early gasoline-powered vehicles would develop what were called "troubles," thereby forcing the driver to "Get Out and Get Under," the title of a popular song. If early motorists had followed the prescriptions of the owner's manuals provided with new vehicles or other mechanical advice literature, they would have been ready for such troubles. Well into the 1920s, in fact, such literature invariably insisted that owner-operators must know the basics about their machine's different systems before they could operate it successfully. To what extent people followed this advice and acquired some measure of automotive literacy is hard to know. But published accounts of auto trips as well as books and articles on maintenance and repair demonstrate that many men and women responded with great resourcefulness to all kinds of breakdowns, which suggests they had acquired a modicum of knowledge.[13] In this context, Jackson's claim that drivers for the early truck fleets knew nothing about maintenance raises an intriguing question. Might there have been a divergence between truck culture and car culture concerning the ability, or at least the willingness, of drivers to get out and get under to make small adjustments or repairs? We can speculate that wage laborers hired to drive trucks for two dollars a day would have had little incentive to acquire mechanical knowledge (or, if they possessed such knowledge, to reveal it to their employer if the vehicle broke down). Car owners and operators, however, would seem to have had many reasons to master their unruly machines and then use that knowledge whenever their cars gave trouble. Many relied on their vehicles to meet business or social appointments, and most wanted to avoid the embarrassment of being stranded and looking helpless in the eyes of passengers or bystanders who might taunt them with the injunction "get a horse." The degree to which such concerns influenced car drivers and truck drivers, and the responses people made to them, require more study.

Although pioneering motorists were often on their own when it came to effecting adjustments and repairs, particularly if out on the open road, from the beginning of the automobile era they could hire others to maintain and fix their vehicles. Indeed, the servicing of automobiles quickly became a gigantic industry. As early as 1925, when Americans spent three billion dollars on new cars, trucks, and tractors, they already spent five billion, almost twice as much, on operation and maintenance, of which one billion went just for labor.[14] We do not know exactly how many individuals were employed in the servicing of cars at that time, but no doubt their numbers rivaled those engaged in manufacturing new cars. Yet despite the economic importance of the maintenance and repair industry, scholars have paid little attention to the subject. Recently, students of the built environment have begun to look at the structures generated by this industry, but there is much we have yet to learn about the evolution and practice of diagnosing automotive troubles, curing or operating on sick machines, and even disposing of their remains when they die.[15]

In this vein, it might be useful to re-examine the occupational origins of the automotive service industry. Automobile historians traditionally assigned a large role in this story to village blacksmiths. Yet bicycle shop owners, electricians, and machinists were just as likely to work on cars and become auto mechanics—so were hardware dealers, who readily added gasoline and automobile parts to their already extensive inventories and moved easily into the new field. All of these groups, in fact, would seem to have been better equipped by skill, knowledge, and equipment to perform many adjustments and repairs on cars than were blacksmiths.[16] While blacksmiths could straighten a bent axle or forge a new spring leaf, there is little reason to think they could adjust the vibrators of an early ignition system, rebuild the main bearings, or even repair a leaking radiator as well as could other kinds of tradesmen.

Many early mechanics also came to the trade from commercial backgrounds. Livery stable operators, for example, often took on the servicing of early automobiles. Some stables may have possessed a forge and could perform blacksmithing, but more likely they captured the auto owner's trade simply because they had the space to garage vehicles (once the horses were pushed out), a necessity in most climates with early cars. Once they had cars in storage, livery stables were naturally drawn into making adjustments and repairs, performing routine maintenance, and stocking auto supplies such as gasoline and oil. In short, the automobile service industry drew on many occupational sources, and the precise story of how practice and knowledge evolved in the field remains to be told.

The later history of automobile mechanics is no better understood. Because the maintenance and repair industry has been so decentralized, auto mechanics have been virtually invisible to historians. Most mechanics have worked alone or with one or two assistants in small shops rather than as part of the gigantic labor forces working in large, centrally administered factories that have interested scholars. Indeed, because mechanics have so often been self-employed, that is, small entrepreneurs, they have been of less interest even to labor historians, who have traditionally identified with employees, preferably union members. Into the 1930s, in fact, many mechanics even lacked a fixed place of business, grinding valves or decarbonizing an engine under a tree behind the car owner's house. These were the "shade-tree mechanics," so styled by new-car dealers, who felt their competition.[17] Other mechanics worked for city storage garages (often former livery stables), gas stations, or the combined gas station–full-service facilities built by major oil companies beginning in the 1920s. Still others were employed by the garages established by dealers who sold new automobiles for particular manufacturers.[18]

All of these worksites matched car owners with mechanics in one of the most psychologically charged relationships of modern consumer societies. From the earliest days of the automotive era, car repairs were costly, and owners, unable for the most part to understand what was wrong with their cars, worried about incompetent work and being overcharged. Changes in the relative numbers and strengths of the three kinds of institutions that made up what can be called the mature service establishment—independent garages, oil company–sponsored service stations, and dealers' shops—therefore significantly affected the experience of car ownership. Theoretically, competition among these three kinds of maintenance and repair facilities ought to have benefitted car owners, but we know too little about the subject to say for sure.

What does seem clear is that in the 1920s and 1930s the competition between the three service providers intensified. Particularly after the downturn in new-car sales and the stock market crash, manufacturers, in league with their dealers, redefined the importance of service to their overall business goals and began to sell service aggressively. This shift is evident in the records of the Ford Motor Company, which alone of the automakers has an extensive archive accessible to historians.[19] As the title for a descriptive booklet for dealers put it, "profits in Ford parts for the garage" had become a major company goal in a decade of reduced profits on new-car sales.[20] Another sign of Ford's new business strategy was that it began to force its dealers to clean up, redecorate, and re-equip their service areas. Oceans of white paint were deployed to transform work spaces, even the grease pits, into imitations of hospital operating rooms, the better to attract car owners away from independent service stations and back to the dealers from whom they originally purchased their vehicles. Service personnel, too, were made to clean up their acts—literally, as white smocks increasingly became mandatory work garb for employees meeting the public, despite their impracticality. In a more functional vein, protective pads came into use to keep grease off seats and other parts of customers' cars.[21]

Another indicator of the automakers' discovery of the profitability of service, or more precisely, of the industry's effort to make more money from that activity, was the invention of the prepackaged rebuild or service kit. These kits included the parts needed for, say, reconditioning a brake, rebuilding a carburetor, or restoring a running board. Ford pushed such kits on their dealers, who were told that, if prominently displayed and combined with advertising and promotion, the kits would add greatly to profits.[22] But increased profits for the dealer and manufacturer only raised the costs of service to the car owner. Furthermore, as a result of the widespread use of these kits, mechanics who were reconditioning a brake, for example, would replace not just the worn or damaged parts but all the parts in the entire component. They did so not necessarily because the parts needed replacement but simply because the parts came in the kit, for which the customer would be billed anyway.[23]

Few save old car buffs care today about automotive parts kits from the 1920s or 1930s. Yet such innovations, for better or worse, played a crucial part in the historical process of rationalizing the work of adjusting, maintaining, and repairing vehicles, work essential to the widespread adoption and use of cars and trucks. Even the much improved and infinitely more reliable vehicles of today, after thousands of refinements by inventors, engineers, and manufacturers, are still not exempt from frequent service. And without service, they would have much less impact on the urban fabric.

What, then, can we conclude about the relationship of cars, cities, and work? There are, I think, three main points worth repeating here: first, for millions the automobile has been an important work tool, a means of commuting to a fixed workplace or moving along an urban delivery or sales route; second, for some people vehicles have been their places of work, as for various mobile tradesmen; finally, for millions, too, the automobile has been an object on which to perform work, whether remedying troubles to reach one's destination, indulging a hobby or pastime, or for pay as a professional mechanic. As Jackson reminds us, instinctively we all know that the car has played a crucial economic role in our daily lives. In a sun-drenched and sea-bathed environment, like Los Angeles, one can easily forget about work, even the many aspects of work related to the life with automobiles. So let us remem-

ber that while vehicles have been labor-saving devices, they have simultaneously been labor-generating possessions. They get the job done, as truck
commercials like to put it, but, when they break down, they become jobs
themselves, messy work for mechanics and repairmen. An appreciation of
these linkages between vehicles and work, then, is the ultimate lesson we can
draw from the past. It is also, I would suggest, a useful agenda for future
study.

# PART 2
## THE AUTOMOBILE, FAMILIES, AND DAILY LIFE

The four essays in this part all relate the automobile and its use to daily life, and several of them emphasize the place of the automobile in family life. Since its inception, the automobile has played an important role in defining expected social behavior in the American family, and it has been associated especially with the definition of gender roles within families.

In the first chapter of this section, urban planner Sandra Rosenbloom looks at the connection between the automobile and work differently than did the authors in part 1. Her point is of great importance for contemporary planners and policymakers. Rosenbloom describes the recent shift of most employment to suburban locations and the entry into the labor force of most women, including the majority of married women with young children at home. She describes the patterns of movement needed to support households having children and multiple workers at suburban locations and concludes that the two-worker family is critically dependent on the automobile for balancing adults' needs for access to work with children's needs for trips to school, child care, social activities, and medical care. Presenting empirical evidence from several countries on the division of responsibility for travel in support of family activities and children, she argues that public transit is not an adequate substitute for the automobile given today's land-use and activity patterns. She implies that there will be great difficulty achieving the goals that Warner espoused in part 1, while at the same time showing the very high costs of current land-use and activity patterns also addressed by Warner.

Historian Michael Berger examines the use of the automobile during its early years in courtship and socialization, and finds that while many can make a case that the automobile contributed to the unity of the family, it is more reasonable to conclude that the car played a greater role in fragmenting the traditional family. The automobile resulted in reduced parental control over children, introduced women to new opportunities for work, recreation, and romance away from the home, and expanded social contacts for many people in rural and urban areas. In response to fears of deteriorating family unity, many political and religious leaders spoke out against the auto, and society sought to limit the freedom of young people by, for example, creating the stereotype of the "woman driver."

Virginia Scharff expands upon the theme developed by Berger. She shows that the electric automobile was light and maneuverable and easy to operate, but that it had limited range and was lacking in power and hill-climbing ability. The electric car, therefore, had many properties which people associated favorably with women drivers, while the more powerful gasoline automobile, with greater range and more mechanical complexity, was more likely to be associated with male drivers. Early manufacturers consciously marketed the electric auto to women, although it is difficult to show that there were any inherent sex-based differences in the ability to master the gasoline auto. After the introduction of electric starters and electric lights into closed automobiles powered by gasoline engines, the electric faded from the scene. Scharff believes that too few historians of the automobile have recognized the importance of gender stereotypes in the evolution of the electric automobile.

Urban planner Martin Wachs argues that the automobile has continued to be one of the most "gendered" objects of twentieth-century technology. The stereotype of the woman driver and the expectation that women would be mechanically inept and thus less interested in the operation of automobiles than men colored early images of the automobile. Later, as women proved equal to men at operating autos and as the automobile industry recognized that the potential for economic growth lay in the sale of second cars to households, the automobile was marketed to women as an extension of their household and family responsibilities. It was portrayed to women as a device to be used in chauffeuring children and for shopping expeditions, while it was marketed to men as a symbol of independence and adventure. It was presumed that women would be most interested in the more domestic aspects of autos such as their colors and upholstery, while men would be most interested in autos' mechanical properties. Wachs argues that gender stereotyping continues to influence the use of autos today and is part of the reason that women drivers' patterns of auto use continue to differ markedly from those of men.

**4.** Sandra Rosenbloom

## WHY WORKING FAMILIES NEED A CAR

In the years since the Second World War, American society has experienced three profound changes. The first is the growing reliance on the car; in ever-increasing numbers we are buying more cars, doing more of our travel in cars, and traveling longer distances with them. Americans traveled almost one-third more miles annually in 1983 than in 1969, although the population increased by only 14 percent.[1] The second profound change is the increasing involvement in the paid labor force of women with young children; in 1985 over half of all married women with children under six and almost half of those with children under one had salaried employment, most of it in the full-time labor force.[2] In 1986 women alone headed almost 20 percent of all families with children, and almost all of those women had full-time employment.[3] The third societal change is the increasing suburbanization of homes and jobs. In 1980 the suburbs already had 60 percent of all jobs in the country; between 1960 and 1980 two-thirds of all new jobs went to the suburbs of cities as disparate as Buffalo and Dallas, St. Louis and Los Angeles, and these trends are likely to intensify.[4] Because of the increasingly dispersed location of both job and home, in 1980 almost 60 percent of all commuters were traveling from one suburb to another for work.

It is rare for anyone to consider how related the first of these trends is to the other two, yet much of our increasing reliance on the car reflects the way that two-worker and single-parent households juggle the complicated responsibilities of home and work in suburban residential and employment locations. The car offers the flexibility and convenience essential to working parents, particularly, mothers who often carry the double burden of working at both work and home. It is hard to see how any other option could serve the complex travel needs of such families.

This essay first explores America's increasing reliance on the private car and examines the other demographic trends that support such reliance. It then looks at how multiple responsibilities influence the travel patterns of working parents, particularly women, and how embedded in those patterns are the needs of children. Overall, the analyses suggest that families who combine trips to work in a suburban environment with other activities—from dropping children off at a day-care center to grocery shopping on the way home—require the convenience and responsiveness offered only by the car.

American travelers have come to depend on the car just as two-worker households have come to depend on the income of the "second" worker—it might be possible to do without either but not without heroic sacrifices. American households have made so many decisions based on the availability of the car (and perhaps on two salaries), that it is simply not possible to reach a majority of their destinations without one.

Studies show that the growth in auto travel over the last two decades has been well ahead of population growth. The U.S. Department of Transportation, in conjunction with the Commerce Department, has been studying American travel patterns for roughly twenty years, conducting three National Personal Transportation Studies (NPTS): in 1969, 1977, and 1983. NPTS data show that, from 1969 to 1977 alone, the number of total miles driven increased 40 percent while the number of licensed drivers increased 24 percent and total population only 8 percent.[5]

The NPTS also show that both absolute and relative use of the car has been increasing since 1969; the number of vehicle trips per household increased from 87,284 million in 1969 to 126,874 million in 1983, or 45 percent over the fourteen year period. Household vehicle miles traveled (VMT) increased 17 percent from 1969 to 1977 and 10 percent from 1977 to 1983, or 29 percent for the entire fourteen years. Between 1969 and 1983 the average household made 39 percent more shopping trips and 40 percent more family and personal business trips in a private vehicle, average trip length increasing 20 percent for shopping and 3 percent for family and personal business.[6]

Table 4.1 shows that in 1983 the private vehicle (cars, vans, trucks, and station wagons) was used by both men and women for more than 80 percent of all their trips. Both sexes were more likely to walk to meet their needs than use transit; less than 3 percent of all trips were made on transit.

Table 4.2 disaggregates overall trip choices by purpose for 1983 trips. The private vehicle accounted for over 80 percent of all trips except to school and church; car use was highest (almost 88 percent) for medical and shopping and lowest (80–82 percent) for visiting and social and recreational trips. Conversely, transit accounted for less than 5 percent of any trip purpose, being highest for work and work-related trips, as well as for trips to school

|                      | WOMEN | MEN  |
| -------------------- | ----- | ---- |
| Private vehicle      | 81.5  | 82.3 |
| Public transportation | 2.5  | 2.1  |
| Walk                 | 9.2   | 7.9  |
| Bike                 | 0.5   | 1.0  |
| Other                | 6.3   | 6.7  |

**TABLE 4.1**

Distribution of Person-Trips by Sex and Mode of Travel,
1983, in Percentage

SOURCE: DERIVED FROM *PERSONAL TRAVEL IN THE U.S.*,
VOL. 2, NATIONWIDE PERSONAL TRANSPORTATION STUDY
(WASHINGTON, D.C.: U.S. DEPARTMENT OF TRANSPORTATION,
1986), TABLE E-73.

*Why Working Families Need a Car*

| | PRIVATE | TRANSIT | BIKE | WALK |
|---|---|---|---|---|
| To/from work | 87.5 | 4.5 | 0.52 | 5.0 |
| Work related | 84.8 | 3.3 | — | 8.4 |
| Shopping | 88.3 | 0.8 | 0.6 | 7.3 |
| Family/personal business | 87.2 | 1.0 | 0.3 | 7.6 |
| Medical | 90.5 | 3.0 | — | 3.2 |
| School/church | 55.9 | 4.7 | 0.6 | 14.9 |
| Visit friends | 82.3 | 1.4 | 1.3 | 10.2 |
| Other social recreational | 80.2 | 1.1 | 1.6 | 10.4 |

**TABLE 4.2**

Distribution of Person-Trips by Mode and Purpose, 1983, in Percentage

SOURCE: DERIVED FROM *PERSONAL TRAVEL IN THE U.S.*, VOL. 2, NATIONWIDE PERSONAL TRANSPORTATION STUDY (WASHINGTON, D.C.: U.S. DEPARTMENT OF TRANSPORTATION, 1986), TABLE E-94.

and church. Walking accounted for over 10 percent of visiting and social trips and almost 15 percent of school and church trips.

NPTS data also show the importance of automobiles to those too young to drive—an indirect measure of the chauffeuring duties required of parents. Table 4.3 shows the distribution of person trips by mode and by selected age categories in 1977 and 1983. Those aged five to fifteen made over 60 percent of their trips in a private car, a figure relatively constant over the six-year period. Transit use by this age group was not high and dropped from 1977 to 1983; instead, the young made the rest of their nonauto trips by school bus and walking.

### THE CHANGING AMERICAN FAMILY

During the same time the car has become a major, and arguably permanent, feature of our society, there have been substantial changes in the structure and activities of the "typical" family. The two most striking changes are the full-time employment of married mothers and the rapid growth of single-parent households.

The United States, like most developed countries, currently has a female labor force participation rate above 50 percent. The fastest growing component of the female labor force is mothers with children under six, over 80 percent of whom are in full-time employment.[7] From 1970 to 1978 employment of married women in the United States with children five and under, whose spouse was present, increased from 37 percent to just under 48 percent. By 1983 almost 38 percent of all women with spouses present and whose children were under three were in the labor force.[8]

It is often assumed that most of the growth in employment among married women at least is in the part-time labor force. While women do make up a significant percentage of the part-time labor force in the United States— 65 percent—most are *not* employed part-time.[9] There is a parallel growth in the number of families headed by women. In 1970 there were 5.5 million U.S. households headed by a woman alone; that number grew by 72 percent by 1983. Today families headed by women alone comprise 14 percent of all U.S. families and 20 percent of all families with children.[10] The female heads of such families are even more likely to have salaried employment than other women. As early as 1978, 65 percent of single parents with children ages three to five and 55.5 percent of those with children under three were employed outside the home.[11]

All indications are that two-worker families and single-parent house-

*Why Working Families Need a Car*

| | 5–15 | | 16–19 | | 65+ | | ALL | |
|---|---|---|---|---|---|---|---|---|
| | 1977 | 1983 | 1977 | 1983 | 1977 | 1983 | 1977 | 1983 |
| Private vehicle | 63.4 | 62.6 | 76.4 | 72.0 | 81.3 | 83.9 | 83.9 | 82.0 |
| Public | 3.1 | 2.9 | 2.9 | 3.3 | 3.1 | 2.6 | 2.4 | 2.2 |
| Walk | 15.8 | 10.5 | 14.5 | 15.6 | 14.3 | 10.4 | 9.3 | 8.5 |
| Bike | 1.8 | 1.8 | 1.5 | 1.6 | 0.2 | 0.3 | 0.6 | 0.8 |
| School bus | 15.2 | 15.9 | 3.9 | 4.8 | — | — | 2.8 | 2.6 |
| Other | 0.7 | 6.3 | 0.8 | 2.7 | 1.0 | 2.8 | 1.0 | 3.9 |

**TABLE 4.3**

Distribution of Person-Trips by Age and Mode of Travel, 1977 and 1983, in Percentage
SOURCE: DERIVED FROM *PERSONAL TRAVEL IN THE U.S.*, VOL. 2, NATIONWIDE PERSONAL
TRANSPORTATION STUDY (WASHINGTON, D.C.: U.S. DEPARTMENT OF TRANSPORTATION, 1986),
TABLE E-72.

The Car and the City

holds display complicated activity patterns in which the travel needs of children are inextricably embedded. Such travel complexity and variability often requires the flexibility of a car.

## THE SUBURBANIZATION OF JOBS

Several recent studies have clearly shown that the "traditional commute," in which a suburban resident travels for work to the traditional core of the city, does not describe the work trip of the majority of American workers.[12] Between 1960 and 1980 two-thirds of all metropolitan job growth went to the suburbs, which now have over 60 percent of all jobs. These patterns are uniform throughout the country, and even in slow-growth parts of the country with declining population (for example, Philadelphia, St. Louis, Pittsburgh, and Buffalo) suburban employment growth far outstripped total employment growth. As a consequence, the majority of work-trip growth, roughly 70 percent, was in the suburb-to-suburb trip pattern. Thus in 1980 almost 60 percent of all commuters were traveling from one suburb to another. Moreover, in the same time period fewer people worked at home (less than 3 percent), and far fewer walked to work (5 percent down from 10 percent in 1960).

The data on suburban travel do not specifically address women workers or employed mothers. Women are, however, the largest component of the change in the total labor force from 1950 to 1980—particularly, women with children. More than three out of five new workers added to the labor force in these three decades were women. Therefore, it is not unreasonable to assume that, in most metropolitan areas, at least 60 percent of all employed mothers work in the suburbs. Moreover, since far more "new" workers added to the labor force in these three decades were making suburb-to-suburb commutes, it is also not unreasonable to assume that roughly two-thirds of suburban women workers are making a suburb-to-suburb commute (that is, both living and working in the suburbs).

The implications of these trends for any worker's use of transit for commuting are staggering, let alone for women workers who often balance many complicated activities with their travel to work. Transit use is difficult for suburban travel because service coverage is poor, due in large part to the lack of concentrated corridors of transit demand and the successful competition offered by the speedier car. As a major report recently commented: "The negative effects on transit of current [suburban employment] trends are clear. Growth is centered where transit use is weakest—in the suburb-to-suburb market, and high levels of [private] vehicle availability severely diminishes the choice of transit."[13] In a 1986 study of suburban employment growth and subsequent traffic congestion, Robert Cervero noted:

> Since 1970, the automobile has strengthened its dominance in the commuting market. . . . Transit's standing could slip even more since buses operating on fixed routes and set schedules are usually ill-suited for delivering workers to dispersed suburban addresses. . . . Even workers in suburban office towers located around rail transit stations are almost entirely dependent on the automobile. Regardless of how conveniently rail transit serves suburban office centers, if only a fraction of the work force lives near a line, most employees will end up driving.[14]

Not surprisingly, in 1980 the smallest transit ridership within metropolitan areas was recorded for suburb-to-suburb commutes; only 1.6 percent of all workers used transit to go to work (compared to 16.1 percent of workers who both lived and worked in the central city).

In short, many (perhaps most) workers have jobs in lower-density suburbs that are not well served by public transit—and perhaps cannot be well served by transit because traditional services, even if available, would take two to three times longer than car travel for the same trip. Again, the use of the private car is a rational response for working families facing an increasingly more difficult urban environment.

The following section shows that the complicated travel patterns of working parents, particularly salaried mothers, are a response to the combination of their household, child care, employment, and chauffeuring responsibilities in suburban environments.

### THE TRAVEL NEEDS OF WORKING FAMILIES

Salaried mothers and their families have to juggle a variety of needs and they do so in ways that make transit or other modes difficult or inappropriate. First, working parents must often *link* trips to or from work, to take children to child care, go shopping, or go to the bank on the way home. Second, many working parents chauffeur their children to an assortment of activities, creating travel patterns that vary daily and weekly. Third, parents, and particularly women, have to be prepared to respond to the needs of sick children; such emergency "preparedness" may require a car.

The following sections present data from small-scale attitudinal and behavioral surveys of married and single employed parents in the United States, France, and the Netherlands undertaken between 1982 and 1985. All respondents described here are full-time salaried workers (35+ hours in the United States, 30+ hours in Europe) with children under eighteen still living at home. Note that all married men described here are married to salaried women who work full-time. Interestingly, while this section focuses largely on U.S. parents, comparable analyses of Dutch families show similar complexity in travel patterns and the need to chauffeur children in spite of safe and widely available alternatives to the car.

Busy families often link trips to or from work in order to efficiently carry out their multiple responsibilities. It is interesting to note that such linked trips are often not broken out or evaluated in urban transportation planning processes because they are difficult to deal with, and they are often assumed to be relatively unimportant. Yet my data from three very different cities around the world—Austin, Texas; Rotterdam, the Netherlands; and Lyons, France—show that most families routinely link trips to and from work. Moreover, employed married mothers in all three countries are more likely to do so than comparable men.[15] In Austin, for example, 42 percent of married fathers and 65 percent of comparable married women with children under six routinely linked trips *to* work; 67 percent of married men and 81 percent of comparable women with older children routinely linked trips home *from* work.

### Chauffeuring Children

Chauffeuring duties are also a very important part of the travel patterns of working parents, and particularly mothers. Figure 4.1 shows that in Austin both parents routinely or frequently made trips solely for their children. Women were far more likely to chauffeur their children; almost 82 percent of all married women with young children did so routinely. While the likelihood dropped as children aged, almost half of all married women continued to routinely make trips solely for their teenagers. Slightly over half of all men made trips solely for their young children, but only 18 percent of men did so for their teenagers.

Figure 4.2 displays the reported frequency of trips made solely for children under six by their parents. The frequency data are illuminating; of the 54 percent of men who reported routinely chauffeuring children under six, the overwhelming number—75 percent—did so less than once per week. However, of the over 90 percent of women who reported such chauffeuring duties, most did so once a week or more, and 16 percent did so more than three times per week per child. Clearly, mothers of very young children are

*Why Working Families Need a Car*

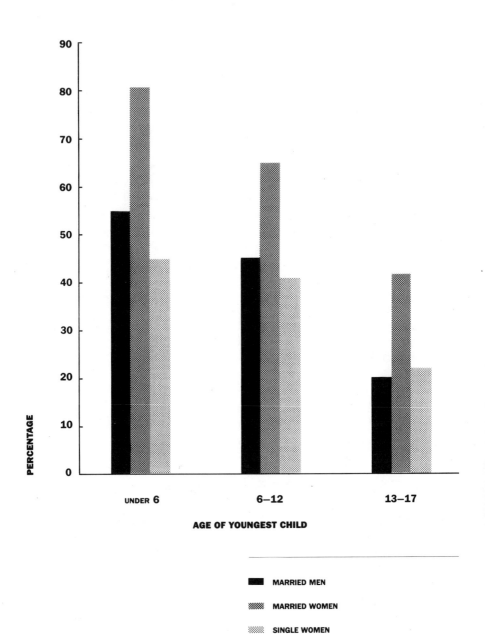

**FIGURE 4.1**

*Percentage of parents who make trips solely for their children, by age of children.*

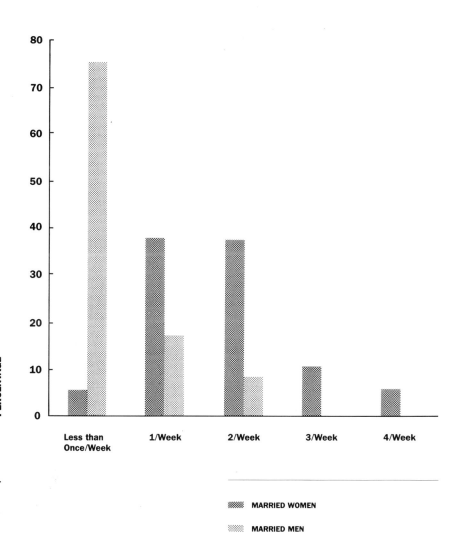

**FIGURE 4.2**

*Frequency of trips made solely for children under six.*

---

*Why Working Families Need a Car*

overwhelmingly the chauffeur for these children. The majority of trips being made by men for children under six are made very infrequently, and they appear to serve a backup or emergency function. Both parents made chauffeured trips less frequently in a week as children grew. Sixty-five percent of mothers and 40 percent of fathers reported chauffeuring children ages six to twelve. The majority of fathers reported making one or two trips per week for each child, and 75 percent of these trips were for recreation.

NPTS data discussed previously showed that over 60 percent of the trips of children under fifteen were made in a car—and figure 4.3 shows more clearly who has the burden of that duty. Both parents agreed that the mother was the most frequent transporter of children of all ages; roughly 60 percent of all respondents reported that the mother was the major transportation provider regardless of the age of the children. More parents of both sexes reported that "other adults" were the primary travel provider than reported that the father was. Note, however, that single mothers, presumably not living with the father of their children, were more likely to report the father as the major travel mode than were married mothers living with the child's father.

It is very clear that, deeply embedded in the travel patterns of salaried parents, and particularly mothers, are the needs of their children. If children had more alternatives, could society relieve employed women of some of their chauffeuring duties and perhaps of the need to drive?

### Dutch Parents and Chauffeuring Duties

To address the issue of chauffeuring responsibilities, a comparable analysis was undertaken of Dutch households in Rotterdam. The data show that, although Dutch working mothers are more likely to make chauffeuring trips than American mothers (because their husbands are less likely to do so than American men), the trips they do make are made less frequently. Dutch families as a unit make fewer trips solely for children than U.S. families.

One possible explanation is that the greater transportation alternatives available to Dutch children free their parents from the need to attend to all their children's travel needs. Dutch working mothers were asked if their children routinely or frequently traveled alone, without adult supervision. Table 4.4 shows the pattern of their responses: 21 percent of mothers reported that their children under six routinely traveled alone; that number rose to 92 percent of mothers of children ages six to twelve and 100 percent of

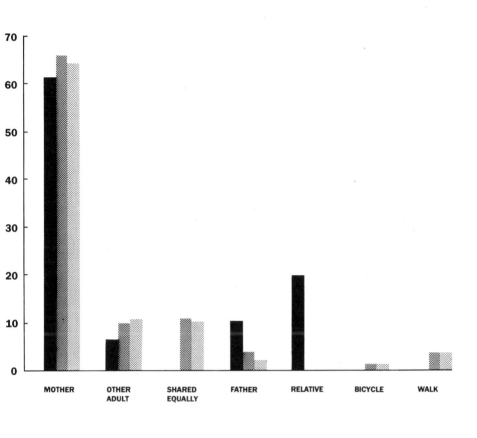

**FIGURE 4.3**

*Children's most frequent travel mode as reported individually by parent for children under six.*

*Why Working Families Need a Car*

| | | MODE OF TRAVEL | | | |
|---|---|---|---|---|---|
| | PERCENTAGE TRAVELING ALONE | MASS TRANSIT AND TRAIN | BIKE | WALK | MOTORCYCLE |
| **Under 6** | 21 | 58 | 8 | 34 | — |
| **6–12** | 92 | 58 | 42 | — | — |
| **13–17** | 100 | 43 | 43 | 9 | 5 |

**TABLE 4.4**

Percentage of Dutch Children Traveling Alone and Most Frequent Travel Mode when Traveling Alone

SOURCE: DATA FROM SANDRA ROSENBLOOM.

the mothers of teenagers. Table 4.4 also examines the modes these children used for the trips they make alone, and it is clear that Dutch children rely heavily on bikes and mass transit. Bicycles are, of course, a major feature of Dutch culture; they are frequently used by adults and account for 25 percent of the Rotterdam home-to-work commute.

Clearly, the existence of viable transportation options that are considered safe and secure enough for fairly young children partially explains why Dutch families make fewer chauffeured trips than American families. Yet, their children's use of mass transit and bikes is hardly a panacea for Dutch women. In spite of extremely good transit facilities and strong support for cycling, mothers still make many chauffeured trips, and their travel patterns are still strongly affected by their children's needs.

Working parents, and particularly single and married mothers, have complex and complicated travel patterns because they must juggle their own employment and household duties and balance them with the travel needs of their children. It is clear that the private car, for all its personal and social costs, is the most useful mode for such families. Conventional fixed-route transit services are not responsive to the needs of working parents, who must link trips, be available on a minute's notice to pick up sick children, or provide a chauffeur service that can vary daily, weekly, and monthly.

### IS DEPENDENCE REVERSIBLE?

Some observers might question whether the preceding discussion really has shown how much families in the United States *need* a car. Perhaps we are simply seeing families forced to use a car because they lack "good" transit services. Can other modes replace the car's disproportionate role in the travel patterns of all Americans?

This section shows that most trips currently made by working mothers and their families could not be made in a reasonable time period by transit— even assuming safe, reliable, ubiquitous services—largely because of significant time differentials between the two modes. Data from the American Housing Survey show that, on average, buses, streetcars, and subways in the United States travel 13.2 miles per hour, less than half as fast as either cars or car pools.[16] Since the average suburb-to-suburb commute in 1980 was 8.2 miles, a direct transit trip—with no waiting or transferring—would take approximately thirty-seven minutes by bus but only sixteen minutes by car.[17]

Moreover, the actual transit time could be 50–100 percent higher because of the inability to synchronize transfers.

NPTS data suggest that, because of these major time differentials, people have made major decisions about the location of their homes, shops, doctors, churches, and playgrounds based on the speed and potential of the car. Even putting other considerations aside, it might not be possible for them to substitute any other mode for the car.

Table 4.5 shows how few current auto trips made as either a driver or a passenger could be made by transit (or walking) even if fixed-route services were ubiquitously available (every two blocks with frequently arriving vehicles). It also shows the percentage of 1983 one-way auto trips that could be made within one hour by walking or transit, assuming a ubiquitous transit system. The analysis shown in table 4.5 takes the distribution of all vehicle trips by purpose and converts the mileage categories into *time*, assuming an average walking speed of four miles per hour and an average transit speed of sixteen miles per hour (with five minutes walking and waiting). Unfortunately, trips were not disaggregated under five miles so the first column clearly overestimates the percentage of trips that could be made within one hour, by walking.

Table 4.5 also shows that no more than 30 percent of any kind of trip could be made by walking, and no more than 53 percent could be made on transit in under an hour—and that only if transit were actually available and did not require time-consuming transfers (both are major assumptions). Over 60 percent of family and personal business trips and visiting trips could not be made in under an hour—one-way. Over 40 percent of medical trips would be forgone. Certainly the current location of some of these trips is a matter of choice and not necessity, and substitutions could be made. But, overall, the use of a mode other than the private vehicle would require substantial restructuring of the entire activity patterns of most households. Moreover, the use of a sixty-minute maximum is questionable because it is unlikely that anyone would be willing to travel over thirty minutes one-way for any except a work trip. If so, over 80 percent of all current auto trips could not be made by any other mode.

These analyses do not suggest that working parents never need transit; clearly, transit is a major travel mode in a few cities and for a few workers in all cities. (Remember that one-third of all transit riders in the country live in New York City, and over 70 percent live in just seven cities.) But in all American metropolitan areas the majority of new jobs as well as new resi-

| | UNDER 5 MILES, COULD WALK | UNDER 15 MILES, COULD USE TRANSIT | MORE THAN 15 MILES, CAN'T WALK OR TAKE TRANSIT |
|---|---|---|---|
| Work | 15.1 | 52.5 | 47.5 |
| Work related | 10.6 | 35.4 | 64.6 |
| Shopping | 29.0 | 63.5 | 36.5 |
| Family/ personal business | 22.2 | 33.8 | 66.2 |
| Medical | 10.7 | 55.0 | 45.0 |
| School/church | 27.9 | 72.4 | 27.6 |
| Visit friends | 11.9 | 36.7 | 63.3 |
| Other social recreational | 17.8 | 46.7 | 43.3 |

NOTE: Assumes a ubiquitous transit system

**TABLE 4.5**

Distribution of Vehicle Trip Mileage by Trip Purposes, One-Hour Walking and Transit Equivalents, 1983

SOURCE: DERIVED FROM *PERSONAL TRAVEL IN THE U.S.*, VOL. 2, NATIONWIDE PERSONAL TRANSPORTATION STUDY (WASHINGTON, D.C.: U.S. DEPARTMENT OF TRANSPORTATION, 1986), TABLE E-41.

dents are locating in the suburbs, which are and will be—because of constraints of the mode—poorly served by traditional transit.

## CONCLUSION

The enormous growth in society's use and dependence on the private car has
closely paralleled the increasing labor force participation of female parents.
Two-worker and single-parent households, struggling to balance their daily
activities and faced by continually decentralizing job opportunities, a dispersing urban infrastructure, and the lack of safe and responsive transportation
options for children, have very little choice—the car is the only practical
option. Not surprisingly, over 60 percent of households earning less than
$10,000 a year owned a car in 1983, and almost 20 percent owned two or more.
These people willingly chose the financial burden of owning a car over their
other options.

It is naive to expect a total reversal in the suburban employment,
housing, and low-density commercial patterns that fuel the growth in use of
the car; it is visionary to expect society to provide working conditions that
offer all parents the flexibility to carry out domestic responsibilities and
respond to children in need without suffering the loss of salary, full-time
benefits, or the potential for advancement; and it seems wishful to hope that
cities could be really safe places in which young children could travel alone.
Failing that metamorphosis of the city, we must accept that the American
"love affair" with the auto is a well-established marriage.

## *5.* Michael L. Berger

# THE CAR'S IMPACT ON THE AMERICAN FAMILY

In the depths of the Depression, the advertising firm of Foster and Kleiser developed and provided as a public service message a billboard display featuring a picture of the "typical" American family: a Caucasian mother and father, two children, and a dog—going for a drive in their car (see fig. 5.1). Two captions, "World's Highest Standard of Living" and "There Is No Way of Life Like the American Way," completed the display. Clearly, the family car and its occupants had been chosen to symbolize the best of American life at a time of acute economic, political, and social distress.

It was not always this way, especially in the early days of motoring. Thus, during the summer of 1904, wealthy drivers were attacked by stone-throwing residents in New York City's lower-class neighborhoods. Such incidents were serious enough to require the assignment of police protection for motorists driving through these neighborhoods.[1] Similarly, in 1906, Woodrow Wilson, then president of Princeton University, announced that "nothing has spread socialistic feeling in this country more than the automobile. To the countryman they are a picture of the arrogance of wealth, with all its independence and carelessness."[2]

The fear that the automobile would exacerbate class divisions was a short-lived one, all but eliminated by the introduction of the assembly line and mass production, which allowed the price of a Model T Ford to drop from an initial $850 to a 1920s low of $290. Such low prices, combined with the introduction and acceptance of installment buying, put the automobile well within the means of the vast American middle class.

Superficially, the motor car can be viewed as just another piece of twentieth-century technology that promised to make life easier and more satisfying. In that respect, it did not differ from the radio, telephone, and vacuum cleaner, all of which had successfully been introduced into the family home. Unlike these other technological artifacts, however, the raison d'être of the automobile was personal mobility away from the homestead. To the extent that forays from home reinforced traditional habits and customs, the family unit and interpersonal relationships within it would remain unchanged. If, however, they introduced alien ideas and customs, they were

**FIGURE 5.1**

*A public service billboard in California's San Joaquin Valley, photographed in 1937
by Dorothea Lange.*

likely to upset the social functioning of the home and modify the very structure of the American family. This chapter will examine and evaluate the multiple social impacts of the automobile on family life in the United States primarily during the interwar years (1918–39).[3]

As indicated, the car created new opportunities for family travel, both within the local community and outside of it. Thus, the 1933 report of the President's Research Committee on Social Trends noted that the car "gave to the owner a control over his movements that the older agencies [rail and water systems] denied. Close at hand and ready for instant use, it carried its owner from door to destination by routes he himself selected, and on schedules of his own making; baggage inconveniences were minimized and perhaps most important of all, the automobile made possible the movement of an entire family at costs that were relatively small."[4]

In a sense, the committee was confirming for the nation as a whole what Robert and Helen Lynd had found earlier in their classic late-1920s sociological study of Muncie, Indiana, entitled *Middletown*. There, the authors had concluded that the motor car was "making noticeable inroads upon the traditional prestige of the family's meal-time at certain points; it had done much to render obsolete the leisurely Sunday noon dinner of a generation ago . . . and during half the year when 'getting out in the car' is pleasant, it often curtails the evening meal to an informal 'bite.'"[5]

While the Lynds were apparently being critical of these developments, they need not have been. In one sense, the car had become an extension of the home. Rather than sitting and talking around the dinner table or in the parlor, the members of the family were choosing to engage in such activities in an automobile—their new mobile, personal "parlor on wheels." As long as the car and the family were inseparable, the former would cause little or no change in the basic structure or functioning of the latter. Certainly, that was the visual implication of the Foster and Kleiser billboard ad cited earlier.

Families soon realized that they had purchased both a new means of recreation and a new, mobile status symbol. In fact, the car soon became an example of what would later be termed "conspicuous consumption." As one early 1920s writer put it: "The motor car has stolen into the vantage-point formerly occupied by the home; it has become the most widely accepted symbol of a man's ability to purchase luxuries. . . . A home is more visible;

but it does not accompany its owner from point to point, and its costs can only be roughly approximated by a layman."[6]

Possession of certain types of motor cars came to have considerable impact on a family's social status. Although automobile ownership cut across all socioeconomic classes, a pecking order of makes and models emerged, ranging from the plebeian Ford Model T to the luxurious Duesenberg Model J. As families traveled more widely and more often, the traditional criteria for attributing status (such as family background or personal qualities) were difficult to apply in cities and neighborhoods where one was unknown. Distance and mobility created a social situation in which people increasingly came to be judged by superficial appearances, and the automobile became a significant contributor to one's image in the outside world.

While motoring trips might further cement family ties and allow for a public display of family wealth, they also could undermine other societal institutions that had been supportive of the traditional family. For example, there was considerable discussion in the 1920s regarding whether or not the automobile was a potential threat to religion, especially in terms of observing the Sabbath. Many sociologists of the period, including the Lynds, noted that the traditional Sunday church visit, followed by a leisurely afternoon meal at home, was often being replaced with a long Sunday drive. The debate over the moral impact of this development, both within the church and the lay community, was to be a long, bitter, and ultimately indecisive one.

Opponents, unable to legally prevent Sunday driving, tried in several cities to deprive the vehicles of the requisite support services by closing filling stations and auto repair shops on the Sabbath. The popularity of Sunday driving was so great by the early 1920s, however, that such proposals were either defeated or proved unenforceable in Atlanta, Birmingham, and New Orleans, and one in Nashville that stood for the entire decade was constantly under attack.[7] An explanation for this opposition was provided in 1923 by a Memphis publication that stated: "Everybody wanted to enjoy a Sunday outing in the automobile, but realized he was taking a big chance [if service stations were closed]. He might run out of gas, have a puncture or break down miles away from home. *Then the whole family would have to walk back* [emphasis added]."[8] Thus, family convenience was to take precedence over religious tradition.

While such local motor excursions were more common, the family vacation automobile trip outside the community was, in many respects, more sociologically significant. Among other things, the educational value of the

**FIGURE 5.2**

*Hamilton Gale, Sr., and family pose in their car on a street in Annapolis, Maryland, during the winter of 1911.*

motor car in this regard should not be minimized. It provided the opportunity whereby families could encounter new experiences together, thus allowing for parental judgment in terms of what was seen and when, and, if necessary, an explanation or censorship of potentially negative experiences.

By 1929 the Aerocar, the first house trailer, had added a new, totally auto-related dimension to such travel, moving it away from institutions that traced their heritage back to the stagecoach and the railroad. The next decade witnessed the appearance of the auto or trailer camp, which proved to be a much more family-based institution than the hotel for which it substituted. A Seattle survey, for instance, showed that only 16 percent of the occupants of hotels were in family groups, while a study of the Puget Sound area and southern California campgrounds revealed that 90 percent of the campers were there together with their families. In both situations the dominant type of family group was the couple without children. The proportion of children among auto campers was, however, eight times larger than that of hotel dwellers.[9]

The ultimate trip, so to speak, was the permanent one to the suburbs. Both the complexity of that socioeconomic phenomenon and the urban focus of this volume mitigate against any lengthy discussion of that point, yet, one aspect needs to be mentioned. The movement of people to the suburbs created a situation in which the husband increasingly commuted to work in the city. As a result, as Ernest Mowrer noted in 1932, the husband's absence from the home from early morning until early evening led to the shifting of additional domestic responsibilities to the mother and the consequent development of a more matriarchal family.[10]

While a 1933 study of sixty-eight cities revealed that the journey to work was more often accomplished on foot or by public transportation, the presence of the automobile undoubtedly increased the willingness of men to live in one neighborhood and work in another.[11] At the very least, it diminished the absolute number of families that could expect the father to return for a workday lunch.

The automobile also was responsible for compounding at least one perennial area of family conflict—money. While the price of a small automobile, such as Ford's Model T, had indeed dipped below $300 by the mid-1920s, still it was a sizable sum for most middle-class American families, and few could afford to pay that amount in cash. Thus, the automobile began to be offered for sale on the installment payment plan. While land/home mortgages had been based on similar arrangements, car installment payments were unique

**FIGURE 5.3**

*Starting out on a family vacation trip via automobile in 1933.*

---

**63**

*The Car's Impact on the American Family*

in that the American family, probably for the first time, was incurring debt for a major asset that was calculated to decrease in value, unlike land or housing, which usually increased in value. While such depreciation was true of sewing machines, vacuum cleaners, or electric washing machines, the automobile would have represented the largest single debt, and, in consequence, a potential source of family strife. Nonetheless, it should be noted that, during the Depression of the 1930s, the family car was often the one tangible asset that was kept at all costs.

Had the automobile influenced the American family only as a unified group, American social history might have been quite different than it has been. The historical evidence shows, however, that there were multiple dimensions to that influence—one was that it affected individual members of the family differently. Therefore, the remainder of this chapter will concentrate on the car's influence on two familial groups: young adults and women.

### YOUNG ADULTS AND THE CAR

The raising of children, particularly during the adolescent years, has often been a source of friction within the American family. The situation was compounded by the introduction of the automobile. In the period under discussion, most families could afford, or chose to own, only one vehicle, and thus there were conflicts resulting from competition for the use of a scarce resource. More significant, however, was the nature of this resource, which, by definition, took young people away from the home and the neighborhood— and the adult control that both provided. In the preautomobile period, parents and the neighborhood community were the dominant force in the character development of youth. Significantly, in their study of Muncie, the Lynds found that approximately 40 percent of the time boys and girls went automobile riding without their parents.[12] More likely than not, they had experiences that were qualitatively different than they would have had if their parents had been along. As noted earlier, the car was more than a means of transportation; it could function as a parlor-on-wheels, without the adult chaperonage usually found at home.

It seems that no age cohort has made greater use of the motor car for social purposes than teenagers. By the 1920s access to an automobile had become a key to peer popularity. Possession of a car, particularly certain models, afforded a degree of social status in itself. In addition, as contemporary psychologists have noted, the automobile often symbolized adulthood through the possession of material wealth and the independence it pro-

**FIGURE 5.4**

*A farm family considers the purchase of a new Chevrolet in Lincoln, Nebraska, in 1939.*

---

*The Car's Impact on the American Family*

vided.[13] Furthermore, the automobile provided a means to meet and maintain friends outside the neighborhood and a degree of privacy in courtship rarely known previously to adolescents (or even adults). It thus threatened to change courting relationships and related moral standards, or so it was perceived.

Interestingly, the perception of this threat cut across racial and class lines. Blaine A. Brownell notes that the Birmingham, Alabama, *Labor Advocate* "attributed the decline of youth to 'night automobile rides, and the consequent and inevitable bottle of white lightning,' while a black writer in Atlanta complained of 'pleasure seeking' among the city's black youth. 'They go automobile riding at nights and all day Sunday, throwing away their hard earnings for a few hours of pleasure.'"[14] Similarly, an Atlanta judge, reflecting on his court experiences in 1921, concluded "that a large percentage of cases are the direct result of too much automobile and too little parental control. It is not too much to ask the parents to throw in the clutch and put on the brakes or our entire civilization will take one last joy ride to destruction."[15] Finally, one widely quoted story claims that Henry Ford deliberately restricted the width of the seats in the Model T so that couples could not have sexual intercourse on them. Ford was clearly a better mechanic than social engineer, and he badly underestimated the ingenuity and physical dexterity of contemporary teenagers and young adults in such matters.

There always have been two schools of thought on the question of whether introduction of the automobile was a contributor to greater sexual freedom or not. On the one hand were people, similar to those interviewed in the 1930s by Albert Blumenthal, who reported that "when it is suggested that the automobile facilitates sex diversions at the present day . . . older residents reply: 'It wasn't very hard to get out of the city limits during the horse-and-buggy days.'"[16] Yet, as the Lynds observed: "Buggy-riding in 1890 allowed only a narrow range of mobility; three to eight were generally accepted hours for riding, and being out after eight-thirty without a chaperon was largely forbidden. In an auto, however, a party may go to a city halfway across the state in the afternoon or evening, unchaperoned automobile parties as late as midnight, while subject to criticism, are not exceptional."[17] Furthermore, as Blumenthal noted, "with the aid of an automobile and the device of leaving the dance an hour or so early, a girl can 'pull a wild party' and still return home at a time which does not arouse the suspicion of her parents."[18] Unfortunately, few statistics are, or will ever be, available to document definitively any change in sexual mores brought on by the motor car.

The desire of young people for automotive mobility, combined with the parental need for control, added a new element to the ageless dynamic of child rearing. Thus, during a period when actual teenage ownership of a car was rare, parents realized that they could categorize its use as a "privilege" that could be granted or withheld depending on the behavioral reinforcement desired. As a result, in time the car key itself came to have symbolic dimensions.

The success or failure of such parental actions is difficult to ascertain. Since other youngsters might have access to cars, however, unless one were prepared to "ground" the child, the punishment was limited in its impact. In fact, one of the overriding principles of the car's impact on American life is that individual families were powerless to stop a societal revolution that collectively they were setting in motion.

## WOMEN AND THE CAR

Although many women expressed an interest in driving their own cars, thus greatly enlarging the radius within which they could travel in a day, they were often stymied by the necessity of hand cranking the motor to start it and the mechanical problems associated with early motoring. Gretchen Sinon, at the time a child in Newark, New Jersey, remembers that, "after Father's death in January 1908, Mother was never without a car, and someone to drive it for her. I'm sure the idea of driving an automobile herself never occurred to her, as in those days cars were apt to break down, and needed a mechanically-minded man who didn't mind getting dirty tinkering with the motor, or fixing a flat tire and pumping it up with a hand pump. I don't remember ever seeing a woman driver at that time."[19]

It was not just the mechanical complexity of early cars that limited the number of ladies behind the wheel. The relatively high price of most pre–World War I automobiles meant that most were bought by the upper class. Since women in such families frequently were accustomed to being transported around town by a coachman in a horse-drawn vehicle, it was natural that the purchase of a motor car was swiftly followed by the engagement of a chauffeur. The latter obviated the need for women drivers—at least among the wealthy.

By the 1920s, however, cars priced at figures that put them within the means of the American middle class appeared and prospered. More important than the diminished cost, at least from the female perspective, was the trend

**FIGURE 5.6**

*Members of the Motor Corps of the National League for Women's Service demonstrate the fine art of automotive repair in 1917.*

*The Car's Impact on the American Family*

toward smaller vehicles and mechanical simplicity, highlighted by the introduction of the electric starter. The First World War, which took men away from the home but left their cars there, created both the need and the opportunity for many women to learn to drive.[20] By the end of the war there existed the real possibility that the automobile could be adopted by large numbers of middle-class women.[21]

Such widespread use of the automobile by American women was viewed with alarm by most men of the time. A 1913 observation by Mrs. A. Sherman Hitchcock, writing for *American Homes and Gardens,* was still pertinent in the 1920s and 1930s. After noting that some husbands did not approve of their wives driving, Mrs. Hitchcock notes: "His real reason is without doubt in most cases a wholly selfish one—he fears her proficiency and doesn't want her to use the car as often as she would wish were she capable of its operation."[22]

Except for the very wealthy, who could afford servants to take care of their households and children, American family life had been grounded in the belief that a woman's place was in the home tending to domestic chores and the needs of her children and menfolk. With "automobility," it was feared that women would fall prey to the lure of the outside world and would neglect their husbands, children, and homes. The car was seen as an instrument that could not only provide freedom for women, but freedom that might not be exercised in the best interests of society and, specifically, the family. Despite a number of articles showing how the motor car could make women more efficient homemakers,[23] the public seemed more concerned about what women might do if they ever finished their housework.

As Geraldine Sartain was to note in a 1939 article for *Independent Woman,* it was not just a question of whether the automobile would provide transportation, recreation, and convenience. Rather, it was the possibility of participation in a richer, fuller life for women that was at issue.[24] Since such a life threatened to radically alter long-established social values, including many associated with motherhood and familial responsibilities, it was feared and resisted in the interwar period. The development and support of a stereotype likely to limit the number of women on the road and the mileage they drove were reasonable developments from the perspective of those who sought to minimize the impact of the automobile as a vehicle for the liberation of women—hence, the emergence of the "woman driver" stereotype and the ridicule that accompanied it.

**FIGURE 5.7**
*A Detroit woman driver behind the wheel of her late 1920s Hupmobile roadster.*

*The Car's Impact on the American Family*

So successful was the stereotype that it would take a number of scientific studies in the interwar period to prove that women were as good, if not better, drivers than men.[25] In addition, *Women's Home Companion, Ladies' Home Journal,* and *Good Housekeeping* felt compelled to employ motor editors to write monthly columns aimed at educating women about better driving habits and undermining the psychological basis for the stereotype. Not until December of 1939 was *Ladies' Home Journal* able to report that a recent survey revealed that a clear majority (65 percent) of the women interviewed felt that they were as good as or better drivers than men.[26]

While it is true that the absolute number of women drivers increased steadily from 1900 to 1940, this fact should not be taken as an indicator of the ineffectiveness of the negative, woman driver stereotype. The per capita number of women drivers prior to World War II never approached that of males, and much of the responsibility for this development must reside with sex-role stereotyping in which the image of women drivers was prominent. Rural women, who were less subject to some of the traditional stereotypical views of femininity and yet had a pressing need for greater mobility, probably were less affected by the beliefs concerning women drivers than their urban counterparts.

### CONCLUSION

The automobile was one of many technological innovations that affected American family life during the interwar period. The telephone, motion pictures (first silent and then sound), radio, and affordable home appliances all coincided with the introduction of the motor car. It is almost impossible to separate out one of these technologies as *the* major instrument of change.

Nonetheless, none of these inventions had quite the same impact as the automobile. For example, as M. F. Nimkoff noted at midcentury; "radio has had less effect on the family because it is not so closely integrated with the family; or, to put it differently, radio leaves the members of a family some choice as to whether they will utilize it or not, and if so, how."[27] This was *not* true of the automobile. While alternate means of transportation continued to exist, particularly in urban areas, the car was unique among them in the number of functions it could perform and the range of personal transport and psychic satisfaction it afforded was both unmatchable and irresistible for most families.

In short, as the President's Research Committee on Social Trends noted in 1933; "imperceptibly, car ownership has created an 'automobile psychology'; the automobile has become a dominant influence in the life of the individual and he, in a real sense, has become dependent upon it."[28] Substitute "family" for the generic "he," and one can conclude that, as early as 1932 and certainly by 1940, the car had permeated every aspect of family life. As historian Kenneth T. Jackson has noted, a careful reading of the Lynds' 1929 study reveals that "in all six areas of social life in Muncie, Indiana—getting a living, making a home, raising the young, using leisure, engaging in religious practices, and participating in community activities—the private car played either a contributing or a dominant role."[29]

In consequence, the following specific conclusions seem warranted. First, the automobile was a parlor, and sometimes a bedroom, on wheels. As such, it performed a number of functions that were very different from those of horse-drawn vehicles, and which tended to detract from the family and the homestead as the center of leisure-time activities.

Second, regardless of which other mode is being compared, the automobile offered the fastest, most direct means of transportation between two points. Parked on the street or in a neighboring garage, the car was "ready when you were," and not limited by a fixed route and/or schedule. Thus, impromptu visits became much more common, and, curiously, those visits always had the potential of being as brief as social conventions would allow. The family, or an individual member of it, was no longer "trapped" by distance and/or a tired horse at a particular location for a set period of time.

Third, for the family as a whole and the individual members within it, the number and range of acquaintances increased, but these probably were not as strong as those that preceded the automobile. Thus, both the concept "friend" and the connotations usually associated with it changed. In addition, as Jesse F. Steiner has noted, the automobile tended to multiply friendships based upon age, sex, and/or common interests, rather than upon kinship and geographical proximity, as was formerly true.[30] Furthermore, the locations where those friends chose to spend their time together for recreation and education were no longer determined by distance alone. Time and geography had ceased to be the social barriers they once were.

Fourth, the car, more than any other transportation device before it, allowed individual members of the nuclear family to have lives of their own, of which the particulars, and sometimes the entire experience, could remain private. No longer need the individual members of a family be dependent on each other for most of their recreational activities. One of the major social reasons for the existence of the family group was clearly eroding.

Finally, the car created a situation whereby the inputs into family life came from sources over which the parents and other adults had little control, and which might view the meaning of life and its values in terms different from theirs. In addition, the very breakdown of isolation fostered by the automobile made it increasingly difficult to control actions by bringing familial and/or community pressure to bear. Thus, the responsibilities of parents increased since the young had to be taught how to analyze and evaluate the contacts and experiences that they might have.

In sum, while the automobile undoubtedly abetted the unity of the family in certain situations, it played a greater role in fragmenting that institution. The car multiplied opportunities for social and economic activities outside the home while at the same time catering to the individual interests and needs of the young and adult members of the family. In consequence, as historian Charles Sanford concludes in "'Woman's Place' in American Car Culture," the "car helped loosen family ties, reduce parental authority over children, introduce women to new opportunities for recreation, romance, and work outside the home; and, in general, expand social contacts between the sexes."[31]

# 6. Virginia Scharff

## GENDER, ELECTRICITY, AND AUTOMOBILITY

By now, it comes as no surprise to even the most ardent car nut that the popular adoption of the automobile has created at least as many problems as it has solved. Sometime-Chicagoan Carl Sandburg wrote of the fog creeping in on little cat feet; in Denver, the city that has the unhappy distinction of having surpassed Los Angeles in some categories of air pollution, there are days when you can watch the Brown Cloud creep down the Platte Valley, hiding the mountains so effectively that you might as well be in Chicago. Contemplating this poisonous vista, one is tempted to blame the machine rather than the society that builds and uses automobiles in the way ours does. I would argue, however, that we cannot understand what our cars do and where they have taken us, let alone figure out how to reduce the social costs of automobility, without examining the cultural and economic values and relations that have shaped our current metropolitan experience.

One particularly critical set of values and relations has to do with the way we carve up the world according to gender. Historian Joan Scott has suggested that, if we view gender as a useful category of historical analysis, we not only illuminate women's lives, but we also discover gender structuring historical developments in ways we might never have expected to find.[1] The history of the auto and what it has meant for the United States would seem to bear out Scott's contention in innumerable ways. Others, notably Dolores Hayden and Martin Wachs, have demonstrated the ways in which developments in housing and transportation systems have been informed by the notion that men and women ought to inhabit separate spheres, substantially to the disadvantage of women.[2] We are all familiar with the stereotype of the incompetent woman driver, and Michael Berger has explored the cultural and political significance of that folkloric figure.[3] At the same time we must always place such ideas in dynamic relation to women's actions, which sometimes defy conventional expectations.[4]

In this chapter I want to address a related aspect of the critical role ideas about maleness and femaleness have played in the making of the car culture and the engendering of automobile design. Manufacturers' notions of masculinity and femininity shaped the very nuts and bolts of the machines

they created, affecting the uses to which cars can be put and the consequences of such use. When women and men failed to act in accordance with
gender scripts, manufacturers revised, but did not abandon, their original
conceptions. I would like to discuss two historical issues in automotive design
and marketing deeply affected by gender ideology: the relation between electric and gasoline cars at the beginning of the automotive era and the adoption
of the electric starter for gasoline vehicles.

### GENDER, ELECTRICITY, AND AUTOMOBILITY

In 1913 *Country Life in America* carried an article explaining "What an
Electric Car Can Do." Author Phil M. Riley promoted electric automobiles in
terms echoing Victorian ideas about women. That he would have done so is
far from surprising, since electric vehicles were marketed primarily for
women. Responding to the criticism that "electric power is weak," Riley
asserted, "It is important with an electric not to waste power needlessly, that
is all." Just as women were admonished to eschew high-powered business and
political activity and conserve their energy for domestic tasks, so the electric
vehicle was to fulfill its mission as "an ever-ready runabout for daily use,"
leaving extended travel and fast driving to men in gas-powered cars. Riley
assured his readers that "[t]he proper sphere of the electric vehicle is not in
competition with the gasolene [*sic*] touring car."[5]

Manufacturers and purveyors of automotive goods were keenly sensitive to (and shared) the propensity to divide up the world by gender, so much
so that for a time even automotive technology and marketing seemed to be
developing within separate masculine and feminine spheres. Magazine columnist C. H. Claudy, a supporter of women's driving, was slow to recommend
gasoline cars for women. Describing the electric as "the car which has a
circumscribed radius," he invoked an image resonantly congruent with the
notion of woman's special, yet limited, sphere. He also recognized that
women might use electrics to accomplish the social and domestic tasks that
were part of the middle-class homemaker's vocation, though he regarded such
work as inconsequential compared to the obligations of professional men
(notably doctors) who also might drive electric vehicles. According to Claudy,
the electric offered a woman the mobility to perform her comparatively trivial
duties without overstepping the bounds of feminine propriety. "What a delight it is," he wrote, "to have a machine which she can run herself, with no
loss of dignity, for making calls, for shopping, for a pleasurable ride, for the
paying back of some small social debt."[6]

Certainly, some women who wanted the increased mobility that came with driving shared the idea that gas cars, being powerful, complicated, fast, and capable of long-distance runs, belonged to men, while electric cars, being simple, comfortable, and quiet, though somewhat short on power and restricted in range, belonged to women. If electrics offered less automobility than gas cars, they offered greater mobility than horses and more independence and flexibility than trolleys. Understandably, some women—most of them upper-class—thus chose to drive electrics. In April of 1904, *Motor* magazine's society columnist noted:

> Mrs. James G. Blaine has been spending the last few weeks with her parents at Washington, and has been seen almost daily riding about in an electric runabout. The latter appears to be the most popular form of automobile for women, at any rate in the National Capital. . . . Indeed, judging from the number of motors that one sees driven by women on a fine afternoon, one would imagine that nearly every belle in Washington owned a machine.[7]

In 1908, the same year he introduced the Model T, Henry Ford bought an electric car for his wife Clara to use for social calls and short trips around town. Ford biographer Allan Nevins commented that "for visits to Dearborn or more distant points she would go with Henry or [their] son Edsel," confirming the assumption that women who drove electrics generally depended on men if they wished to travel any distance from home.[8]

In the years before World War I, articles on electric vehicles, or women drivers, and advertisements for electrics in such publications as *Motor* and *Country Life in America* featured photographs of women driving, charging, and otherwise maintaining electrics, reflecting both a marketing strategy and an ideology that continued to divide automobility by gender.[9] In advertisements for electric vehicles in which drivers were pictured in illustrations, manufacturers including the Anderson, Woods, Baker, Borland, and Milburn companies featured women almost exclusively. Another ad identified the Detroit Electric as "the last word in luxury and beauty, as well as efficiency" but also noted its particular value as a closed car:

> To the well-bred woman, the Detroit Electric has a particular appeal. In it she can preserve her toilet immaculate, her coiffure intact. She can drive it with all desired privacy, yet safely—in constant touch with traffic conditions all about her.[10]

Thus, very early on, women's automobility was identified with vehicles that offered comfort and cleanliness, but which men spurned because "they did not go far enough or fast enough."[11]

At the same time there was beginning to be considerable doubt as to whether women really were satisfied to leave long-distance touring and high-speed driving to men. In 1912 Claudy seemed to recognize the disintegration of the separate-spheres ideology when applied to motive power in automobiles, stating that "the time has gone by when motor cars had sex—when the gasolene [sic] car was preeminently for the man, and the electric, because of its simplicity, for the woman." Still not quite able to completely abandon the idea that "motor cars had sex," he contradicted himself almost in the same breath, predicting that, "of all the types of self-propelled vehicles, the electric is now, and seems likely to remain, the simplest to handle on the road and to care for at home, whereby it still is, and seems likely to continue to be, the ladies' favorite."[12]

The author himself, in the very same article, provided evidence to undermine the latter statement. Relating the story of a bride who told her young husband, "I don't want an electric. I want a car that can go a long distance. I want a car that can go fast, and an electric can't go either far or fast," Claudy commented incredulously, "The lady was right in one thing— she did not want an electric. What she wanted was a six-cylinder touring car!"[13] He nevertheless set about trying to convince women drivers that, rather than demanding the speed, range, and hill-climbing power of gasoline vehicles, they would be better off accommodating themselves to the electric's limitations. This promotional strategy certainly made very little business sense in an economy in which consumers, male or female, had some choice and families buying only one vehicle were likely to have to accommodate male drivers who were presumed to want to go farther and faster than their female counterparts.[14]

Neither was such a pitch calculated to appeal to women motorists in places where distances were great and paved roads rare. In Tucson, Arizona, in 1914, for example, twenty-three women owned autos; twenty-one of them owned gasoline-powered vehicles, and none of the four hundred and two male car owners listed owned electrics. Only one vehicle listed could be definitely identified as an electric, and one other might have been an electric.[15] The economic folly of such advice was compounded by the fact that, particularly after the introduction of the Model T, numerous gasoline cars were available for prices under $1,500, but electric auto prices appear to have remained high.[16]

Claudy admitted that a "practical electric vehicle cannot be built so that it can go fast *and* far *and* climb hills. *Speed* you can have, or great *radius* you

| YEAR | MANUFACTURER | PRICE IN DOLLARS |
|---|---|---|
| 1903 | Pope-Waverly | 850–900 |
| 1909 | Woods | 2,100–2,700 |
| 1910 | Bailey | 2,400–2,600 |
| 1910 | Hupp-Yeats | 1,750 |
| 1912 | Waverly | 2,250 |
| 1912 | Standard | 1,850 |
| 1913 | Argo | 2,500–3,100 |
| 1913 | Detroit | 2,550–3,000 |
| 1916 | Milburn[a] | 1,285–1,685 |
| 1917 | Milburn[a] | 1,885 |
| 1918 | Milburn[a] | 1,885 |
| 1919 | Milburn[a] | 2,385 |

[a] Prices given are for the "Milburn Light Electric," a model that apparently became more expensive between 1916 and 1919.

.

### TABLE 6.1

Selected Prices of Electrics, 1903–19

SOURCE: *MOTOR* MAGAZINE, ADVERTISEMENTS FOR ELECTRIC VEHICLES INCLUDING PRICE INFORMATION, 1903–20.

*Gender, Electricity, and Automobility*

can have—but not both at once and still keep down weight and cost."[17] Yet he insisted that women had no need for speed:

> It can be roundly stated without fear of contradiction that the times a woman wants to run an electric 30 miles an hour, are few and far between. . . . It is an unnecessarily fast speed for pleasure driving . . . if the car you select has a maximum speed of 25 miles on the level, it goes quite fast enough.[18]

Claudy further insisted that "a radius of 60 to 80 miles is ample for any electric car," stretching somewhat the capabilities of the average electric vehicle and clearly implying that women had no need to go farther.

Some historians of the car culture have noted that electric vehicles failed the test of the marketplace, mentioning in passing that women seemed to prefer electric to gas-powered motorcars.[19] In *America Adopts the Automobile*, James J. Flink wrote: "The silent, odorless electric car came to be especially favored by women, who were concerned foremost with comfort and cleanliness and had a hard time controlling a spirited team or learning to shift gears."[20] Yet, given the fact that more and more women learned to drive as time passed, these statements are contradictory; if women drivers had truly preferred electric cars, then the demand for such vehicles would have grown far more than it did over time. These historians confuse manufacturers' expectations about the gendered nature of the auto market with women's choices and then dismiss those choices as unimportant. The early assumption that gas cars ought to be for men and electric cars ought to be for women, given the different "spheres" of gas and electric autos, obscured the fact that drivers of both sexes approved specific components of each type of vehicle. Moreover, in adopting a competitive economic model based on the technological determinist idea that the gasoline car "defeated" the electric simply because the former provided what the (male) public wanted in an automobile, investigators trivialize women's participation in the car culture and misconstrue the interaction between these two early branches of automotive technology, a relation deeply affected (though not determined) by gender ideology.[21]

Even the simplest automobiles are collections of solutions to technological problems, including motive power, body design, safety systems, ease of maintenance, comfort, and relative need for physical strength in operation. As more and more Americans took to motoring, electric and gasoline vehicle technology both competed and converged, a historical and economic process conditioned by both women's actions and the cultural identification of electric vehicles with women.

A few gasoline auto manufacturers recognized early that there was a female market for their product. Moreover, the ways in which such manufacturers promoted their wares suggest that they had begun to see that the automobile was unlikely to supercede the horse as a mode of popular transportation until it became a family utility vehicle. The Maxwell-Briscoe Company, for example, made an effort to market gas-powered cars as economical and dependable vehicles for families, including women drivers, in 1909, and sending Alice Huyler Ramsey and three women passengers on a highly publicized cross-country drive and mounting an advertising campaign based on the notion of the inexpensive family car.[22] In praise of its Model AA, a "reliable business runabout" priced at $600, the company asserted: "Everyone should own this car, because it fills the universal need. As easy to drive as an electric. Your wife, daughter, or son can run this MAXWELL and care for it—a chauffeur is unnecessary."[23] The ad copywriters also described the multiple ways in which their product might be used: "For errands, shopping, calls, meeting trains, taking the children to school, for business or pleasure, this automobile is the gateway to outdoors and health. Picture yourself in it—how would you use it?"[24] For readers not imaginative enough to conjure up such an image, Maxwell illustrated its ad with a picture of a woman dropping off a man at the gateway to a building obviously designed for business.

The notion that auto technology was composed of separate, gender-appropriate spheres defined by weak electricity and strong gasoline faded entirely from view as manufacturers of gas-powered cars began to incorporate more and more features deemed appropriate for women drivers, options and systems often inspired by electric vehicle design. Electric cars, which one historian dismissed as "the most conservative form of the automobile," led the way in two important areas of automobile technology: electric starting and closed vehicle design.[25]

To start electric cars, drivers had only to turn a key or flick a switch that started electrical current flowing. Early gasoline cars, however, required complicated multistep procedures to accommodate start-up and warm-up of "cold" engines. For one thing, gas-powered vehicles generally needed to be cranked to start, a job John B. Rae has aptly described in *The American Automobile* as "backbreaking, frustrating, and risky."[26] Historian Frank Donovan pointed out the perils of cranking, noting that the proper way to hold the crank was with the four fingers around it and the thumb tucked against the index finger: "One never put the thumb around the crank, because when it kicked back, as it often did if the spark was not properly adjusted, the result might be a broken thumb or wrist."[27] Men who cranked automobiles certainly had reason to hope for some innovation that would take the physical hardship and danger out of the act of starting a car, particularly when drivers wished to be neat, clean, composed, and punctual upon arrival at their destinations, preferences that would have negatively affected the hand-cranked auto's usefulness as a way of getting to work.[28] Yet cranking was seen as a kind of masculine rite offering proof of a man's fitness to motor. The perception that the crank limited the gasoline auto's usefulness arose only when assumptions about gender-appropriate automotive technology collided with an effort to accommodate a prospective clientele composed of both men and women, forcing adjustments in automotive design as well as in the gendering of technology.

Manufacturers' adoption of the self-starter redefined the boundary between men's and women's automotive spheres, no longer identified as the distinction between gas and electric motorcars but, instead, seen as the adaptation of gas cars to "feminine" standards. Coinciding with the recognition that women were not confining themselves to the electric's circumscribed sphere, automatic starting mechanisms for gasoline vehicles were early and often treated not as innovations furthering the efficiency of men but as concessions to feminine convenience, as accessories on par with luxurious upholstery and doors designed to accommodate long skirts. Rae has called the electric starter "a major factor in promoting the widespread use of the automobile, particularly because it made the operation of gasoline cars more attractive to women."[29] Surely the electric starter also made gas cars more attractive to men. Moreover, the application of electricity to the problem of starting an automobile was a relatively simple engineering problem, particularly when compared to the complexity of the internal combustion engine and the amount of creative energy that went into its design and modification in the years before 1910. Technological know-how was not the chief reason that manufacturers took so long in doing away with the crank.

If, in these years, the self-starter was often depicted as a gallant automotive bow to the ladies, it could also be seen as the chivalrous male motorist's defense against the dangers posed by female weakness. Rae related the tale of how two pioneers of the auto industry, Henry F. Leland and Charles F. Kettering, working for the Cadillac Motor Company, decided to tackle the problem of designing an automatic starter for gasoline cars. According to a story that has achieved the status of folklore in the history of the automobile in the United States, Byron Carter, designer of the Cartercar and a friend of Leland's, "went to the assistance of a lady whose car had stalled; he suffered a broken jaw when the crank handle kicked back, and gangrene subsequently caused his death."[30]

The story is interesting in several regards. First, it offers us a picture of a woman already at the wheel of a gasoline car, driving despite the lack of an automatic starter.[31] Second, it demonstrates that cranking was a risky business even for the most seasoned male motorist; Carter, after all, was an auto manufacturer. In relating the same story, Donovan noted that Carter's fatal accident had happened while he was holding the crank properly.[32] Third, the anecdote reveals the gender ideology associated with the act of starting a car. Carter might just as easily have been killed cranking his own car; somehow, though, the helpless and anonymous woman driver in this story is implicitly to blame. Another version of the story, related by Theodore F. McManus and Norman Beasley, clearly found the woman driver at fault. According to these authors, the crank kicked back and struck Carter in the jaw because, "unthinkingly, the strange woman had not retarded the spark."[33]

The necessity of cranking balky, stalled automobiles, particularly in bad weather or heavy traffic, surely encumbered men driving their own cars. Doubtless, men also sometimes forgot to retard the spark and did themselves some damage as the price of their absent-mindedness. In this story, however, the development of the self-starter appears not as an innovation based on convenience and safety for all drivers, male or female, but rather as a response to the perils presented by women's weakness and flightiness. The story thus conveys the impression that, left to themselves, men would not have bothered with such mechanical fripperies as the automatic starter but that they did so out of loyalty to gallant brother motorists who endangered themselves through chivalrous concern for less hardy (and potentially lethally incompetent) women drivers.

McManus and Beasley reported that the other Cadillac engineers scoffed at Kettering's idea of using an electric storage battery to start a gasoline engine. Perhaps responding in part to the widespread practice of identifying electricity in autos with feminine frailty, these other engineers predicted that an electric battery would be too weak and would cause the engine to knock.[34] Ignoring such reasoning, Kettering persisted, and by 1912 the Cadillac engineering department, led by Leland and paced by Kettering, had worked out the design of an electric starter; such devices were subsequently installed on Cadillac cars.[35] Within a year, according to Allan Nevins, electric self-starters had replaced cranks on one third of the models in the

Madison Square Garden auto show.[36] Moreover, the electrical battery used for starting made way for the development of an electrical system that could also be used for lighting, making night driving easier and safer.

The concept of gender as a defining category of auto technology, however, endured. Despite such meteoric success, the electric starter continued to be advertised as a feminine convenience. "WOMEN WON'T WORRY," said an ad for the Electric Auto-Lite Company, "if their cars are equipped with Auto-Lite starting motors and lighting generators. They are an open-sesame which removes the last obstacles from the pleasant and successful operation of gasoline motor cars by women."[37]

Electric vehicle technology had a significant and heretofore unacknowledged influence on the development of gasoline-powered cars, particularly as the idea that the latter vehicles were appropriate for all drivers regardless of gender became widely accepted. With some hesitancy, manufacturers of gas-powered vehicles began to include electrical systems and, more broadly, features associated with safety, comfort, and convenience, attributes deemed appropriate to women drivers. Innovations such as the self-starter doubtless served the interest of male drivers as well, helping to change driving from elite sport to popular transportation mode to everyday necessity for a broad middle-class constituency. Partly because of popular assumptions about proper masculinity and femininity, the American car culture took rather longer in coming than it might have. In other words, some of the very items that gasoline car manufacturers, dealers, and consumers had considered feminine frills, at length incorporated as standard automotive equipment, would transform the automobile from a quirky novelty useful only to those with enough leisure to enjoy an unreliable and physically taxing hobby to a tool of middle-class workers.

### CONCLUSION

What can we learn from this history lesson? New challenges confront us now—traffic congestion and environmental degradation. It seems to me that solving these problems will require a heightened consciousness of both the gendering of our technology and our landscape and a clearer idea of where women are and where they need to go.

Throughout the history of the automobile, innovations designed to enhance safety, comfort, convenience, and cleanliness, no matter how useful to all drivers and passengers, have been coded as feminine and touted as concessions to female frailty. At the same time we have tenaciously preserved those attributes of the automobile regarded as masculine, no matter how foolish and, at times, against heavy odds. As a proponent of automotive safety, Ralph Nader has often been treated as a killjoy whose masculinity is suspect. The gasoline shortages of the 1970s prompted the federal government to promote fuel conservation by reducing speed limits on the interstate highways, a law many motorists regarded as an insult to their manhood and the Reagan administration eagerly reversed in 1988. Denver's Brown Cloud has impelled the state of Colorado to experiment with mandatory use of cleaner-burning, oxygen-enriched fuels. Nobody actually *likes* air pollution, but, despite the almost universal desire to clean up the environment, many motorists worry that oxyfuel will damage their vehicles and result in a loss of power.

Whose power? What kind of power? In a recent episode of "Miami Vice," Don Johnson, playing detective Sonny Crockett, meets his bride, a rock singer played by Sheena Easton. As the embodiment of masculine cool, he drives a Ferrari Testarosa. As he opens the passenger door for her, she subverts his attempt to impress her with his vehicular macho, sneering, "So this is your Testosteroney, eh?"

The history of electric vehicle technology provides evidence for the contention that there is nothing inevitable about the masculinity of technology, even where the automobile, often considered a kind of metallic phallus, is concerned. However, as long as we continue to define drivers as he-men who are solely concerned with speed, distance, and display, to the detriment of safety, convenience, and cleanliness, we will be slow to design automobiles that get us where we want to go with a minimum of damage to ourselves and our world. Women as well as men will hesitate about adopting features deemed feminine, denigrating such innovations even when they prove valuable. If, however, we can develop a more pluralistic view of who uses motorcars, and how, and why, we might find ourselves imagining anew how to make our car culture cities livable for everyone.

## 7. Martin Wachs

# MEN, WOMEN, AND URBAN TRAVEL:
## THE PERSISTENCE OF SEPARATE SPHERES

### TRAVEL PATTERNS AS A GENDERED PHENOMENON

Metropolitan areas have been shaped by transportation systems, and daily life is structured by access and travel. There is a registered motor vehicle for every 1.3 people in the United States, and the average American household has twice as many automobiles as it has children under the age of twenty. Families order their daily lives on the basis of their car pools, business trips, or the time at which they must pick up grandma at the doctor's office. Cars are as much a part of our identity as homes and careers. They are, in fact, the critical link between our homes, jobs, and social lives. Marriages are proposed in cars, and children conceived in them. A parent tells a child about his or her birth by relating the story of a hurried trip to the hospital in a snow-storm, and the end of life is marked by the solemn ride to the cemetery.

It is surprising, then, that scholars have paid so little attention to the relationship between autos and gender. Since Simone de Beauvoir's *The Second Sex* and Betty Friedan's *The Feminine Mystique*, millions of pages have been written about the way gender has structured social relationships in the home, workplace, politics, education, and religious institutions, but very little has been said about gender differences in travel, despite the fact that mobility and travel are essential to fulfilling every role we play.

Looking closely, we begin to see that the automobile is one of the most clearly "gendered" aspects of American urban life. Throughout the auto's hundred-year history, women have experienced the relationship between the car and the city differently than have men, and the differences remain surprisingly persistent. The National Personal Travel Survey (NPTS) of 1983 showed, for example, that the average male licensed driver drove 13,962 miles per year, while the average female driver drove only 6,381 miles per year.[1] In her study, "Public Transportation and the Travel Needs of Women," Genevieve Giuliano examined many data sets from regional transportation studies and found that women traveled in total much less than men in most American cities, yet they used public transit more.[2] Geographers Susan Hanson and Ibopo Johnston reported that working women, depending upon the city under study, make journeys to work that vary from half to two-thirds the length of the average man's journey to work.[3] And even casual observation makes it clear that, when men and women travel together in cars, the man is far more likely to be the driver while the woman is in all probability in the passenger's seat.

I believe that urban planners and policymakers have generally misunderstood the differences between men's and women's travel patterns and have failed to grasp what those differences signify. It frequently has been suggested that the huge differences in travel between men and women will soon decrease or completely disappear because women are entering the labor force in larger numbers than ever before. When equality is achieved in employment, it is said, female travel patterns will more closely resemble male patterns. I do not believe that this is so, and my position is derived from a historical analysis of urban form and travel. The city was deliberately structured to place men and women in separate spheres, and, as the city adjusts over time to the universal mobility provided by the automobile, it is doing so in a social environment that ensures the continued existence of those separate spheres.

More than 70 percent of American men over the age of seventy are licensed to drive, while only 30 percent of women over seventy hold licenses. This huge difference is a residual of differences in access to autos fifty years ago and clearly is changing rapidly. More than 90 percent of both men and women between the ages of twenty and fifty are licensed to drive, and there is essentially no difference in licensing rates by gender among young and middle-aged Americans.[4] This data is used as evidence to indicate that gender will soon cease to be a factor affecting driving patterns, but that evidence is incomplete. Younger women, for example, though licensed in equal proportions to younger men, travel for different purposes, and they drive different distances. In a 1988 report to the Rockefeller Foundation, Sandra Rosenbloom has shown that women continue to make most shopping trips and family business trips, and men travel more for work and recreational purposes, even in households in which both spouses work.[5] I believe that these patterns have deep historical roots and that the form taken by the twentieth-century city reflects the gender division of space to at least as great an extent that it reflects efforts to conquer space through improved mobility. If this is so, women's increasing use of the automobile can continue to involve a pattern of social relationships based more on gender than on mobility.

For most of recorded history a majority of people worked at home. Most households produced food, shelter, and clothing under their own roofs, and merchants, blacksmiths, crafts people, and others who offered services for sale did so at their homes. This was true in the United States until well into the nineteenth century, but it began to change slowly as capitalism matured and the industrial revolution gained momentum. Factories reached sufficiently large scale that they required more workers than could be provided within a household and needed separate buildings and special locations, for example, providing access to waterways and railroad lines.

By 1850 a substantial proportion of the population—but still a minority—worked outside of the home. Virtually all of those workers were men, and most walked to work. The first metropolitan transit services, horse-drawn omnibuses, began in the 1830s through the 1850s, reflecting increases in travel to and from work and the need for economic transactions during the workday.[6] The availability of the first public transit services made it possible to consciously separate home and workplace in space, and it is clear that the separation that took place was based on ideological commitments that were gender-based.

In the United States during the last century, men and women pursued what historians have come to call "separate spheres." Man's arena was economic production and public life (politics and scholarship), and woman's sphere was the care of children, the nurturing of husband, the comfort and tranquility of home, and the moral guardianship of the family.[7] Feminist scholar Aileen Kraditor has called this "the cult of domesticity," and Barbara Welter has labeled it "the cult of true womanhood," and it led to the cultural and social definition of women's work and women's roles that were separate from men's, taking place at different times and different places. By the second half of the nineteenth century, home had become more than an economic unit of production. It slowly became a symbol of the ideal of goodness and morality, and it provided material comfort and status. Above all, the home had become the domain of women to a far greater extent than of men.

The technological advances in urban transportation that took place in the second half of the eighteenth century—from horse cars on rails to electric cable cars and streetcars, suburban railway systems, and, finally, the automobile—all made it possible for the workplace to be located at ever-increasing distances from the home. But it is important to remember that these technological advances took place in a culture that was dominated by the growing separation of men's and women's spheres. Men's workplaces and homes *could* be located apart because of advances in transport technology, while the *desirability* of residential suburbs removed from the business quarters of cities resulted from the cultural norm of separating man's economic sphere from woman's domestic sphere. And the rapid spread of low-density, single-family suburbs, which is often cited as a result of transportation technology, was equally a result of widespread preference for the separation of the economic sphere from the domestic sphere. This preference is clear, for example, in Charles Horton Cooley's explanation of the social role of public transportation in American life, which he wrote in 1884:

> Humanity demands that men have sunlight, fresh air, grass, and trees. It demands these things for the man himself and still more earnestly for his wife and children. On the other hand, industrial conditions require concentration. It is the office of urban transportation to reconcile these conflicting requirements; in so far as it is efficient it enables men to work in aggregates and yet to live in decent isolation. The greater its efficiency in speed, cheapness, and convenience, the greater the area over which a given industrial population may be spread.[8]

As Cooley's quotation illustrates, one hundred years ago Americans aspired to lower densities and larger individual homes, which were designed largely to be women's domain. Streetcar suburbs of low-density, single-family homes were built in most urban areas well before the arrival of the automobile, but they were available to only a small proportion of the population who could afford them. Those who used public transit had to pay roughly 20 percent of their average daily wages in fares. Thus, only the rich could live in the suburbs and commute by transit, while most people remained in the inner cities and walked to work.[9] This arrangement remained the case as urban densities increased precipitously around the turn of the century with the flood of migration from Europe. By 1910 population density on the east side of Manhattan reached nine hundred people per acre and was growing by 40 percent per decade.[10] In Pittsburgh steelworkers lived in crowded tenements in the shadow of the mills because they could afford neither elegant single-family suburban housing nor the cost of commuting.

Social reformers saw high-density urban living as the source of disease and maladjustment, and progressives called for suburbanization and the lowering of transit fares to permit it. Their distinctions between suburb and city perpetuated the notion of separate spheres, for they identified the crowded inner city with masculine images of commerce and vice while describing residential suburbs in terms associated with feminine virtues of domesticity. Feminists and settlement workers joined with real estate developers in calling for lower density and greater separation of home and workplace, which meant more transit lines and lower flat fares. Mrs. V. G. Simkhovitch, for example, a New York settlement house worker who was the only woman to address the first National Conference on City Planning in Washington, D.C., in 1909, joined with male speakers in advocating a lowering of transit fares, universal free transfers, and the construction of low-density residential suburbs as the solution to the urban crisis.[11] The new subway in New York was designed to operate with the flat fare and free transfers that still exist in order to promote suburbanization and lower densities by separating man's sphere from woman's sphere in space as well as function.

### WOMEN AND THE EARLY AUTOMOBILE

The automobile appeared before the new transit systems were fully built, bringing with it an enormous variety of social changes. As is well known, the auto was for a time the plaything of the rich, and, while at first one's class determined one's access to the auto, gender did so to a far lesser extent. Autos fit most naturally in low-density, spacious surroundings, and that meant the suburbs, which were women's domain during most of the workweek. The unconventional Mrs. August Belmont, who had already shocked society by marrying a Vanderbilt before that family was considered socially eligible and divorcing him when divorce was unheard of, also blazed the trail by appearing in public at the wheel of her new car in 1897. Later, she financially supported the National Woman's Party, one of several groups that used automobiles extensively in campaigns for women's rights and suffrage. Suffragists held auto parties in town squares at which speakers would arrive in automobiles draped with banners, carrying mobile podiums and literature to distribute to the assembled audiences. In 1912 the pugnacious and portly Mrs. Belmont made national headlines by leading a "monster parade" down Fifth Avenue in support of the feminist cause, and she did so at the front of an impressive "automobile contingent."[12]

Before the turn of the century and until the First World War there were women's auto races and automobile gymkhanas. Many books were published recounting cross-country automobile adventure trips by women, including one by Emily Post, who was accompanied by her son.[13] On January 2, 1900,

Florence E. Woods, at the age of seventeen, merited front-page headlines as she became the first woman to drive her automobile through New York's Central Park.[14] There is ample evidence that women could crank-start a car, replace flat tires, and disassemble carburetors as effectively as men. In her 1908 book about motoring, for example, Hilda Ward describes in detail how she patched tires, fixed fuel leaks, and corrected the functioning of cylinders that were misfiring.[15] Similarly, the daughter of Laura Ingalls Wilder, while herself motoring across Europe with a female companion, wrote to her father, Almanzo, giving him detailed instructions on what he should do to clear clogged fuel lines, including blowing into them and using the tire pump should exhaling fail.[16] She joked about how mechanically inept her father seemed to be, while the technical details of auto maintenance came so easily to her.

Society women before 1910 drove for recreation quite as freely as wealthy men, and were called "cheauffueses," but effects of the doctrine of separate spheres was evident in their travel patterns. Women drove downtown more rarely than men; typically, they stayed within their suburban communities, driving to social events, shops, and school functions. And, as Virginia Scharff has shown, the electric automobile was clearly marketed in recognition that woman's sphere gave rise to different automotive needs and patterns of use than did man's.[17]

### NATIONAL ADOPTION OF THE AUTOMOBILE

The first three decades of this century saw enormous political, economic, and social change, and the automobile was emerging in the midst of that change at an almost unbelievable pace. While it was still a phenomenon that turned heads in 1900, by 1910 there was one auto for every two-hundred sixty-five people in the United States. As mass production lowered the price of the automobile in relation to income, by 1917 the ratio stood at one car for every twenty-two people, and in 1919 it was reported to be one per sixteen people. The proportion of our population engaged in manufacturing, servicing, selling, and insuring automobiles had grown so large that the general prosperity that encouraged auto ownership was in large part explained on the basis of the growth of the automobile industry itself. By 1929, with new-car financing universally based on credit, we had one car for every six men, women, and children in the country, ownership extended to middle- and even lower-class families, and almost literally we could accommodate the entire population had it wished to take to the roads at once.[18] By now, as one author put it, a "new car means more to the clerk in the chain grocery store, who never owned one before, than it means to the president of the company whose garages have housed a dozen for years."[19]

As auto ownership grew by leaps and bounds, inner-city population densities declined, and suburbs grew in every metropolitan area. In response, transit use increased for work trips but declined dramatically for recreational and social trips, which were increasingly the domain of the automobile.

The enormous growth of the automobile industry in the first part of the twentieth century was the most important factor in the prosperity of the 1920s, yet economists and businessmen began to worry about the future. With the number of automobiles approaching the number of families in the United States, industry spokesmen and social commentators wondered aloud whether or not we were approaching "saturation" and whether that meant that the future demand for replacement automobiles would be much lower than the annual demand for "first cars," which had fueled the early growth of the industry. If so, would manufacturers be left with idle capacity in the coming years, and would the economic growth of the country be impaired?[20] The answer came as a conscious and vigorous effort by the industry to promote the ownership of more than one car per family, and the advertising of the 1920s clearly indicates that the second car was marketed to households whose first car was largely man's domain but whose second car would be used mostly by the woman of the house.

### GENDER STEREOTYPING AND THE AUTO IN THE TWENTIES

Given that the auto industry had decided to market cars to a growth market consisting primarily of women, it is interesting to examine the manner in which it both presented women and attempted to appeal to them. After all, during the First World War women had entered the work force in unprecedented numbers, and in 1920 they had won the right to vote. American women had gone to Europe to aid in the war effort by serving as ambulance drivers, and they had freed men for military service by working as truck and bus drivers at home. The image of the flapper was dominating the media, as girls bobbed their hair, wore short skirts, and were seen drinking and smoking in public. The 1920s are often described as a time of increasing female independence and assertiveness, and the automobile could be seen as a machine that could liberate women from their traditional roles and help break down the barriers between the separate spheres of gender.

But established values were also very strong, and the flapper was more a countercultural image than the typical housewife of the period. Indeed, opinion leaders seemed to have a greater need than ever to reinforce the traditional roles of women against the threats of change. They spoke out against the declining importance of family and home and transformed the very meaning of the liberation of women from a change in their roles to a release from drudgery by applying technology to the reinforcement of women's traditional roles.

Feminist scholars have shown that the introduction into the home of such technological devices as electric washing machines and dryers, vacuum cleaners, and electric and gas ovens and ranges resulted for most women in little or no decline in domestic responsibilities or even the time spent in household work. Households invested capital in acquiring these machines and subsequently became used to clothes more frequently laundered, rooms more thoroughly cleaned, and meals more elegantly prepared; women's chores became more mechanized but no less demanding.[21] Such was the case with the automobile, which permitted women to expand their domestic sphere to a much greater extent than it ever permitted them to abandon it.

In "The Emergence of the Modern Woman," Barbara Peterson, for example, describes the emergence of the modern woman in the 1920s in these terms:

> The decade of the 1920s wanted its women soft and pliant and condoned aggressiveness only in sex and sports. . . . In the era which glorified that "the business of America is business," every woman was told through the media and advertising that she was entitled to an automobile, radio, washing machine, vacuum cleaner and a "total electric kitchen." This was to be her true liberation; with her new leisure she could be a better mother and more beautiful wife.[22]

It is not surprising that in a world of jazz, rouge, and short skirts, women were deliberately portrayed in extremely traditional roles by those writing the ad copy for the automobile industry. A General Motors advertisement of the 1920s typical of hundreds of ads placed in magazines and newspapers, shows a middle-class woman picking flowers with her children; their car is visible in the background. The text reads:

> "When I was a child it was easy for mothers to keep in touch with their children," says a woman in Illinois. "Today the members of the family must make a real effort to keep united. I thought a great deal about this as my children began to grow up. I decided that the most important thing I could possibly do would be to plan ways in which they and I could have good

times together. My husband agreed, and for that reason we bought a second automobile, since he had to use his car in getting back and forth to business. I can't begin to tell you of the happiness it has given us—picnics together, expeditions for wildflowers in the spring, and exploration parties to spots of historic interest. It's our very best investment. It has helped the children and me to keep on being pals." Every year thousands of families decide that a second car is a saver of time, a great contribution to family happiness and health.[23]

The text suggests that traditional roles may be harder to achieve than in the past, but it glorifies them and recommends an automobile as the path to their attainment.

In a long series of advertisements that ran throughout the 1920s the Chevrolet was portrayed in each using a different appeal to the traditional feminine role model. One advertisement, entitled "Where Town and Country Meet," states that a Chevrolet enables the city housewife to buy eggs, vegetables, poultry, and small fruits, direct from the farmer's wife, fresh and cheap.[24] Another ad, entitled "Shop With a Chevrolet," begins with the words: "Chevrolet Utility Coupe is proving a wonderful help to many housekeepers, more than paying its low cost of upkeep through economies of time and money saved in cash and carry shopping."[25] Another ad in the series is entitled "See the Children Safely to School" and starts with the text: "Why worry about the safety of your little ones on the highways or crossing city streets on the way to school?" while a similar ad is entitled "Motor to Church in Comfort."[26]

In response to threats of new economic, social, and political freedom for women during the 1920s, the automobile increasingly became a means by which woman's sphere of home and family was reinforced. Women's opportunities to use the automobile became more and more limited through symbolism and social convention, as their actual physical access to the auto increased.

The popular literature of the 1920s began to present exaggerated descriptions of a women's world as compared with men's, and the automobile constituted a central part of the imagery. In a widely quoted treatise, *The Suburban Trend*, Harlan Paul Douglass advocated that decentralization and suburbanization continue as the solution to urban ills, though he was well aware of the extent to which suburban life differentially affected men and women. He noted, for example, that, in several suburbs where commuters were surveyed, women constituted only between 8 and 15 percent of the commuters to the central city. He described women's role as driving their husbands to and from the train stations, driving children to school, and driving to shopping locations.[27]

While women who drove in the first decades of the century were assumed to have at least some interest in the mechanical properties of automobiles, during the 1920s the mechanical traits of cars came to be associated more with man's domain. Women were increasingly important as a market for automobiles, but it was asserted that they had little interest in the engines, brakes, or tires and instead were devoted to the properties of cars that were more associated with feminine roles: color, styling, upholstery, and comfort. An article in *Automobile Topics*, a trade journal read by auto dealers, stated: "One of the first things a woman thinks of when the purchase of a new car is considered, is whether the color of the upholstering will harmonize with her personality, coloring, and clothes." The article goes on to state that if she thinks the car will not complement her looks, the salesman "might as well try to sell his cars to an Eskimo."[28]

In a popular book on consumers, Walter Pitkin reported on a study that showed that in 1929 men were the principal buyers of 59 percent of the automobiles sold, while women had become the principal buyers of 41 percent of all new cars. Despite women's increasing influence on car purchases, in a section entitled "Woman, the Economic Imbecile," he quotes Alice Hamilton's column from the *New York World Telegram* to describe how women go about selecting automobiles:

> When a woman views a motor car and looks as if she were pondering weighty matters the automobile dealer grows elated. "Ah," he thinks, "she is considering our wonderful new floating power. She is enchanted by our full pressure engine lubrication.
>
> That puzzled look is deceptive. She is not thinking of free-wheeling, of automatic clutches. She is wondering if the car is sufficiently impressive to serve as a frame for her as she sits, viewed through the glass by passing admiring multitudes. She considers how her foot, ankle, and calf will look as she steps smartly down upon the running board. . . . Does this fawn gray upholstery go with most of her clothes?[29]

As the lines between men's and women's roles regarding the automobile were drawn increasingly sharply in the 1920s to limit woman's place, the

---

stereotype of the woman driver as indecisive, erratic, and unsafe became ever more common. In a study of women drivers, Michael Berger, for example, quotes one writer who stated in the *New Statesman* in 1927 that women "do not very commonly possess the nervous imperturbability which is essential to good driving. They seem always to be a little self-conscious on the road, a little doubtful about their own powers. They are too easily worried, too uncertain of their own right of way, too apt to let their emotions affect their manipulation of the steering wheel."[30]

Women's domestic roles are frequently described in the literature of the 1920s as more suited to their temperament and motor abilities than such mechanical tasks as driving a car. Walter Pitkin, for example, states that women differ from men in motor ability, primarily in that "boys and men on the average greatly exceed women and girls in the ability to manipulate mechanical contrivances," and, as a consequence, "women shrink from acting when facing a crisis," "work by fits and starts" when under high pressure, and work consistently only when there is no pressure. Consequently, Pitkin concludes, women are overcautious, they make poorer drivers than men, and "they cause accidents on the part of their fellow drivers." He goes so far as to state that "owing to their inferior motor outlets, women succeed best in outer behavior in relatively simple motor activities, such as sweeping, washing, and ironing" rather than in more complex motor tasks like driving.[31]

The 1920s were the decade in which the automobile fully assumed the functions it has in today's society, with most households having at least one automobile that is central to their economic and social lives. Yet, despite the increasing universality of automobile transportation and the prospect that women and men might have equal access to autos by each having one, this period was also characterized by a solidification of gender roles with respect to cars. Women were clearly defined as more restricted in their access to autos, as their roles as homemaker and nurturer of children were reinterpreted and applied to their status as automobile operators. Their mechanical competence and driving skill were portrayed as limited in order to maintain social boundaries on women's access to transportation for fear that otherwise women might use this access to step beyond their traditional sphere of activities.

### GENDER AND THE AUTOMOBILE SINCE WORLD WAR II

The process of suburbanization and expanding motorization of the population, and their reinforcement of the doctrine of separate spheres, were severely interrupted for fully fifteen years by the Depression and World War II. First, economic distress and then shortages, rationing, and military service brought great discontinuities in families' patterns of residential location and travel. But after the war Americans resumed the previous pattern of suburbanization with renewed commitment, as if to make up for lost time. Suburbs grew more rapidly than ever, and autos became the nation's primary mode of commuting as highway building and single-family housing subsidy programs reinforced our shared commitment to this pattern. Home remained the separate sphere of women, and, in keeping with that image, the design of suburban residential tracts stressed built-in cabinets, versatile kitchen appliances, and the provision of play areas for children.[32] Suburbs were still designed as dormitories for downtown workplaces, and freeways were built to replace commuter railroads and trolley lines as connections to the traditional downtowns. In *The Feminine Mystique*, Betty Friedan criticized the physical environment of the suburbs nearly as vigorously as she did the anachronistic cult of domesticity, which had been carried to new extremes in postwar America.

### THE NATURE OF RECENT CHANGES IN WOMEN'S SOCIAL ROLES

During the past two decades it has become obvious that the place of women in the economic life of America has been changing substantially. While some would credit the women's movement for increasing participation of women in the labor force, the changes might be more attributable to a transformation of the economy, as services, information processing, finance, and retailing have eclipsed manufacturing and heavy industry as the sources of most employment. Because work in these types of jobs does not require downtown locations, and the labor force is now increasingly concentrated in the suburbs, a growing proportion of all jobs have come to be concentrated in the suburbs. Indeed, the 1970 census showed that more people traveled to work from suburb to suburb than from suburb to downtown or entirely within the central city.

The automobile has become the overwhelmingly dominant mode of commuting, and urban transit systems have steadily lost passengers despite major infusions of public subsidies and the construction of new rail systems in several cities. Service and retailing establishments located in the suburbs to take advantage of lower-cost land, proximity to their markets, and proximity to a low-priced labor force, consisting increasingly of suburban women. In the early 1990s the suburbs are home to a variety of families, many of which do and many of which do not match the traditional stereotypes. Most suburban women are in the labor force, and many single-parent, female-headed households reside in the suburbs alongside two-parent households. Suburban households often have as many automobiles as they have licensed drivers, and yet differences in roles and travel patterns persist as an echo of the past. Women still make the vast majority of the household's trips for the purposes of shopping, and taking children to school, doctors, dentists, and childcare, and their work trips are predictably shorter than men's in part because the demand of these household roles persists and must be considered as women contemplate employment alternatives.

## CONCLUSION

For a hundred years we have associated the city with male characteristics. Cities epitomize assertiveness through their economic activity, intellectual creativity, and centrality in world affairs. Simultaneously, we have associated the suburbs with woman's sphere. We have thought of the suburbs as places of domesticity, passivity, repose, closeness to nature, and spiritual values.[33] Scholars have frequently noted this dichotomy when describing the place of the home and house in American society. They have noted less often the central role that transportation has played in both creating and maintaining this dichotomy and the utility of travel data for measuring its extent.

By permitting the spatial separation of home and workplace within the bounds of reasonable expenditures of time and cost, public transit and the automobile encouraged cities to develop spatially in response to the image of separate spheres that was so central to American culture. And current studies of transportation patterns provide us with measures of the extent to which that image still dominates family and economic life. The automobile did not create the separation of gender spheres, nor has any technological innovation been sufficiently powerful to lessen the influence of this cultural norm in American life.

Women have entered the work force in very large numbers but still make work trips that are on average substantially shorter than men's. Whether they are working or not, women make many more trips for the purpose of "serving passengers," for example, delivering someone else to a destination of importance to that person. While women today have nearly universal access to automobiles and the labor market, they continue to inhabit the domestic sphere and their travel patterns reflect this.

Lower-paid workers have always made shorter work trips than higher-paid ones. Poorer workers a century ago lived near their places of employment because the cost of transport would deplete their earnings if they moved farther away. Today we find that women live closer to their jobs than do employed men in the same households. There are three factors that, taken together, might explain this phenomenon. First, women are substantially lower paid than men. While more women are in the labor force than ever before, they tend to hold the same types of jobs as they did in the 1950s. Women are overrepresented in what is called the secondary work force, consisting of part-time or seasonal workers, and are concentrated in job classifications in which the vast majority of employees are women, especially in clerical and sales work. These positions pay lower wages than the positions traditionally held by men, and it is argued by some that women select jobs closer to home because searching farther away yields no wage advantage among the jobs for which many women qualify. Second, women might work closer to home because the recent suburbanization of service and retail activity has resulted in "women's" jobs being more evenly distributed across the urban landscape than the professional and technical jobs that are more typically held by men. In other words, women are filling the jobs that moved to the suburbs in the first place in order to take advantage of a proximate low-paid work force, and those jobs involve shorter commuting distances for just that reason. Third, women work closer to home and drive shorter distances in part because, even as they enter the work force, they retain their family obligations as nurturers, shoppers, and homemakers. Because of the time commitments involved in these activities, and the need to be nearer to children in case of, for example, a school emergency call, women choose work locations in order to minimize travel and maximize productive uses of their time.[34]

In her 1980 study on "Masculine Cities and Feminine Suburbs," Susan Saegert has written that men who enter the work force rely on their wives for support, and few male workers have no wives to rely upon.[35] Even as women enter the economic world of work in record numbers and drive cars in record numbers, they retain the traditional role for which the suburbs were designed in the first place. The structure of suburban life—the low population densities and the greater distances that must be traversed—continue to limit women's full entry into what has traditionally been man's sphere, which is not surprising since they were built with distinct gender roles in mind. Surveys have shown that men continue to prefer suburban living, but working women who value both their family roles and their work have reported that they find it easier to juggle their dual responsibilities in urban rather than suburban environments, where child care, shopping, and services are available at shorter distances from the home. It is not surprising that this is the case, since women are now exerting extra effort and energy to blend roles that were consciously planned to take place in spatially separated locations.

Many people have predicted that in the near future women's travel patterns will come to resemble men's, but that prediction has been based mostly on the simple expectation that differences between men and women's travel were primarily derived from their different levels of participation in the work force. If, however, we accept travel patterns to be a reflection of a much broader pattern derived from the cultural norm of domesticity and we note that women's domestic roles are persistent because the cultural stereotyping of gender roles is persistent, it follows that women's travel patterns will continue to differ substantially from those of men. The family with two cars and two workers is not necessarily a family in which men's and women's roles are equalized. Our society's expectations regarding women's and men's roles gave rise to the land-use transportation system that we have today, and, while evolution of transportation technology and urban form have changed travel patterns in marginal ways, it remains to be seen whether America is ready to adopt new models of gender roles. Travel patterns of men and women will not create those changes in cultural norms but, rather, will be an indicator as to whether or not they have occurred.

# PART 3
## THE AUTOMOBILE
## AND DESIGN

*In this part five authors address ways in which the automobile has affected architecture and urban form and concepts of modernity and luxury in design thought. Different aspects of the car—as a designed object, a vehicle from which we perceive the city, and convenient, personal transport—have played roles in creating and transforming building types and urban spaces and the car itself. Many of these changes are obvious, but, as several authors show, the evolution rarely has been linear, and the cultural and social implications are often complex.*

*David Gebhard, an architectural historian, traces the evolution of the garage in relation to the single-family house. Noting the complex and nonlinear development of the type, he attributes its one-step-forward, one-step-back history to the struggle between functional and symbolic considerations. The basic options and issues of domestic automobile storage appeared early in the century; the succession of a completely separate structure by the semidetached, then completely attached, garage hidden away at the*

*back of the lot or pushed forward to serve as a main entrance. The rich preferred auto courts with multiple car garages, often disguised as picturesque outbuildings, while middle-class home owners could order prefabricated structures to assemble themselves. Few major innovations occurred until the postwar appearance of the open carport. Its popularity did not last long, however, since its openness excluded many of the functions of earlier garages, such as storage, workshop, laundry space, and, most important, easy conversion into an extra room. Today's norm, the three-car, attached garage, continues the pattern of accommodating practical and aesthetic needs.*

*Drummond Buckley expands on this formal history by exploring the social implications of architectural changes in the garage and house. He argues that the garage's move from the backyard to the front of the site indicated a significant change in leisure and domestic activities. Instead of sitting on the front porch to socialize with passing neighbors, families retreated to more privatized spaces taking*

drives in their automobiles and enclosing their backyards as a se-
cluded extension of the house. The
configuration of house plans reflected this change by moving public
rooms to the rear of the house,
focusing on the backyard, with bedrooms facing the street. The garage
served as an additional barrier, a
buffer zone between the domestic
realm and the public realm of the
street. As automobiles extended the
range of each family's work and social contacts, the importance of the
neighborhood as a community
lessened, and the front porch disappeared along with the front yard
and the sidewalk culture it represented. Buckley concludes that, although other technologies such as
the telephone, radio, and television
also affected these social changes,
the automobile radically altered
American concepts of the house and
its relationship to the surrounding
community.

Architectural historian Richard
Longstreth traces the ups and
downs of a new building type produced by the automobile, the drive-
in shopping center. Although the
city's earlier acceptance of the car
ensured its role as a hotbed of experimentation in auto-related architecture, drive-in markets were
the first buildings to provide retail
services based on concepts of land
use and interior space derived from
the automobile. By replacing the
prototype of street-facing shop
fronts with a forecourt for off-street
parking, these markets recognized
that convenient automobile access
to one-stop shopping was a key
component in increasingly
motorized lives. These markets not
only attracted the attention of both
conventional and modernist architects but also became a popular for-
mula for retail development across
the country. Ironically, by this time
Angelenos had embraced new retail
formats, such as monumental supermarkets and linear storefronts,
as along the Miracle Mile, which
emphasized street frontality, while
still offering parking in the rear.
Longstreth shows that these configurations represented even more
complex responses to the automobile, providing traditional metropolitan images whose street-front
drama was best perceived from a
moving car, while still satisfying
the need for convenience.

In his chapter, automobile industry historian James J. Flink explores the custom coach-built
luxury car as a status symbol, examining both the technological advances that allowed production of
spectacular and unique auto bodies
and the social trends that led
people to seek out automobiles that
would constitute the ultimate in
conspicuous consumption.

*Alan Hess, a historian and architect, also comments on the connection between image and design, arguing that postwar automobile design and roadside architecture developed a common vocabulary of forms and symbols that interpreted rapid cultural changes of the period to a mass audience. The exaggerated tail fins, floating cantilevers, and angled glass walls visible in a 1959 Chevy or in Ship's Coffee Shops presented an aesthetic that evolved by exploiting rather than avoiding the dictates of the commercial marketplace. Architects and auto stylists transformed the world of jet planes, television, and the atomic bomb into symbolic but communicable images; floating geometries, flames, lines, and starbursts, in disjointed combinations. Architecturally, the apparently incompatible forms of mobile car and immobile building were brought together into a single, continuous space of glass walls and dramatically minimal supports. Indoor and outdoor space eased the transition from driver to pedestrian to diner and back. Hess claims that, although design theorists of the period attacked these products as inappropriate, bizarre, and unfunctional, their expressive styling functioned as poetic metaphors for their time.*

# *8.* David Gebhard

## THE SUBURBAN HOUSE AND THE AUTOMOBILE

In 1911, the New York journal *American Architect* published a volume with the title *Garages: Country and Suburban.*[1] Though the automobile was still new, the editors of the journal were openly enthusiastic about this new machine and its impact on suburban residential design: "The coming of the automobile has introduced a new phase into the architect's daily work. The smart, shining, highly developed machine, quick, accurate and efficient, full of the very essence of modernity . . . seems to require more 'chic' accommodations than did even the smartest horse and vehicles of the last generation."[2]

The history of the single-family suburban dwelling, and its accommodations for the car, has been looked upon generally as a simple, linear, step-by-step evolution from the late nineteenth-century suburban horse stable to the open carports of the 1950s, which showed off the family's gleaming "chrome-plated bathtub." As often is the case in the history of building types in the nineteenth and twentieth centuries, actual historical "tales" are usually far more complex than is usually realized; it is especially true in regard to the on-again, off-again battle between purely functional considerations and symbolic/aesthetic implications of the suburban garage.[3]

The story of the residential garage starts out in the early 1900s in a seemingly uncomplicated, pragmatic fashion. At first the place for the automobile was within or attached to the horse stable and barn, but by the mid-1900s it had been separated and had become a distinct building type in its own right. Clients and architects were intrigued by the numerous approaches that could be taken not only to the design of the garage itself but equally to how it could be located in relation to the house and its landscaped grounds. The literature of the years 1905 through 1918 is filled with discussions of siting, fitting the driveway and the garage into the overall landscape design of the site, and, of course, the many possibilities of imagery that could be used in garage design.[4] In addition, there were a series of "practical" considerations to be dealt with and responded to. Questions of a safe place for storage of the car, insurance, and the new and growing local building regulations pertaining to the garage and its location were addressed.[5]

By the early 1920s there was a wide variety of solutions "on the market" for the siting and design of the garage. These solutions varied according to the nature of the dwelling, whether it was a true country house and estate, an upper-middle-class suburban house, or a more modest middle-class speculative dwelling. Solutions for these three suburban building types ranged from the completely separate complex, which might be realized elaborately on a country estate, to a one- or two-car garage attached directly to a middle-class suburban dwelling.[6]

In the third decade of this century the garage was frequently coupled in the client's and architect's minds with the kitchen and bathroom as an essential, practical, machine-like element that was fully incorporated, akin to plumbing and heating, into the dwelling. In this atmosphere of rational planning, the ideal garage was to be situated at the family entrance to the house.[7] And since the automobile was perceived of as *the* prevalent symbol of the machine age, there was no reason for it to be hidden away. Thus, by the end of the 1930s, the open carport was increasingly incorporated into modern image houses, ranging from the designs of Frank Lloyd Wright's Usonian houses to innumerable examples of the popular Streamline Moderne style. The very term carport, which came into popular jargon in 1939, bespeaks the essence of the Streamline Moderne—the storage place for the car thought of in terms of the nautical streamlined ship.

After World War II the carport fully caught on for upper-middle-class as well as for modest spec houses. The carport often was maneuvered so that it became both the private as well as the public entrance to the house. The visible presence of the car became a plug-in component of the house: It was a room on wheels, an enclosed capsule, that provided the connective link between the stationary element, the house and its gardens, and the world beyond—the supermarket, parking lot, or drive-in theater.[8]

If one considers what geographic region of the country should provide the "perfect" history of the garage and its evolution, one would normally turn to southern California and its dominant metropolis, Los Angeles. The quick, open, and passionate adoption of the automobile in southern California indeed provides us with an excellent case history of how the automobile was absorbed and housed within suburbia. Surprisingly, though, Los Angeles was not the locale that in an experimental, avant-garde sense, ever led the way. In every instance, ranging from the attached garage to the later carport, the initial "invention" occurred elsewhere in the country and, after the new innovation had entered the scene, then and only then was it taken up in California's Southland. Los Angeles' quick adoption of new approaches to the auto, the garage, and the suburban residence coincided with its taking over of other automobile-induced innovations gathered from outside the region— drive-in theaters, drive-in supermarkets, and freeways.

Before turning to the specific case history of the development of the suburban garage in Southern California and within Los Angeles, we should be aware of several other aspects of the design history of the garage during its earliest years. With this material as a background, we will be in a better position to understand and to appraise Los Angeles' response to the car within the suburban scene. We should not only be aware of the detached stable and its eventual evolution into the free-standing garage but we must also plug in the late nineteenth-century fondness for the porte-cochere, the carriage vehicular entrance, into the dwelling.

The symbolic implication of the porte-cochere went far beyond simple utility. It created a new vehicular entrance into the house, which in many instances openly competed with or even supplanted the usual pedestrian front porch entrance. In many of the larger suburban or country houses, the porte-cochere emerged symbolically as the entrance of prestige into the dwelling. In many instances in more modest middle-class dwellings, a porte-cochere was attached to the house purely as an image; no actual entranceway into the house was provided. In relationship to the twentieth-century automobile garage, the porte-cochere by far had more of a symbolic import than the detached stable.

The Chicago architect Charles E. White, Jr., who wrote frequently about the suburban garage, remarked in a 1911 article, "Housing the Automobile," that

> keeping pace with automotive growth, modern garages and garage appa-
> ratus are up to a very high standard of practical utility. There isn't much
> room left for improvement . . . every conceivable kind of plan and every
> form of construction has been tried out, so that now garage design is more
> or less standardized.[9]

White laid down for his readers three basic solutions for the suburban garage: (1) the completely separate, detached garage, (2) the semi-attached garage, and (3) the attached garage. For his illustration of these different types, he employed examples designed by three of his Chicago colleagues: a detached garage by Frank Lloyd Wright, a semi-attached garage by Spencer and Powers, and an attached garage by George W. Maher. According to White, the advantage of the detached garage occurred at both ends of the economic spectrum: for the large estate, an independent complex of garages, stables, utility buildings, and servant's quarters, and, for the family of limited budget, "nothing is better than one of the little portable garages built at the factory and shipped in sections to the owner, who can erect the building himself with the aid of a few bolts and screws." He emphasized that portable garages of this sort were best built away from the dwelling since, more likely than not, they had little to contribute to the aesthetic quality of the house and its landscaped grounds.[10]

The garage semi-attached to the house via a porch, pergola, trellis, or wall, according to White, had not only the functional advantage of proximity, but it then could add appreciably to the aesthetic impact of the landscape and the dwelling. The Minneapolis firm of Purcell, Feick, and Elmslie often used a "breezeway" to connect the house and the garage, as in their 1912–13 country house for E. W. Decker at Holdridge, Minnesota, or in their suburban, upper-middle-class house for E. S. Hoyt in 1913 in Red Wing, Minnesota.[11] In his 1911 article White illustrated an example from the work of Spencer and Powers (McCready House, Oak Park, Illinois, 1907) as an excellent solution for the semi-attached garage.[12]

Another visually effective way of attaching the house to the garage was to connect the two buildings together by a wall pierced by an arch opening or a pergola and to have the driveway pass through and under these connected coverings. This arrangement not only tied the two units together, but it went a step further and suggested that one was entering the private realm of the house through a traditional porte-cochere.[13]

In a 1917 article, "The Garage in the House," John Taylor Boyd, Jr. noted: "No new feature such as this typical twentieth-century device [the automobile] can come into our lives without making a place for itself, causing readjustments in our scheme of things."[14] One of our "readjustments" to the car was "to make the garage a part of the house."[15] The typical approach was to design the fully attached garage so that it read as a low, secondary extension of the house but equally it could be contained within the body of the house or placed under the house in the basement. The arguments advanced by Boyd for the attached garage covered both functional considerations to "be located where the owner . . . may reach it easily without going outdoors in bad weather," and aesthetic considerations (the average house would "gain immensely in appearance if [it could] be stretched out by adding a low garage building.")[16]

The drive-through garage, with its advantage of not having to back out the car, had come onto the scene in free-standing garages before 1910.[17] In the very early 1910s this fixture was taken up by the Prairie School Chicago architect Walter Burley Griffin. In his 1912 Melson House at Mason City, Iowa, the double drive-through garage was placed at the front of the house, and it served as the family's principal entrance to the dwelling.[18]

The carport also emerged at this time, although this solution of car accommodation was not to become a fashionable solution until the years after the Second World War. Again Griffin was in the forefront with his 1909 open-carported Sloan house in Elmhurst, Illinois.[19] One approaches the entrance to this house via one of the two ribbons of the concrete driveway, and, after reaching the carport, the visitor turns right to enter the house. The service area to the rear was entered by going through the carport. Another example of the early occurrence of the carport was in the 1913 Lockwood Lake dwelling in northern Wisconsin, designed by the Minneapolis firm of Purcell, Feick, and Elmslie. They slipped in a carport as a porch extension of the dwelling, and they labeled it the "Auto Space."

The primacy of the automobile as the one and only mode of entrance into the larger country houses was firmly established by the mid-1900s. The well-defined entrance auto court formed an essential architectural and landscape feature of these designs, especially within the popular Mediterranean and Georgian country houses of designers like Charles Platt, Mellor, Meigs, Howe, Dwight James Baum, and their contemporaries.[20]

Whether conceived of as a separate or semi-attached building or as part of the dwelling, there were two approaches that could be taken to the design of the garage. Either the garage could be openly declared for what it was—in a sense, glorying in and drawing attention to the new machine—or its presence could be hidden. The receptacle for the auto could be an independent unit, posed as a picturesque outbuilding in the garden (in some grand examples, as the illusion of a distant village) or it could be created as a nonbuilding completely encompassed within a pergola, trellis and vegetation, or hidden within a hillside.[21] A similar approach could be taken if the garage was semi- or fully attached to the house. If the garage directly faced the street, its entrance could be asserted, or it could mischievously hide behind a door designed as a portion of a wood wall (with window and all); it could pose as a treillage wall, or it could be recessed far back within a porch or pergola structure. If there were enough room on the suburban site, the driveway might lead around the house so that the garage doors faced the side or the

rear. With this half-hidden approach, the garage wing would appear as simply a traditional wing of the house.

From its inception in the early 1900s the garage was pressed into many other uses, ranging from storage for boats, to a work or garden shop, and as a play area for the children on a rainy day. There were complaints, even in the 1900s, that the demands on the space of the garage were such that the poor car, for which all of this supposedly had been built, might end up forlornly parked outside.

The purely functional considerations for the garage in its early years were both different from and the same as later considerations of the 1920s into the 1960s. Distinct during the early years were the concerns for being able to service the car and for its safe storage. Maintaining and tinkering with this new machine simply to keep it in running order could demand a virtual service garage, with hoists, oil pits, work benches, and space for all the needed tools. Since service stations and auto garages were none too plentiful in the first two decades of the century, an underground tank for gasoline storage was frequently provided, even in modest, middle-class establishments. These tanks, plus the general feeling that the car posed a real danger from explosion and fire, meant that the ideal garage building should be as nearly fireproof as possible, and, if it were attached to the house, it should be separated from the dwelling by a concrete or hollow tile wall and a metal-clad fire door.

Purely mechanical inventiveness abounded in these first years, ranging from varied methods of heating and lighting to the use of motorized turntables that could be placed within the garage or in the drive area to the front.[22] By the late 1910s all of the garage door types we are now familiar with had come into existence: hinged, accordion, horizontal track, and overhead (sectional or single) types. Thus, Charles E. White, Jr., was correct when he observed in 1911 that "there isn't much room for improvement"[23] as far as the garage, parking, and its driveway were concerned.

In its first years the designers of garages were highly inventive when it came to the use of materials and structure. Their resourcefulness was due to the notion that the garage should be fireproof, but it was also an outcome of the receptivity at the time to the use of new materials and structural forms. In his little book, *Making A Garage* (1913), A. Raymond Ellis discusses how the ideal garage might be made of poured concrete, concrete block, or hollow terra-cotta tile.[24] For those who did not wish to go to the expense of concrete or terra-cotta, there was also, Ellis points out, the "Pipe Frame Garage":

**FIGURE 8.2**

*Advertisement, Dellamore turntable, Pasadena, California, 1914.*

"This construction consists of a framework of pipes . . . set in a base of concrete, and the walls are covered with wire and mortar."[25] The dramatic mechanical improvement of the automobile in the 1920s and the development of service stations so that gasoline need no longer be stored at home meant that normal wood-stud construction could replace the earlier fireproof materials. Thus, when Dorothy and Julian Olney outlined the approach to structure in their 1931 *The American Home Book of Garages*, they assumed that the structure would be wood frame, and the only major questions had to do with whether one sheathed it in brick, stone, stucco, or wood.[26]

California participated in these early years of garage design before 1918, realizing all of the varied and inventive approaches. In 1903–6, when Bertram G. Goodhue planned his Mediterranean country estate, "El Fureidas," for J. W. Gillespie in Montecito, he laid out the auto court as the courtyard entry to the house.[27] By the end of the 1920s the entrance auto court had become a standard item for California's upper-middle-class suburban and country houses—regardless of whether the imagery was Mediterranean, Spanish, English, French, or Anglo-American Colonial. At the other end of the economic spectrum, a middle-class homeowner did not need to order a prefab garage from as far away as Sears Roebuck and Company in Chicago or an Aladdin ready-cut garage from Bay City, Michigan. He or she could pick up the telephone and order one from Pacific Ready-Cut Homes, Inc., at 1300 South Hill Street in downtown Los Angeles.[28] From Pacific Ready-Cut the homeowner could obtain garages whose designs might convey a Mission Revival style or perfectly complement the rustic wood-shingled image of a California bungalow.

Several southern California geographic peculiarities ended up encouraging the preeminence of the automobile in relation to the suburban house. One of these had to do with the hilly terrain in many areas of the Los Angeles basin, which, as Lillian Ferguson noted in 1916, led to "the practice of placing the garage before the home located upon the hilly lot."[29] A second influencing factor was the general tendency in the design of suburban subdivisions of all types to eliminate the traditional eastern and midwestern alley. Each dwelling then had to have its own driveway leaving from the street, and, while many of these led in a conventional fashion to separate garages situated near the rear of the lot, increasingly, it was argued that it was much more sensible to bring the garage as far forward toward the street as possible (considering the cost of a long driveway, the garden space that would be lost, and the convenience to the owners). Even the negative aspects of the smell of gasoline and exhaust easily could (supposedly) be dealt with cosmetically in the Southland. According to a 1921 article in *Touchstone* magazine, "Californians do not fear its [the odors associated with the car] close proximity, for it is an easy matter for them to conceal its presence, aromatically as well as aesthetically, with roses, honeysuckle, jasmine and many other fragrant vines."[30]

In a 1916 *Sunset* magazine article, "What is Home without a Garage?" Lillian Ferguson illustrates how quickly California took over many of the basic garage types established in the East and Midwest, ranging from the free-standing garage to one placed within the house.[31] The free-standing garage built into the hillside effectively posed as a traditional gatekeeper's cottage at the entrance to the steep hillside driveway of architect John Parkinson's own 1906 house in Los Angeles. Mead and Requa in their 1915 Shrader House in Hollywood, and George Washington Smith in his own 1916 house in Montecito attached their garages to the service areas—a solution often repeated in the 1920s and 1930s.

The San Diego and Los Angeles architect Irving J. Gill played the entire field in his pre-1920s solutions to the suburban house, its site and its garage. In the South Pasadena Miltimore House (1911), Gill took the driveway under one of the handsome pergola structures, which posed as an open porte cochere that extended across the front of the house to the front entrance. In the Lee House (1911) and the Teats House (1911–12), both in San Diego, the garages were attached to and were placed right at the street front of the houses. In the famed Dodge House, Hollywood (1915–16), the mission-arched porte cochere front entrance facing to the side, away from the street, was the entry for both guests and the family. At the rear of the house Gill injected a three-car drive-through garage between the servants' wing and the elevated, out-of-doors swimming pool. Finally, in the design for the unbuilt Olmstead House in San Diego (1911), a pergola (as a carport) was situated in front, directly connected to and adjacent to the front entrance.

The receptivity to the car of California bungalows of the period 1900 through the 1910s represented at best a mixed affair. In the large-scale, upper-middle-class "ultimate bungalows" of Charles and Henry Greene and others, circular drives, porte cochere, and beautifully designed separate garage buildings were carefully integrated into the landscaped site. But in the average modest spec or pattern-book, single-floor bungalows with their narrow forty- or fifty-foot-wide lots, the garage was almost always separate and placed near the rear of the property. The drive itself frequently was planned to emphasize one's entry via the car by having the front entrances to the house approached off the driveway, taking the driveway under and through an attached pergola entrance, or creating a simplified form of an extended porch—acting loosely as a diminutive porte cochere.

Probably Los Angeles's most flamboyant acknowledgment of the auto and its relation to an upper-middle-class suburban dwelling in the second decade of this century was the Japanesque Bernheimer House (Franklin M. Small, 1913), which was set on top of one of the south-facing Hollywood hills. The house was sited in the center of an oval, 360-degree drive that completely surrounded the house, and the curve of the drive was repeated through a succession of terraced walls descending down the hillside.

The unreserved acceptance of the car in the post–World War I years, as an essential feature of the suburban house, was eloquently summed up in Theodore Baer's comment in the September, 1922, issue of *House Beautiful*: "my heart is architecturally singing with delight at the host of fresh new problems the garage has opened up."[32] By 1920 the innovative phase of the suburban garage was over; the task of the designer was to study how the garage could be fully integrated into the suburban site and the imagery of the dwelling. Henry W. Rowe wrote in 1927: "The commonplace garage is fortunately being supplanted by a unit of grace and charm, one that takes its place properly in the supporting entourage; it is only fitting that this last act in domestic accessory architecture should be played in a consistently romantic manner, and that the garage should receive its due in the general plan."[33] Though writers at the time spoke of giving the "garage its proper place in the house machine in accordance with the dictates of efficiency," the real interest then was with the sense of its "picturesque" imagery.[34]

By the end of the 1920s the garage was completely absorbed into the suburban southern California dwelling and its landscape. Even in the innumerable acres of inexpensive tract houses that began to cover portions of the Los Angeles basin where the garage was still placed to the rear of the lot, the driveway (usually of two parallel ribbons of concrete) generally served both as the paved pathway for the auto as well as the pedestrian walkway leading up to the front door. Increasingly, even in these small spec houses, the garage became attached or semi-attached to the house. With the passion for the Hispanic and Mediterranean style in California during the decade of the 1920s, the driveway and the garage frequently came to be used as a visual device that helped to establish picturesque walled courts and gardens, or they posed as extended pergolas or arched loggias. The Long Beach–based Roy Hilton Company, "A House Plan Service and Special Architectural Designing by Mail," offered a number of inexpensive Spanish designs with integrated garages.[35] Numerous other designs, some Spanish, others French and English, were offered by the Angelus Home-Plan Service Company and by numerous builders of spec houses throughout southern California.[36] When, in 1922, the Santa Barbara architect George Washington Smith designed three spec houses for the Maravilla Company of Ojai, he designed their attached garages and driveways as integral features of the house and its garden.

The driveway and garage organized on a small scale to create an auto court that gave entrance to the house was an increasingly popular theme throughout the 1920s. In one of his designs of 1925, the Los Angeles architect Henry C. Newell brought both the family's and visitors' cars through a roofed portion of the house and then into a paved auto court. He separated the two-car garages into two buildings, which helped to establish and define the seclusion of his Mediterranean-inspired court. A few years later Palmer Sabin created a similar, though somewhat more open, auto court as a forecourt for one of his 1928 Spanish Colonial Revival houses at Emerald Bay.

California's contingent of avant-garde architects—R. M. Schindler, Richard J. Neutra, and Lloyd Wright—were, like their European counterparts, enthralled with the car as a fact and symbol of the new age. As with those who utilized traditional imagery, these California designers brought the garage fully into the house, either in the basement of a hillside house or, as in Schindler's well-known Lovell beach house of Newport Beach (1923–26), under the raised first floor of the dwelling.

At the very end of the 1920s and into the early 1930s, there were a few new wrinkles that came about in the suburban dwelling and its garage. One of these had to do with size and flexible use of space. "With the increase in motor car transportation," wrote Marc N. Goodnow in 1928, "has come also the double garage. . . . One family of my acquaintance had a wall partition built through the center of a two-car garage and devoted the extra space to toy engines, building clocks, kiddy kars, electric trains."[37] In the area of function, electronically operated garage door openers came into use by the mid-1920s and by 1930 radio devices were available so that the garage doors could be opened and closed from the interior of the car itself.[38]

Though the Spanish Colonial Revival style continued into the 1930s in Los Angeles and throughout California architecturally, it was replaced by a renewed interest in the Anglo-American Colonial. This 1930s phase of the Anglo-Colonial Revival style came into its own in the Los Angeles region in the purest way with spec builders and architects producing versions of the

**FIGURE 8.3**

*Spec house for the Maravilla Land Company, George Washington Smith, architect;
Ojai, California 1921.*

New England, the Cape Cod, the stone Pennsylvania farmhouse style, and even a few instances of dwellings conveying the Williamsburg image. The "native" Hispanic architectural tradition absorbed the fashionable Anglo-Colonial into its own regional styles, the Monterey and the California ranch house. The 1930s in Los Angeles turned out to be a vigorous period for the popular Streamline Moderne style as well as for the high-art modernist.

Despite these shifts in architectural and landscape images in Los Angeles and southern California in the 1930s, the approach to the automobile and its relationship to the suburban dwelling did not change radically from that of the late 1920s. The contingent of older and younger Los Angeles modernists advanced the connective link between the car and the suburban house most forcibly when their images spilled out into the popular Streamline Moderne style. Neutra's streamline metal-clad ship, the Von Sternberg House (1936), Northridge, brought visitors and its owner in underneath the searchlighted bridge—just as a motor launch might bring passengers up to an ocean liner. In the 1937 house for John Entenza, Harwell H. Harris played with segments of circles, with a semicircular drive bringing one under the circular, disk-covered carport and entrance to the house. Schindler opened up both ends of his attached garage in his 1933 projected prototype concrete 4-1/2-room house so that the garage could be used to house the auto, or it could function as a semi-enclosed, out-of-door porch room. In his Van Patten House, Los Angeles (1934–35), the three garages are all that is visible from the street.

The modest, small, single-floor spec houses, which began to be built in ever larger numbers from the mid-1930s on in Los Angeles, now had their garages attached either to the side or in some instances to the front of the house. Whether the family might settle on the "Bermuda," the "California," or "Colonial" model in the 1935–37 Westside Village in Los Angeles, each of these two-bedroom houses had an attached garage, plastered inside, equipped with overhead sectional doors, and having a small door at the rear.

For the upper-middle-class traditionalist image houses of Los Angeles, the favored form of the auto court increasingly became the norm. In the January, 1936, issue of *House and Garden*, Gerald K. Geerlings pointed out that the auto court was not simply a functional solution for entrance and parking, but it was equally important aesthetically. "It is not exaggeration," he wrote, "to state that a garage entrance court can change the aspect of a house."[39]

Cliff May let the auto court and garage decidedly alter the play between

garden, courtyard, and the many single-floor California ranch houses that he designed and built in West Los Angeles. In the 1934 "Modern Ranch House," one of Los Angeles's most successful domestic architects, H. Roy Kelley, laid out a low-walled "Motor Court," which dominated and took over the street facade of his idealized Colonialized ranch house.[40]

How the auto court could be maneuvered from the formal to the informal in these upper-middle-class Los Angeles houses can be seen in Wallace Neff's Miller House (1938) in Bel Air and Roland E. Coate's Rupple House (1938) in San Marino. The informal mood of the rural English image is sustained in the loose layout of the auto court of Neff's Miller House while the precise balanced symmetry of facade—walls, clipped plants, and hedges—reinforce the eighteenth-century French image of Coate's Rupple House.

Though the drive, auto court, and garage declared the presence of the auto, delightfully illusionistic games still were being played with the entrance of the garage. It was the great period, especially in spec houses, for garage doors to hint that they were not openings but were simply walls with their own shuttered windows. The modernists, too, played a similar game; Schindler's Walker House (Los Angeles, 1936) presents its single-element garage door as a sheet of painted plywood that matches the plywood panel to the side, which illusionistically hides the fact that it contains the front door. In Gregory Ain's 1937 Edwards House (Los Angeles), the face of the garage is a recessed plane of horizontal boards that continues as a connective treillage to the house.

The post–World War II years witnessed the acceptance of the open carport.[41] In a feature article in February, 1955, the editors of *House Beautiful* illustrated the latest, "the Drive-in House": "Here is the first reception room for formal car arrival, where you drive within the walls of the house, yet enter the front door ceremonially."[42] The carport came into its own after 1945 for varied reasons. Practically, the post–World War II auto had arrived at such a state of mechanical perfection that it could be left outside, and, in contrast to the "machines" of the first two decades of the century, it no longer needed to be maintained and tinkered with by its owner. Auto agencies, repair garages, and service stations were in profusion. At least in theory it was now a clean object, not smelling of petroleum products and not leaving drops or pools of oil hither and yon. Architecturally, the sense of structure and materials could be enhanced in the design of the carport by the elimination of some of the surrounding walls. There was a symbolic feeling of modernist functional minimization conveyed by the form of the carport, even though the construction of its roofing system and supports and the enclosed storage area might in the end cost more than simply building a fully enclosed garage with doors.

Finally, there was the crucial aesthetic question; the carport, with its hovering, cantilevered roof, looked modern. The importance of this feature was pointedly summed up in an article, "Not Just Any Port in a Storm: Carports," in the January, 1953, issue of the Iowa-based *Better Homes and Gardens:* "Carports offer unusual freedom of design. Their crisp open structure[s] are the perfect counterpart for today's house."[43] For California the most extensive presentation of impact of the automobile on the suburban house was a long, seventeen-page article, "Life with the Auto," published in the June, 1956, issue of *Sunset.*[44] The article posed a series of questions: "What happens when all our millions of cars reach home? What happens when they regroup and cluster later in the evening, for dinner parties, for teenage parties, for swimming? Where do we park them, store them, shelter them, enter them, leave them?"[45] It then set out to answer them. As one would expect of a California-oriented publication such as *Sunset,* the auto was seen as an object as natural to the landscape as the nineteenth-century imported eucalyptus trees, and the solutions suggested dealt with general suburban planning problems, landscape architecture, and, only after these issues had been settled, the architecture of the garage and the suburban dwelling.

The many solutions to the car and the suburban house were published in a couple of popular California publications of the time: Cliff May's *Sunset Western Ranch Houses* and Paul R. Williams's *New Homes for Today.*[46] Los Angeles's traditional establishment architects—Roland E. Coate, H. Roy Kelley, and Paul R. Williams—continued to relate the garage to the garden and dwelling in a fashion similar to their pre-1941 work. The growing contingent of Los Angeles modernists did the same, only they employed the carport with increased frequency. The steel post and beam Case Study Houses (sponsored by *Arts and Architecture Magazine*) of Craig Ellwood and Pierre Koenig were themselves so open that their carports were only differentiated from the house because they lacked glass walls and sliding glass doors. Gregory Ain, in his projected single-family housing, such as his Park Planned Homes in Altadena (Ain, Johnson and Day, 1946–47), created small-scale auto courts for each dwelling by arranging the semi-attached carports and their extending walls in relationship the house and screens of planted vegetation.

What certainly looked like a long-term life for the open carport in fact did not come about. By the opening years of the 1960s the enclosed garage, generally situated at the front of the house, had returned. The reasons for the demise of the open carport were many. The visual demands placed upon a family living in a carported house were hefty. The space would have to be kept puritanically clean at all times, including the shining automobile. Generally, the storage areas provided were not only limited in size, but they too demanded a puritanical sense of organization. Then, too, by its very nature, the open carport could not easily accommodate other activities. As early as 1943, O. G. Soderstrom had observed that "Dad goes to the garage, but not for the car! A room for Dad [to work], and a laundry for Mother."[47]

One of the prevalent do it yourself family episodes of the late 1940s and beyond was to convert part or all of the garage into a family room or den. The demise of the carport can be understood quickly today by driving down the streets of the 1946–48 Park Planned Homes in Altadena, California. Carport after carport have been enclosed, and in their design a vivid clash occurs between the modernist intention of the architect and the casual aesthetic of the middle-class, do it yourself world.

The final blow directed against the carport was the marked increase in the number of cars owned by a single family and their acquisition of numerous other possessions. There was now a need to store the family boat, the power lawn mower, and other large pieces of equipment. By the mid- to late 1960s, the typical middle-class California project house was introduced to the street by three-car garages, one of which could easily be converted (according to promotional advertising) into a family room or workshop.

As many of the eye-catching automobile ads of the 1920s indicate, the car was romantically and pragmatically viewed as a sort of H. G. Wells time machine, which not only could fulfill mundane needs but could also wisk one off to imaginary worlds of the past and the future. In these 1920s ads a Pierce Arrow or Auburn Speedster was typically posed on a driveway or within a motor court in front of an upper-middle-class California Spanish Revival or English Tudor Revival style dwelling. The car had the capacity to bring the members of the family back to their suburban world of a romantic-historic-inspired house and garden, or it could take them off to other adventures. As the intervening receptacle posed between the open beyond and the suburban dwelling, the garage ended up expressing how the auto was seen and, above all, how it was ideologically and emotionally responded to in these years. In a 1921 article in *Touchstone*, Eloise Roberts commented: "The Bell gives to the Cathedral its soaring and distinctive tower. The fireplace gives to the roof of the home its comely and expressive chimney. The motor car has had fully a revitalizing and lasting effect upon the domestic architecture of this age."[48]

## 9. Drummond Buckley

# A GARAGE IN THE HOUSE

In his 1976 article "The Domestication of the Garage," J. B. Jackson outlines the vernacular tradition of housing the automobile in America. He divides garage history into three distinct periods: (1) the "romantic garage," ostentatious as the estate it stood on, where early motorists parked their expensive pleasure vehicles; (2) the "practical garage," barely larger than the car itself and usually prefabricated, where middle-class Americans parked their Tin Lizzies; and (3) the "family garage," often with room for two cars and always attached to the house, where postwar families both parked and performed various domestic activities.[1] Thus, Jackson illustrates how caring for the car became one of the main functions of the American house.

As the garage evolved, other household spaces were also transformed by the car. The incorporation of the automobile into everyday life between 1900 and 1950 placed physical demands on the shape and configuration of the single-family home. As the garage made its way into the forefront of the suburban house, it provided more than shelter for the automobile; it replaced the front door as the symbolic and functional entrance. Meanwhile, during the same fifty-year period, the front porch disappeared and the popular conception of "backyard living" was born. Suburban dwellers retreated from the street as the car became their main mode of transport. Where the porch had provided an intermediary space between public and private, the garage served as a barrier. Changing floor and site plans, together with the attitudes expressed in contemporary magazines, document these adjuvant purposes and effects of putting the garage up front in the American house.

From the automobile's early appearance on American streets, observers noted the strains it placed on traditional house forms. A 1907 writer for *Harper's Weekly* found that "finance, art, homes and automobiles are arrayed in bloodless but no less real and serious battle against the horse, sloth, architectural traditions or difficulties and the fire insurance underwriters."[2] The author proposed to "domesticate" the automobile by incorporating the garage into the body of the house. One need only look to France for precedent, the author noted, where stables had been incorporated into urbane rowhouses since the sixteenth century. Most Americans were not ready

**FIGURE 9.1**

A 1907 observer looked to this "French Dwelling house of the Sixteenth Century combining the
Functions of Residence and Stable" as a prototype for the attached garage.

A Garage in the House

to accommodate the automobile into their carefully ordered domestic spaces. It would take another forty years before the car would be fully domesticated. But even in 1907 suburban and country dwellers who could afford the car had already begun to fit it into the architecture of their homes by building personal garages on their estates to match their domestic architecture. There was nothing really new in this solution, for the carriage house had long complemented the architecture of the upper-class estate.

As the motor car became more than a plaything for the wealthy, the middle-class began to deal with the parking problem. The initial reaction was to treat the car as an important family tool, housing it in a backyard shed. "Hastily thrown together boxes, corrugated iron affairs and even tents began to dot the landscape," according to one account. Both the convention of the horse mode of transport and caution toward the new technology of the auto influenced car owners in their decisions to keep the garage separate from the house. Practical considerations included fire hazard, narrow lot size, and an existing housing stock designed only to accommodate the pedestrian and the streetcar.[3]

Rather than hire a local carpenter to construct these early garages, many preferred to buy them ready-made. As early as 1911, an architect advised the readers of *House Beautiful* that the "portable garage," purchased in sections from a manufacturer and usually constructed on-site by the owner, was the most convenient and inexpensive solution to housing the motor car.[4] Popular throughout the 1910s and 1920s the portable garage shared much in common with the automobile it housed; both were built in a factory, available in a wide range of styles, and facilitated a mobile lifestyle.

The rear of the house was a practical place for the detached garage. Most backyards were served by alleys that provided access for the butcherboy, ashman, ice company, and various other delivery services. Often completely covered in asphalt or gravel, the backyard was a utilitarian space where trash was burned, clothes were washed and hung up to dry, and unneeded household items were left to rust.[5] A garage facing the alley preserved traditional service-oriented functions in the back and left the front of the house exactly as it had been without the automobile. Sidewalks did not need to be cut up in order to accommodate motor cars, thus keeping the area between house and street a pedestrian-only zone.

Even before the automobile began to exert a powerful influence on daily life, critics attacked the practical backyard as incongruous with suburban ideals. Magazines like the *Craftsman* called for the beautification of the "unsightly backyard" through both ornamental and productive gardening. The goal was to create a personal retreat where one rejected the opportunity to "become acquainted with the faces on the street" for a chance to be "where the corn is growing and the souls of men and women are not hidden beneath the complexities of life."[6] Like many Progressive Era reformers, the editors of the *Craftsman* saw the backyard as a place where individuals could commune with nature while escaping the ills of the city.

In the 1920s, the suburban household had three main choices for outdoor recreation: sitting on the porch, motoring on the open road, or gardening and relaxing in the backyard. Each had different ramifications for the suburb and each was affected by widespread automobile ownership.

Throughout the early twentieth century, the view from the front porch was rapidly changing; the noise and dust of motor traffic infringed on the passive nature of porch sitting, while the distance and speed of the motorist made personal contact with passing neighbors difficult. Some lamented the dying tradition of porch culture in the middle-class suburb. Others fled it for the exhilaration and varied scenery of the open road. "I hate to see those desert wastes that once were great piazzas," wrote one commentator for *House Beautiful* in 1915:

> House after house, along any great summer highway, shows its porch, gay with all the trappings of outdoor elegance—vacant. They have hung their harps upon the willows and gone a-motoring. There is companionship, and there may be (though I doubt it) conversation in the automobile; there is surely pleasure, exhilaration, the uplifting of heart at the sight of the beauty of the world. But we need the piazza just as much as ever. There are peace, and quiet talk, and the touch upon the soul of a dear familiar view.[7]

As a connection to community, the porch represented the best and worst of suburban living to contemporary observers. Many regarded it as the setting for gossip, idleness, and intrusive curiosity. Seven years after bemoaning the decline of the front porch, *House Beautiful* rallied for its extinction: "In the town and the suburb, the increase in motor-traffic, the dust and proximity of other houses tend to make the front porch less desirable each year. . . . One prefers [porches] turned away from the trivial drama of the street with its hucksters and milk wagons and gossip, to the serenity of trees

**FIGURE 9.2**

*As this 1920 advertisement illustrates, early recreational motorists socialized from the car as an alternative to socializing from the porch.*

and flowers in the back yard." A popular play and novel of the early 1920s, *Miss Lulu Bett*, epitomized this attitude, using the front porch as a setting of endless adult ennui.[8]

Motoring was in some ways analogous to sitting on the porch. The car offered a place to sit, socialize, and watch the passing scenery. In *Middletown*, the 1929 sociological study of Muncie, Indiana, Robert and Helen Lynd commented that the car replaced the porch as a place for "cooling off after supper."[9] Like the porch swing, the car seat offered a semi-private space from which to see and be seen. Because it was also a form of transport, the automobile offered a new experience of privacy to the middle class. It allowed its owners to extend their semi-private domain beyond the house to wherever the road might lead, which put less pressure on the actual house to provide a transition zone between public and private space.

In contrast to the front porch and the car, which were constantly providing opportunity for public interaction, the backyard could become an entirely private space. When surrounded by a fence or other enclosure, the backyard was often referred to as an "outdoor living room"—in other words, an extension of the house's private interior rooms. For the first time, large numbers of the middle class could languish like royalty in their own private sunshine rather than share the public open spaces of parks and streets. In the beginning, suburbanites were encouraged to use their backyards productively, such as during the national crusade for Victory Gardens during the First World War. But this use soon gave way to entirely recreational pursuits. Ornamental gardening, badminton, and lounging became common backyard activities. Neighbors might be invited to share the garden, but they could not arrive unannounced as they had on the front porch. By 1929 a speaker at the Tenth National Conference on Housing would declare that the "outdoor living room" represented a progression "from the enforced privacy of pioneer or rural living, through front porch promiscuity to a new voluntary privacy that has in it the charm of sanctuary from a too noisy world."[10]

As the "cult of the backyard" grew, the utilitarian garage seemed increasingly out of place there. Fashionable suburbanites tried either to disguise it behind a barrage of vines and flowers or emphasize it as an architectural feature of the garden. In the 1920s, the alley entrance gave way to the personal driveway. Now the garage could be seen clearly from the street, increasing its value as a status symbol. George Babbit, the hero of Sinclair Lewis' suburban satire, had a driveway leading from the street to his corrugated-iron garage and once remarked that there was "no class to that

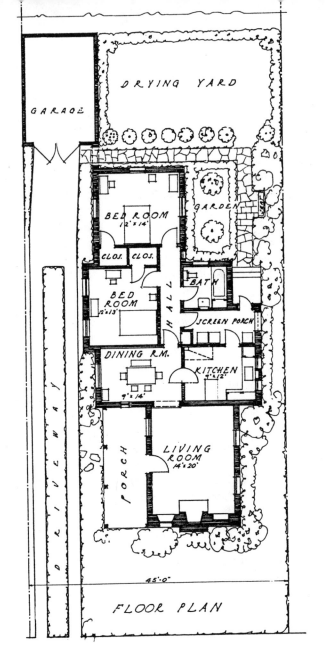

DRYING YARD

GARAGE

GARDEN

BED ROOM
12' X 14'

CLOS. CLOS.

BED ROOM
12' X 13'

HALL

BATH

SCREEN PORCH

DINING R.M.
9' X 14'

KITCHEN
9' X 12'

PORCH

LIVING ROOM
14' X 20'

DRIVEWAY

45'-0"

FLOOR PLAN

**FIGURE 9.3**

*The front driveway became a prominent feature of the suburban house in the 1920s, providing both convenient access to the street and a visual link to the garage.*

tin shack. Have to build me a frame garage."[11] As the decade progressed, suburban residents would have an ever-increasing number of styles to choose from, ranging from Craftsman to Richardson Romanesque. Yet, whatever the style, all the prefabricated garages of the 1920s seem intended to convey the image of permanence that Babbit longed for.

A survey of pattern books from the 1910s and 1920s underscores the ever-increasing influence of the car on the dwelling. The *Bungalow Book* of 1910, published in Chicago by "Bungalow Man" Henry Wilson, is indicative of the general pre-automobile suburban house, with nearly all renderings and photographs depicting a walkway leading from sidewalk to stoop. Plans reveal bedrooms at the rear of the bungalows, with the public rooms looking out over the front yard. In all of the plans, the only entrance from the rear is through a service porch that leads to the kitchen, while the front door generally opens onto the living room from a relatively spacious porch. In addition to full plans, the reader of The *Bungalow Book* could also order from a wide assortment of prefabricated front doors, indicative of their importance as the main entrance to the house.[12]

A decade later the automobile was beginning to exert national influence at a rapidly accelerating rate. In 1921 the national average was one vehicle for every 10.1 persons, by 1929 there was one vehicle for every 4.5 persons. Regional variation was dramatic, with about twice as many cars per person in California as the nation as a whole.[13] Pattern books and advertisements for single-family houses in southern California show signs of the automobile's increasing presence. As early as 1918, the *Los Angeles Times* featured an advertisement for an inexpensive "Colonial Home and Garage." In the early 1920s driveways are pictured as prominently as walkways. The 1925 pattern book *Spanish Homes of California* includes twenty-one plans, only two with a front porch. Many of the plans have living rooms with narrow windows on the street side and double glass doors opening to a patio in the backyard.[14]

By the 1920s many commentators began to doubt the practicality of keeping the garage in the backyard. In the previous decade it had become fashionable for the nouveau riche to attach their garages to their homes, leading a 1920 writer for *Country Life* to note that, "in many fine neighborhoods, real estate restrictions prevent the building of isolated garages on the property." Not only did the attached garage demonstrate the owner's progressive attitude about the motor car; it showed that the resulting increased fire insurance premium was of no concern to the owners. Moreover, the garage had "few of the drawbacks of the stable . . . [and] chauffeurs, as we all

*A Garage in the House*

## You can now have a garage with less fuss and at a lower cost.

This Togan Garage comes to you ready to assemble and erect. The building complete, even to painting, is done for you at the factory.

Togan Garages are roomy, generously lighted; interiors are smoothly finished. Service doors carefully fitted, equipped complete with selected garage hardware. Windows are made in casement or sliding sash with side entry doors to match. Styles of windows optional, also location of side entry.

Built in a variety of designs, there's one that agrees architecturally with your home.

In addition, a price comparison will convince you that the Togan way is the less expensive way.

### SOLD BY DEALERS

## TOGAN  GARAGES

Manufactured by Togan-Stiles, 1606 Eastern Ave., Grand Rapids, Mich.

*An interesting brochure concerning Togan Garages, with illustrations, will be sent for fifteen cents; also name of nearest dealer.*

### FIGURE 9.4

*The "portable garage," constructed in a factory and delivered to the customer in sections, was often designed to give the illusion of homelike permanence.*

---

know, rank infinitely higher than grooms in the social classification of the household." The greatest advantage of an attached garage, according to most accounts, was the easy access it allowed from house to car.[15] Still, the attached garage was so rare in 1919 that one writer commented, "putting a garage in a house may sound like a joke, but it is not." When it was attached, it was usually in the basement, at the back, or in a projecting wing, rarely with a door directly to the house.[16]

By the late 1920s the attached garage had become a more accepted feature of the middle-class house. An extensive feature in a 1929 issue of *Architectural Record* notes the increasing tendency to attach as "a development that has followed the changed attitude toward the motor car. . . . The discovery that the garage was not a stable has made it common practice to include it in the house and express it externally." The "customary treatment" of putting the garage in the backyard was seen as inconvenient and unnecessarily expensive because it required a long driveway, a separate heater, and the construction of a fourth wall.[17]

While architects seem to have been in agreement by the late twenties that the attached garage made good sense, they all did not concur on its placement in relation to the rest of the house. Two schools of thought predominated, those who sought to add the garage to the house while maintaining the dominance of the pedestrian entrance and those who sought to use the attached garage as a tool for the privatization of the backyard regardless of its effect on the pedestrian orientation.

The editors of *Architectural Record* took the conservative position. They acknowledged the garage as a necessary feature of modern domestic life, while seeking to maintain pedestrian relationships and human scale. The editors turned to Henry Wright and Clarence Stein's "Town for the Motor Age" of Radburn, New Jersey, as a model arrangement. Radburn is acknowledged widely as a model development, progressive in its provisions for public open space and planned community orientation. Its most noteworthy feature is the careful separation of pedestrians from automobiles, achieved by isolating pedestrian paths from vehicular roads.

Like the entire community plan, the floor plan of the Radburn House is full of tensions between pedestrian and car, public and private, and front and back. The house chosen by the editors of *Record* has four entrances yet only three rooms, because it is designed to accommodate pedestrian traffic on one side and automobiles on the other. "The house has two front yards, no back yards," wrote Louis Brownlow, a consultant to the nonprofit corporation that

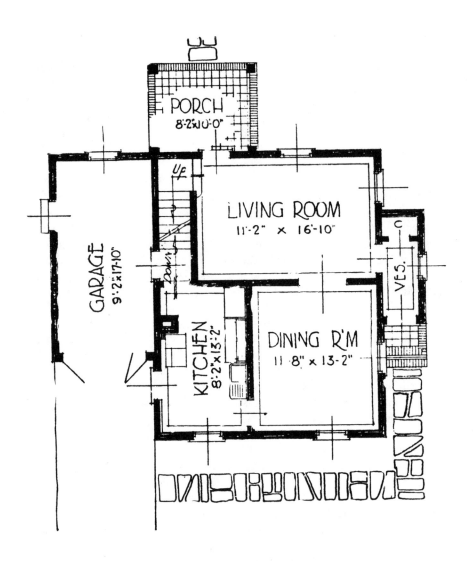

**FIGURE 9.5**

*In the Radburn plan of 1929, porches faced pedestrian paths at the rear of houses, and access to the garage was from a cul-de-sac reserved for automobile access.*

built Radburn. He continued: "It has two principal entrances—a motor entrance and a pedestrian entrance." Even though Brownlow considered the garage "as much a part of the house as the dining room," he was not trying to promote a car-oriented lifestyle. To the contrary, he predicted that Radburn would "open the way for a revival of pedestrianism" in the United States.[18] Despite its innovative features, Radburn was essentially a reactionary response to the automobile—an attempt to turn back the clock to a time when pedestrians were unthreatened by vehicles on neighborhood suburban streets. In plan, Radburn is similar to the alley-garage configuration of the 1910s. The cul-de-sac behind the Radburn house is nothing more than an inverted service alley for cars, while the path on the opposite side is intended to serve a community function similar to that of the pre-automobile sidewalk. Even though the porch had long been on the decline in the auto suburb, Stein and Wright's design features a prominent front porch facing a pedestrian path. The Radburn plan was basically a last-ditch effort to protect the Victorian suburban community from destruction by the automobile.[19]

Two years later *Record* again pushed for an arrangement that preserved a traditional house-to-street relationship, though boldly claiming that the garage "should be considered the main entrance to the house." Here the pedestrian entrance was left intact by placing the garage in the rear by means of a loop driveway, thus "making available entire house frontage for living rooms" rather than focusing public areas of the house on a garageless backyard. The author also attempted to preserve the hall as the main entrance to the house by making it directly accessible from the garage, as if the resident who must enter through the kitchen or the back was somehow undignified.[20]

The Small Homes Plan Bureau, an influential lobbying group for small architects, took the alternative approach to the attached garage, embracing the new kind of suburb facilitated by the automobile. Here the effort was to use the garage as a way of shutting out the surrounding community and emphasizing the private garden. Through architectural competitions, plan books, and advice columns in newspapers, the Small Homes Plan Bureau and a companion group, the Better Homes in America Association, attempted to convince home buyers and builders about the virtues of the porchless house, which had living rooms facing the rear yard. In a 1929 *Los Angeles Times* column, one architect with the bureau argued that the garage's "importance in the daily scheme of life, coupled with the desire to give more space to the garden, is bringing it forward as a feature of the front elevation . . . it may be

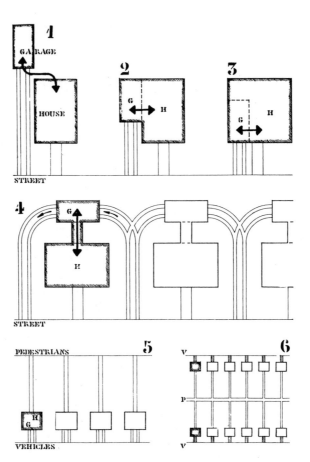

**1.** Detached garage, an arrangement suggested by the stable which was separated from house for sanitary reasons.

**2.** Same garage unit attached to house in order to attain convenience of entry. There is no valid reason as in case of stable to separate the two elements.

**3.** Final step in evolution. The garage is here incorporated in house plan and is most directly accessible from entrance hallway and from street.

**4.** An arrangement with garage at rear making available entire house frontage for living rooms. Cars may drive into and out of garage instead of backing out to street. One driveway serves two garages.

**5./6.** A desirable separation of pedestrians and vehicles with grouped houses. Garage entrances face highways. Hall entries for pedestrians and the living rooms front gardens.

**FIGURE 9.6**

*The history of the garage, according to* Architectural Record, *including recommendations for proper placement. The authors were most concerned with accommodating the car while preserving an amiable relationship between the house and the street.*

handled in such a way as to further the need for shielding the patio or garden from the noises of the street."[21]

The argument for the privatized house eventually proved highly persuasive to most Americans. In their advice, the editors of *Architectural Record* and the builders of Radburn underestimated the growing importance of the isolated backyard as a feature of the postautomobile suburban house. Their designs were rarely followed in either vernacular or architectural house construction. Instead, people put the garage at the front of the house, leaving the back free for private pursuits and buffering the entire house from the noise of the street and the public realm of the neighborhood.

Separated from the sounds and activities of the street, the enclosed and spacious backyard had important repercussions on suburban life. In the 1929 *Middletown* study, one woman reminisced about the diverse functions of her by-then defunct front porch: "In the nineties we were all much more together. People brought chairs and cushions out of the house and sat on the lawns evenings. We rolled out a strip of carpet and put cushions on the porch step to take care the unlimited flow of neighbors that dropped by. We'd sit out so all evening." This kind of spontaneous interaction was purposely discouraged in the private backyard, completely enclosed by a fence on three sides and the house and garage on the fourth side. A *Los Angeles Times* article of 1927 found the walled backyard "almost a necessity" for the house on a small lot, for "it provides a definite area for garden treatment, and gives the effect of shutting out the surrounding stretches of barren country or adjoining houses."[22]

The retreat to the backyard was not merely a response to the automobile. It was also part of a broad suburban trend toward privatization. The trend is best explained by looking at the use of the private backyard as a safe, easily controlled play area for children. In *Middletown* youngsters protested being driven from the street to the sidewalk in the 1920s. Ten years later a newspaper editorial claimed that even "Sidewalk Play is Dangerous."[23] Certainly this was a reaction to the danger posed by automobiles. But the push to keep children in the backyard was also part of the basic suburban ideology, which placed a greater emphasis on the family than on the neighborhood. The single-family home long had been considered a haven for bringing up the right kind of children, and a growing self-consciousness about their needs led to increasingly specialized, child-oriented spaces like the enclosed backyard.

The mobility allowed by the car altered neighborly relations and, as Folke T. Kihlstedt points out, "broke down formal barriers, acting as a level-

*A Garage in the House*

ing force by bringing into intimate contact sections of the population which normally would never meet." This "leveling" did not last for long; people soon found new ways to be segregated by class, race, and age. The sheer scale of the automobile suburb was perhaps the biggest contribution to new forms of segregation. In the interim, domestic spaces that had been used to buffer classes from each other lost their importance. If a visitor to a pre-auto house was not welcome inside, he might be left standing on the porch. In the postauto house, one was much less likely to have such a visitor because, for many miles around, everyone was of the same socioeconomic background.[24]

Despite being more homogeneous, the post-auto neighborhood was no longer a cohesive whole. In *Middletown* the Lynds found that: "instead of a family's activities in getting a living, making a home, play, [and] church-going . . . overlapping and bolstering each other, one's neighbors may work at shops at the other end of the city, while those with whom one works may have their homes anywhere from one to two-score miles distant."[25] In this fragmented community, people welcomed the private backyard.

The importance of the automobile in family life continued through the depression years. A 1934 article in *Woman's Home Companion* noted that the remodeling loans available through the National Housing Act could be used to construct an attached garage. The government further sanctioned the attached garage in 1936, when the Federal Housing Administration distributed four sketch plans of ideal subsistence housing on 50-by-100-foot city or suburban lots. One plan includes a semi-attached garage and a living room oriented toward the backyard. The attached garage, however, had yet to become a standard feature of new houses on a national scale. A sample of eighty three- to four-bedroom house plans published in a 1936 edition of *American Architect* reveals only twenty with attached garages.[26]

Only after World War II did the attached garage become a standard feature of the suburban house. By this time the automobile had become so central to national policy that the Bureau of Labor Statistics listed it as a "necessity of life" along with food, clothing, and shelter. A flood of do-it-yourself home planning books were published in anticipation of a boom in new-house construction by postwar families. All seem to have been in agreement on the necessity of attaching garages and improving backyards. "The old practice of having a relatively deep front lawn [and] tucking the garage away at the rear by means of a long driveway," wrote one of these house planners, "meant that the most private and usable area of the plot was shrunken into a sort of glorified drying yard." In popular home magazines, other advisors discussed the benefits of enclosing the "useless porch."[27]

The typical post-war house plan included a garage with direct access to the kitchen, a living room oriented to the backyard, and two or three bedrooms at the front or side of the house. If a porch was part of the plan, it was either ornamental (a narrow roof overhang over a narrow strip of cement) or in the rear. The last remaining connection with the street was the picture window, which fell out of favor by the late 1950s. By the mid-1950s, many large-scale developers used varying patterns on garage doors to distinguish otherwise identical houses.

In what J. B. Jackson calls the "family garage" of the postwar period, the space became a less specialized area for men and women's housework and other family activities. In 1945 *Better Homes and Gardens* took a somewhat radical stance on the multipurpose garage: "rather than waste [the] heated and high-cost attached garage on their car and garden tools, we suggest that the Adamses keep their car in a low-cost shelter and remodel to gain the twenty uses below," including "corralling the baby," "after-work showers," and "pattern cutting." Ironically, many of the activities suggested for the garage were once performed on the porch. Like other contemporary proposals for improving on the multipurpose garage, *Better Homes and Gardens* emphasized the benefits to the wife: "Look, Mr. Husband—don't let the little woman down when you plan your post-war home. Give her a room like this to save her energy and to ease the sag of her metatarsals."[28]

Perhaps women had a say in the use of the postwar garage because they frequently used the automobile as workers during the war. Their input might explain the rapid acceptance of the attached garage in the postwar house. "The war taught us a great lesson," according to one account. "It taught us how deeply you and I and John and Mary and Pete had incorporated car driving into our personal workaday lives." It was especially true for "Mary." A Los Angeles poll found that 70 percent of the workers at the "big new war plants" commuted in automobiles.[29]

In 1955 Cornell University did a study of homeowner motivations in Buffalo, New York. Although their sample of 773 families was hardly representative of the nation as a whole, the attitudes reflected national trends as seen in both popular magazines and house plans. The researchers found that 50 percent chose their house to be "free from traffic noises," and a little more than that wanted "enough room outside the house for personal enjoyment";

only 27 percent felt it was important to be "near houses of good friends"; over half disliked or were indifferent to neighbors being able to see in the house; and over half were indifferent or disliked being able to see the street from the inside of the house.[30]

With the construction of vast suburban tracts like Levittown, post-war builders set the pattern of suburban development for thirty years to come. We live with the results today, as Kenneth T. Jackson notes in *The Crabgrass Frontier:* "the life of the sidewalk and front yard has largely disappeared, and the social intercourse that used to be the main characteristic of urban life has vanished. Residential neighborhoods have become a mass of small, private islands, with the backyard functioning as a wholesome, family-oriented, and reclusive place."[31] A difficult question remains: did qualities inherent in the car cause Americans to retreat into their "private islands"? Jackson suggests that the "drive-in culture" is at the root of community decline in the suburbs. Yet any mention of a technological "culture" must not be limited to the car. The cultures of the telephone, radio, and television have also had a great effect on the evolution of the privatized house.

The automobile was not the only catalyst for the retreat to the back-yard, nor did it merely facilitate suburban trends. As with other technologies, a direct causal relationship is difficult to discern. Popular attitudes and house plans demonstrate, however, that the automobile radically changed the way suburban Americans thought about the house and its relationship to the surrounding community. The garage's evolution from back-yard shed to front entrance clearly reveals the impact of the car on domestic space. As the automobile became the dominant mode of transport in the United States between 1900 and 1950, the front porch vanished, the backyard came into its own, and the vernacular suburban house became a place where the family and the car could reside as equals.

# 10. Richard Longstreth

# THE PERILS OF A PARKLESS TOWN

The early months of 1920 were traumatic ones for anybody who invested, worked, or shopped in downtown Los Angeles. After weeks of deliberation amid much controversy, the city council enacted a parking ban in the commercial core, which had been plagued by massive traffic congestion for some time. The new provision would ostensibly enable streetcars, and, hence, many people who came downtown, to move freely. Soon after the ordinance took effect on April 10, however, merchants witnessed a sharp decline in business. The earlier forecast of the *Los Angeles Times* had been correct in its depiction of the "perils of a parkless town." Denied ready access by automobile to the central shopping district, residents would not shop there at all, and soon major shopping districts would emerge in outlying areas to address the shifting market. Opposition to the ban swelled, and it was substantially modified less than thirty days after its inception. But the lessons of this episode left an indelible impression on Angelenos. To remain competitive, retail services must accommodate the motorist.[1] Indeed, having adequate places to park came to be seen as essential to the future health of the city. Such traffic problems were by no means unique to Los Angeles in the post–World War I era but they were more intensely felt, and efforts to rectify them often occurred earlier than in other places.

The factors contributing to the automobile's pivotal position in the city's development are not difficult to identify. Los Angeles was experiencing an enormous population boom from 319,000 people in 1910 to 576,000 in 1920 (an 80 percent increase) and then to 1,238,000 in 1930 (a 115 percent increase), which made it the fifth largest metropolis in the nation. This surge in growth, paralleling that of major eastern and midwestern cities during the nineteenth century, occurred concurrently with the introduction of the automobile as a major conveyance, used by the middle class as well as the rich and for everyday business as well as recreational outings. The region was especially conducive to this widespread reliance on the car. Roads were generally straight

The material presented in this essay was gathered in the course of research for a forthcoming book that examines aspects of the automobile's impact on retail development patterns in southern California from the 1920s to the early 1950s.

and flat, and the salubrious climate facilitated driving year round. Many people had recently moved to the region—by car—from small cities, towns, and rural areas where public transportation was more limited and driving taken more for granted than in densely populated centers. As a result, by 1924 Los Angeles enjoyed the highest percentage of automobile ownership in the world; automobile registrations in the county multiplied five and a half times between 1919 and 1929, from 141 to 777 thousand.[2] The nature of development also contributed to extensive automobile use. For decades the region had been heralded as a place of free-standing, single-family houses, and, as Los Angeles was transformed from a small city to a very large one, this ideal not only persisted, it was a major attraction to the middle and prosperous working classes alike. Abundant and hence comparatively cheap land further contributed to Los Angeles having the lowest population density and by far the highest percentage of single-family houses in the United States by 1930.[3] These conditions were well known to Angelenos, who were quite conscious of how and why theirs was a great city in the making.

Under the circumstances, it is hardly surprising that the Los Angeles area became a seminal proving ground for architectural experiments to accommodate motorists' needs. No other metropolis in fact contributed in so many ways to the reconfiguration of commercial development that began to occur during the interwar decades as a result of widespread automobile usage. As early as 1921, an alternative to the downtown tourist hotel, called the Motor Inn, was erected in Boyle Heights, providing a model for the more famous Milestone Mo-Tel in San Luis Obispo, begun three years later, and countless subsequent examples. The region also rightfully can claim the world's first drive-in bank, constructed in 1937.[4] Other types of facilities, including drive-in restaurants and drive-in laundries, did not originate in the area but did appear early, were developed in as ambitious a way as could be found in the country, and soon became closely identified with southern California's rapidly expanding urban landscape.[5]

As significant as such experimental work might be, it was not central to the evolving structure of new commercial districts. Motels remained in peripheral locations; other drive-in facilities were relatively few in number or were anomalies prior to World War II. Throughout the metropolitan area, the overwhelming majority of retail development followed a traditional pattern of buildings occupying all or most of the front portion of their lots along well-traveled streetcar and automobile routes. By virtue of its extent, dispersed over a vast, primarily residential area, this development eased the plight of the motorist. Services were close to home, and the grid of wide boulevards facilitated traffic flow. Nevertheless, there was nothing new about the underlying physical order to which these linear precincts conformed.

Decentralized retail services offered a partial solution to the problems of the metropolis in the automobile age, but they also generated difficulties. Large outlying centers, such as those along Western Avenue, soon became congested themselves, albeit far less so than downtown. The volume of traffic, combined with its rapid pace, rendered many sites, once considered prime retail locations for a streetcar-oriented populace, of lesser value. These circumstances, coupled with extensive overbuilding of commercial facilities during the speculative real estate frenzy of the 1920s, intensified competition among merchants and, no doubt, the willingness of some to try alternative courses.

Among the most significant undertakings to devise a fundamentally new configuration of both external and internal space tailored to address the routine of the motorist was a long-forgotten type known as the drive-in market. These complexes in fact comprised the first common retail building type, not catering to the automobile itself, to make such a design departure. Unlike most analogous experiments of the period, the drive-in market became a ubiquitous feature in the metropolis. The earliest known example was erected at Glendale in 1924. After several subsequent years of sporadic trial ventures, the type rapidly gained popular acceptance. By the opening months of 1928 dozens of examples were being constructed; four years later over two-hundred of them existed in the region.[6]

The change in configuration that the drive-in market represented seemed radical at that time; most of the valuable frontage area was given over to parking and the building itself straddled the rear of the lot on one or, more generally, two sides. Instead of lining the standard shoebox form of grocery and other stores, goods in the drive-in market were oriented to the incoming patron in an open, light, and airy setting. Another key difference lay in merchandising. The relatively large lot required to incorporate a forecourt induced builders of drive-in markets to employ a nascent practice of combining related facilities whereby the presence of each would reinforce the appeal of the others. Thus, these markets had at least several departments—for groceries, fruits and vegetables, meats, a delicatessen, and a bakery. Often other basic services, such as a florist, drug store, or cafe, were included

**FIGURE 10.2**

*Billie Bird Market, 1929; 2311–2321 West Main Street, Alhambra, California (altered).*

*The Perils of a Parkless Town*

in one or more end units. Each department was leased to an individual merchant, but the entire food-selling area was designed, and in effect operated, as a unit.

Convenience was key to the concept's success. The forecourt allowed motorists to park right next to the store rather than searching for curbside space. The range of items sold attracted more customers and fostered increased purchases per customer. Greater sales permitted longer hours of operation, which generated additional revenue and enabled a pricing structure that gave these independent operations a competitive edge over chain stores. Once the type had demonstrated its profit-making capacity, the demand for leases seemed insatiable; units were occupied almost as fast as speculators could construct them during the peak years of 1928–30. The diffusion process occurred through neither large corporations or special-purpose syndicates, but rather from the work of scores of individuals who adhered to a more-or-less standard pattern, each seeking to profit from what had become a lucrative form of real estate development.

The merchandizing strategy found at drive-in markets had already been applied with considerable success to auto service centers, called super service stations, the first of which appears to have been built in Los Angeles in 1914. Many such facilities erected after World War I utilized a configuration and the idea of one-stop shopping—in this case, for all basic automotive needs—that developers of drive-in markets adopted a few years later.[7] Thus, the markets' major contribution lay not in originating the concept, but in adapting it to non-automotive retail functions and demonstrating that, even when the car itself was not the primary object of attention, breaking from a traditional mode was advantageous.

Once that demonstration was made, the design of drive-in markets became relatively standardized. Variations in size, range of goods, configuration and siting for the most part encompassed a limited spectrum.[8] The most conspicuous differences tended to be in outward appearance. Some examples were simple and cheap, others quite elaborate. On occasion, exotic imagery was employed, as with the Clock Market in Beverly Hills or the Mandarin Market in Hollywood (both 1929), to secure a memorable impression and, it was hoped, a larger clientele.[9]

With or without exotica, drive-in market design revealed an underlying aim of creating work that was more distinct than the pervasive, plain, boxlike buildings characteristic to most retail facilities in outlying areas—work that would be more compatible with surrounding residential neighborhoods.

**FIGURE 10.3**

*Plaza Market, 1928, Morgan, Walls and Clements, architects, 4651–4663 West Pico Boulevard, Los Angeles (no longer standing).*

---

**147**

*The Perils of a Parkless Town*

While this concern became widespread for commercial architecture generally during the 1920s, designers of drive-in markets were especially conscious of the need to create schemes conducive to attracting the attention of customers in moving vehicles. The designs most admired at that time, such as the Plaza Market on Pico Boulevard by Morgan, Walls and Clements (1928), possessed a simple, clear arrangement of forms and elements so as to register a memorable impression of the complex at a fleeting glance. However intricate the details might be, it was believed that they should remain subordinate to an overall effect tailored to the motorist more than the pedestrian.

In pursuing these aims, the architects of most drive-in markets employed traditional imagery, yet the field attracted several leading modernists as well. Lloyd Wright's work, such as the Yucca-Vine Market in Hollywood (1930), was among the most striking and became a prototype for the bold, exuberant, abstract vocabulary of roadside architecture in the region after World War II.[10]

Equally influential in this regard were some of Richard Neutra's schemes for drive-in markets, such as a hypothetical study (circa 1928) in which, at a very early date, the building is a minimalist interplay of vertical supports, roof slab, and glass walls. A solution that seemed almost as radical at that time was realized by George Adams with the Mesa-Vernon Market in Leimert Park the same year, a design that was among the most widely publicized and highly regarded examples of the type, and which exhibited qualities that would remain current in retail design at least through the 1940s.[11]

Drive-in markets attracted national attention among real estate developers, retailers, planners, and architects. The type's influence was considerable in scope. Frank Lloyd Wright adapted the idea for market centers in his Broadacre City plan of the early 1930s.[12] Of far more immediate consequence, however, was the work of a Washington, D.C., real estate firm, Shannon and Luchs, which erected the Park and Shop in 1930 after some two years of market and planning studies. This complex was larger than most drive-in markets, but the main difference was that it combined the drive-in concept with that of the neighborhood shopping center: the market was only one of ten stores encompassing a full range of everyday retail services.[13] Previously, the few such centers that had been developed in the United States had a traditional street-front configuration. The Park and Shop proved that the forecourt afforded a distinct advantage and the open front, so important to drive-in markets, was not an essential feature. The scheme served as a

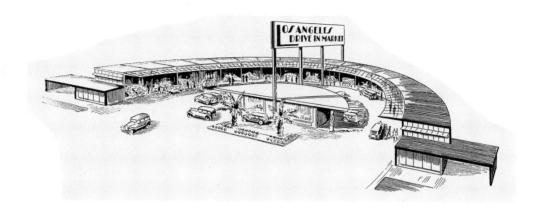

model for dozens of other planned shopping centers erected during the 1930s and hundreds more built after World War II.

Even by 1941 drive-in neighborhood centers could be found from Buffalo to Atlanta, Houston to Tacoma, but *not* in southern California. The circumstances contributing to the absence of such work in the place that had given rise to its market progenitors are too numerous and complex to address fully here, but a few key factors deserve attention. During the 1930s Angelenos felt they had better alternatives. One was the supermarket, which itself was a child of the region, pioneered by the Ralphs Grocery Company in the late 1920s, and which had completely usurped the drive-in market as the preferred retail outlet for food by the mid-1930s.[14] The two types had some attributes in common, but the supermarket was not only much larger, its rectangular configuration proved more effective in inducing shoppers to circulate throughout the premises. Both factors were essential to high-volume sales, which, in turn, became important to business survival during the worst years of the Depression. By the time the economic picture began to improve, the supermarket's advantages were regarded as transcendent. Examples continued to be built in great numbers, collectively becoming one of the most distinctive features of the urban landscape in southern California and an increasingly prominent one in other parts of the country toward the decade's end.[15]

Much like the earlier drive-in market, the supermarket was often sited somewhat apart from concentrated retail nodes so that adequate land could be secured at a reasonable price for both the building and the adjacent car lot. Creating additional retail facilities as part of the scheme almost never was undertaken because the supermarket was viewed as a destination point unto itself; customer draw remained sufficient without a supporting cast. To attract such patronage, however, it was believed that the building must abut the sidewalk so that it could stand as a prominent local landmark to motorist and pedestrian alike. Offstreet parking was situated to one side rather than in front. Side entrances leading directly from the lot became ever more standard by the late 1930s, yet the supermarket's architectural treatment in most cases continued to emphasize the street facade alone. In visual terms, the parking area was thus residue space rather than an integral component of the design, as it had been with the drive-in market.

The street orientation of supermarkets reflected a common outlook in the region. Through the 1920s, boosters nurtured the ideal of the great metropolitan core as much as they did neighborhoods of detached houses. Repeat-

**FIGURE 10.5**

*Ralphs Supermarket, 1929, Russell Collins, architect, 171–181 North Lake Street, Pasadena,
California (no longer standing).*

———

**151**

*The Perils of a Parkless Town*

edly, visions of the future depicted not one but a multitude of skyscraper centers scattered about the Los Angeles basin. While little such development was realized until recent decades, the local passion for a metropolitan image, coupled with one for scenographic drama while motoring, had a profound effect upon the nature of commercial development. Downtown Hollywood embodied this sentiment to a certain degree, but the key examples were found along Wilshire Boulevard in the blocks around Western Avenue and in the precinct known as the Miracle Mile. Here at once was the skyscraper city and the dispersed linear city.[16] Off-street parking was provided on some of the Wilshire properties, but only at the rear where it would not ruin the big-city allusion or the excitement of the urban landscape as it was seen from behind the wheel.

Wilshire Boulevard set the standard for countless smaller retail precincts in the region during the 1930s and 1940s. Planned shopping centers developed during this period maintained a sense of street-front drama by adhering to the pattern of showing facades and offering rear parking. Such complexes were often conceived and operated more as an agglomeration of stores than as a fully integrated facility. On the whole, merchants showed a persistent reluctance to abandon their traditional sidewalk orientation. Food retailers whose supermarkets formed the anchor units of these centers were especially adamant on the matter.[17]

Only in the 1950s, with the planning of much larger and more centrally organized shopping complexes, did the local street-front pattern begin to erode. The first significant departure came with the Lakewood Center (1950–53) near Long Beach, which was also among the earliest regional shopping malls in the nation.[18] Given its immense size (occupying a 165-acre tract and containing over sixty units) and internally focused configuration (with a pedestrian way as the organizational spine), the parking lot, planned to accommodate over twelve thousand cars, could no longer be relegated to either the sides or the rear; it had to be circumferential if all stores were to enjoy ready access. Such circumstances made the mall the generator of its own physical order, responding little if at all to that of the environs. By this time, too, the street no longer held so much appeal as a showcase for architectural display. The boulevard, defined by tangent buildings as much as by its own spatial openness, became, as it were, the commercial strip, a much more loosely organized panoply in which open space tended to dominate and free-standing signs often assumed a more important role than buildings as the means by which the motorist's attention was secured.

The development of architecture to accommodate the motorist is not always the neat, linear sequence it is often depicted as being, whereby space devoted to the car steadily is given increased primacy. Rather, the process can be complex and filled with diverse, sometimes divergent, strains. Regional factors also may be crucial to understanding the sequence. Los Angeles gave birth to the drive-in market, then spurred its rapid demise after about five years. New developments, stemming in part from the drive-in market, were ignored locally in favor of others, equally new, but also revealing a persistence of tradition. Not until the advent of the mall, which permitted no reference to long-standing, street-oriented patterns, were local conventions discarded.[19]

The drive-in markets that helped to start it all have long been forgotten. Yet recent work in the region demonstrates that the process also can be somewhat cyclical. As the demand for regional malls has become saturated and driving to them on the freeway becomes ever less appealing, as escalating land values have tended to render the supermarket an ever less profitable enterprise, as the city's boulevards approach ever more a gridlock, and as finding a place to park—anywhere—becomes ever more a problem, Angelenos have created the microcenter.[20] It is not quite the drive-in market again, and it is not at all fashionable to like them the way people enjoyed drive-in markets, but they are a new success story for the convenience they afford to a populace ever conscious of the perils of a parkless town.

James J. Flink

# THE ULTIMATE STATUS SYMBOL:
## THE CUSTOM COACHBUILT CAR IN THE INTERWAR PERIOD

Reynold Wik has observed that more has been written about Henry Ford and his Model T than anyone could read in a single lifetime. In sharp contrast, the literature on the true luxury car is sparse. Richard Burns Carson calls "the Olympian luxury cars [of the 1920s and 1930s] the finest and most fabulous automobiles in American automotive history." They were the cars of the super rich in an era of expanding middle-class motoring. As such, they exemplified the most advanced engineering and styling of their day—emulated, sometimes decades later, in moderately priced production cars for the masses. Not only were these cars at the cutting edge of technological and stylistic innovation, the chassis manufacturers and custom coach builders responsible for them also form the critical link bridging the transition from a pioneering auto industry headed in the main by amateur inventors and practical mechanics to the mature post–World War II industry dominated by professional stylists and cost-cutting accountants. Carson's 1976 *The Olympian Cars: The Great American Luxury Automobiles of the Twenties and Thirties* offers an excellent introduction to the topic.[1]

Yet much remains to be done. As Paul Brennan complained in 1982 in *Automobile Quarterly*, "Anyone who makes even a cursory examination of the literature devoted to custom-built luxury automobiles can find a number of fine, detailed articles about an individual prestige chassis or single coachbuilder. But the body of more comprehensive studies is small and self-contradictory, and there is virtually nothing that gives a systematic overview and analysis of the luxury car phenomenon itself."[2]

As I demonstrated in my 1970 book *America Adopts the Automobile*, the automobile never was in concept or in fact exclusively "a plaything of the idle rich."[3] From the very beginning of its development, the automobile was portrayed in the popular circulating media both here and in Europe as a potentially practical road vehicle that would come to be lowered in price and would supersede the horse in the near future. And early auto enthusiasts, especially in the United States, included many middle-class persons with a mechanical bent.

Lynwood Bryant has called the 1901 Mercedes "the first modern motor-car in all respects."[4] It featured a honeycomb radiator, a pressed-steel chassis, mechanically operated intake valves, and an improved gate gearbox. Its thirty-five-horsepower engine achieved a speed of fifty-three miles per hour. This Mercedes was technologically light-years in advance of the contemporary American 1901 three-horsepower curved-dash Oldsmobile, the first gasoline automobile produced in significant volume, for the "Olds" was in all respects merely a motorized horse buggy, and it rattled apart in a short time. The Mercedes sold for ten times the price of the $650 Olds, not because it was a luxury car but because the best artisanal methods of the day made any reliable car expensive to produce. As late as 1909, at the most integrated automobile factory in Europe at Stuttgart, Germany, seventeen hundred workers produced annually fewer than one thousand Mercedes cars. So, too, in the United States, as late as 1913 and after Frederick Winslow Taylor's principles of "scientific" management of labor had been adopted to rationalize production, at Packard in Detroit it still took 4,525 workers to produce only 2,984 cars, an annual production rate of about one car for every 1.5 workers.

Reconciliation of the quality of the 1901 Mercedes with the low price of the 1901 curved-dash Olds was achieved by the Ford Motor Company first with its 1906–7 Model N, then more spectacularly with its 1908 Model T through mass-production techniques, most notably the moving assembly line, innovated at Ford's Highland Park plant in 1913–14. The Model T was an exceptional car for its day, and Ford's advertising boast was essentially correct: "No car under $2,000 offers more, and no car over $2,000 offers more except the trimmings." By its withdrawal from the market in 1927, its price had been lowered to only $290 for the coupe, and some fifteen million units had been sold, making mass personal automobility a reality in the United States.

Elsewhere, I have demonstrated that, in contrast with Ford and other early American automotive entrepreneurs, the early European automobile industry was dominated by formally trained engineers, who sought the technical perfection of the car at the expense of not standardizing design to produce in volume so that unit prices could be lowered.[5] Artisanal production for a very limited upper-class market also was encouraged in Europe by low per capita incomes and inequitable income distribution relative to the United States. Additionally, European roads were vastly superior to American roads, which were until the mid-1920s too primitive to accommodate powerful, fast luxury cars. These factors combined to give European automakers a decided lead in the development of the true luxury car in the years immediately preceding the First World War, from about 1909 to 1914, while American automakers, led by Ford, were developing a mass market for motorcars in the United States.

Paradoxically, however, the American luxury car market, the largest luxury car market in the world by far, depended upon the development of the mass market for the Model T as well as on the better roads provided by the 1916 Federal Aid Road Act and the 1921 Federal Highway Act, which led to an interconnected system of state highways by the mid-1920s. As Carson points out, "The luxury car's rise depended on acceptance of the basic motoring experience as commonplace, and this condition had been met by 1925. As long as an automotive journey seemed rare and exotic in itself, there was little demand in refining that experience, but, when riding in a car became an everyday event, the jaded and affluent began to expect new and more specialized pleasures from their vehicles."[6] Concrete interstate highways and the tourist services that came with them—the result of mass motorization—made long-distance travel by luxury car an attractive alternative to the Pullman compartment for the American elite.

"The first signs of a coming luxury consciousness in America were given by the Importers' Salon, which was founded just before World War I," Carson relates. "Presented annually in New York City, the Importers' Salon brought before an elite and moneyed audience the very finest of European motorcars."[7] Rolls Royce and Mercedes were both prominent marques. The most technologically advanced chassis of the day, however, were the Milanese-built Isotta-Fraschini and the French-built Hispano-Suiza.

The Isotta-Fraschini Tipo 8 light-alloy engine was the first production straight-8, and the car featured four-wheel brakes. Its merits remain largely academic, however, for despite the fact that the Tipo 8 was designed with the American market in mind, only nineteen Tipo 8 chassis were shipped to the United States between 1919 and 1932.

The 1919 overhead cam engine that powered the Hispano-Suiza H6 model chassis in the 1920s was half of the V-12 airplane engine produced by the firm during the war. Its capacity was increased from four hundred cubic inch displacement (CID) to 423 CID in the mid-1920s, giving it 10 percent more displacement than the American Duesenberg Model J. At $14,500 per unit, the Hispano-Suiza chassis was the most expensive produced on either side of the Atlantic. "While no more than 2,614 chassis in the H6 series were produced—perhaps a quarter of these were exported to the United States—their impact was profound," relates Brennan. "Strother MacMinn has epitomized the judgment of other authorities in calling this Hispano concept 'the most innovative and significant design of the [1920s] decade.'"[8] Hugo Pfau comments that "Hispano built only chassis, and these were fitted with bodies from the finest coachbuilders the world over. Rarely was more than one of a design built, since the clientele constituted the elite of the world who wanted individuality above all else." Pfau concurs that "many experts consider the Hispano-Suiza, especially the H-6 models, the finest automobile of all time."[9]

The first American chassis able to compete with these European chassis were introduced in 1920—the Lincoln on September 25, and the Duesenberg a few weeks later. Carson points out that the popularity of other luxury marques notwithstanding, "together, the Duesenberg and the Lincoln defined the new objectives of chassis development that Americans would pursue for the next two decades. . . . Leland's theme of using engine power to increase smoothness, ease, and reliability of operation was always more popular than Duesenberg's of increasing over-the-road speed potential."[10]

Henry M. Leland initially had developed the Cadillac, which won the prestigious Dewar Trophy of the Royal Automobile Club of England in 1908 for previously unparalleled parts' interchangeability and again in 1912 for innovation of the self-starter. The 1914 Cadillac was the first American production car powered by a V-8 engine.

Leland and his son Wilfred left General Motors (GM) following an altercation with GM founder William C. Durant over their desire to switch Cadillac production entirely over to the Liberty Aircraft engine as a patriotic duty. The Lincoln Model L was envisioned as America's first "permanent car," a car so well designed and built that it would never need to be replaced. The Lincoln V-8 engine had a larger cylinder capacity than the Cadillac and a sixty degree rather than a ninety degree angle of V between the cylinders to reduce synchronous vibration. The Lincoln L, in Carson's words, "inspired other marques toward a luxury standard of performance that was refined in operation and enduring in quality."[11]

Fred Duesenberg developed the Duesenberg Model A prototype after doing work during the war on a huge French aircraft engine designed by Ettore Bugatti. The Duesenberg Model A was the first American car powered by a straight eight-cylinder engine, and it was the first American car to feature the sensitive handling and excellent braking found on the Isotta-Fraschini and the Hispano-Suiza. The Model A was America's earliest high-performance passenger car. It was surpassed in 1932 by the Duesenberg Model J, which developed 265 brake horsepower (bhp), about twice the horsepower of any car on the road. The supercharged Duesenberg Model SJ developed 320 bhp, and, fitted with an aerodynamic body in 1935, it set International Class B speed records of 135.47 miles per hour for twenty-four hours and 152.145 miles per hour for one-hour running times. Only some four hundred eighty J and SJ Duesenbergs were produced between the J's debut in 1928 and the company's failure in 1937. The Duesenberg J models marked the zenith in development of luxury car chassis.

Durant-Dort and Studebaker are the prime examples of leading carriage and wagon manufacturers who became large-volume producers of moderately priced automobiles. So too did many of the builders of custom horse-drawn coaches make the easy transition to providing custom automobile bodies for luxury car chassis. Early automobile bodies closely copied horse-drawn body types—such as the phaeton, the brougham, and the landau. However, whereas for a variety of reasons the manufacture of automobiles came to be centered in southern Michigan by 1905, the overwhelming majority of custom coach builders remained located in the East, in close proximity to their wealthy patrons. Indeed, the early market for luxury cars was so limited geographically that until after 1920 few cars were purchased at the Importers' Salon by persons living outside the environs of New York City. Pfau lists a total of one hundred-sixteen American firms that made custom automobile bodies prior to the Second World War.[12] Among the more prominent Eastern old-line custom coach builders—those who made the transition from making custom bodies for horse-drawn to motor vehicles—were Brewster, Brunn, Derham, Fleetwood, and Judkins. While the volume production of passenger cars in Detroit rapidly developed after 1910 into an oligopolistic, mass-production industry, the custom coach builders were very small businesses that relied on outmoded artisanal production methods and were controlled by master craftsmen from the shop floor. Furthermore, while Ford, General Motors, and Chrysler Corporation returned huge profits to their stockholders, the coach builders survived from hand to mouth, even during the prosperous 1920s. Although custom bodies generally sold for between $5,000 and $15,000, the profit margin was slight.

During the 1920s the American coach-built car came to rival the European. By 1928 the Importers' Salon had become the Automobile Salon, with annual exhibits in Chicago, San Francisco, and Los Angeles as well as in New York. American custom coach builders were invited to participate, but their creations bore only their identification because American chassis manufacturers still were barred. In general, one day of the exhibit was set aside for potential buyers, invited from the social register and plied with champagne, one day for chauffeurs, who were expected to influence their employers and were tipped accordingly, and one day for automotive engineers representing the makers of production cars.

"Prior to the First World War," writes David H. Ross, "American coach-building was a conservative affair. The automobile bodies built by the old-line custom coachbuilders . . . were as staid and formal in their designs as was the clientele who bought them." The luxury car market, however, not only expanded greatly as the rich became still richer with Coolidge prosperity, but its nature changed fundamentally as movie idols sought to display their newly gained wealth and status. From the introduction of the automobile in the United States, southern California had been known in the auto industry as "a bottomless pit" for new-car sales. With the rise of the movie industry in the 1920s, it was inevitable that southern California, which led the nation in the ratio of cars to people, become the mainstay of the market for custom-built luxury cars. Duesenberg, Lincoln, and Cadillac were the favored chassis in southern California, where taste in bodies often ran to garish extremes. Eastern coach builders found that outlandish designs, impossible to dispose of at any price elsewhere, found ready buyers in Hollywood. And the cars of the stars began to set trends in luxury car design. One result, according to Ross, was that "the younger generation in families of long-established wealth wanted a new approach to automotive design with more fleet and graceful lines, an expression of power and motion—even when the car was standing still. And the newly rich wanted more flash, more ostentation. . . . Both groups were demanding that the cars, the bodies, be styled—not merely engineered to a set of formal shapes."[13]

The new demand that custom-built bodies be styled was met in particular by LeBaron, Inc., Carrossiers in New York City, Don Lee in Hollywood, and Walter M. Murphy in Pasadena. Each of these firms made unique and significant contributions to the development of automobile styling.

LeBaron was formed in 1920 by twenty-six-year-old Raymond H. Dietrich and twenty-four-year-old Thomas L. Hibbard. Both had been drafts-men at the old-line coach-building firm of Brewster and Company, which began building custom automobile bodies in 1910. "As draftsmen," Carson explains, "their talents were totally subservient to those of the master wood-workers and metal shapers, just as they would have been at . . . any other coachbuilding house of the time . . . making full-scale drawings of component body parts to aid in the construction of templates." But at LeBaron, Dietrich and Hibbard turned the tables to establish the primacy of the designer, innovate the "free form designing idea" of conceptualizing the design of the car as a whole, and develop "a larger new theme of 'automotive architecture,' which amounted to applying the architect's traditional role to the field of luxury auto building. . . . The customer didn't buy an automobile from Dietrich and Hibbard; what he bought were the complete plans with which an automobile body could be built."[14]

Hibbard left in 1923 to go into the custom body business with Howard "Dutch" Darrin in Paris, and most Hispano-Suiza chassis imported into the United States in the 1920s were fitted with Hibbard and Darrin bodies. By 1923 LeBaron too was making custom bodies at Bridgeport, Connecticut. Pfau, who worked at LeBaron, recalled that "we kept in our office a copy of the current social register. Most of our customers were listed in it." He also noted that LeBaron's "major clientele were not impressed by movie stars but only by fellow members of the '400.'"[15] Nevertheless, Rudolph Valentino and Gloria Swanson were among LeBaron's earliest customers, and the bodies built for them on Isotta-Fraschini chassis remain probably the best-known LeBaron creations. LeBaron designs characteristically emphasized long, low lines.

Walter M. Murphy came from a Detroit family that had made its fortune in lumbering. An uncle, William H. Murphy, had first been a backer of Henry Ford's early automotive ventures, then a stockholder in Henry M. Leland's Cadillac. Walter Murphy began selling Simplex and Locomobile cars with custom bodies in Los Angeles in 1916. He became the California distributor for the new Lincoln car in 1920 and was forced into the body business by the Lincoln's stodgy styling and poor body engineering. The Lincoln possessed a near perfect chassis, but Herman C. Brunn relates that "the bodies were so poorly engineered that people got out and walked home from demonstrations because of uncomfortable seats and body rumbles."[16] The body sat so high that one could enter it with a hat on without stooping. And the car came only in dark green, dark blue, and black. To sell the car in southern California, Murphy had to lower its roof six inches and repaint it in brighter colors. He also made custom bodies for Lincoln chassis. The second one produced, a phaeton, was for Douglas Fairbanks, newly married to Mary Pickford.

The problem of Lincoln styling ended with the acquisition of Lincoln from the Lelands by Ford in 1922. Edsel Ford, the new Lincoln president, had an impeccable aesthetic sensitivity and set about immediately to improve the styling of the production Lincoln.

Murphy then turned to building custom bodies for a variety of chassis at his Pasadena plant, and he swapped his Lincoln distributorship for a Hudson distributorship in 1926. His "most inspired design proposals" were made for the Model J Duesenberg, which Strother MacMinn claims "undoubtedly had a greater impact on the international car market than any other American car before or since. . . . Murphy built more bodies on Duesenberg chassis than any other marque. Likewise, more Duesenbergs carried Murphy bodies than from any other coach builder. It was the peak of an era.[17] Murphy's forte was in designing convertibles and roadsters in an era when the open touring car was rapidly being replaced by the closed sedan, and he innovated the system by which the convertible top folded down into a well behind the driver's seat. Like LeBaron, Murphy designs featured long, low, functional lines.

Upon Murphy's retirement in 1932, Christian Bohman and Max Schwartz, two of his workmen, took over the business under the name Bohman and Schwartz, with the initial aim of completing the rebuilding of cars then in the shop belonging to Eddy Peabody and Gary Cooper. They remained in the customizing business until 1944. Clark Gable's 1937 Bohman and Schwartz restyled Rollston-bodied Duesenberg JN Roadster, now in the Behring collection at Blackhawk, California, is probably the most famous southern California coach-built car.

Don Lee was the West Coast Cadillac distributor. The Earl Automobile Works did custom bodywork on Cadillac chassis for Lee. The owner's son, Harley J. Earl, became Lee's chief designer. As MacMinn says, "Earl's dramatic designs for prominent members of society and the movie colony . . . hit the market's bull's-eye and, simultaneously . . . burnished Cadillac's West Coast prestige and acceptance to perfection."[18] Earl used modeling clay in developing his designs instead of the then-conventional wooden models and hammered metal parts. This approach permitted him to conceptualize more fluid, rounded shapes. Like LeBaron, he also departed from common practice, in Alfred P. Sloan, Jr.'s words, by "designing the complete automobile, shaping the body, hood, fenders, headlights, and running boards and blending them into a good looking whole. This, too, was a novel technique."[19]

As early as 1921, the General Motors product policy had stressed "the very great importance of style in selling," and, in a letter dated July 8, 1926, to Harry H. Bassett, the general manager of Buick, GM president Alfred

Sloan, expressed his "general views about the need [for GM] to develop a styling program." His views about the importance of styling were shared by Lawrence P. Fisher, the general manager of Cadillac, who had been impressed by the special Cadillac bodies designed by Harley Earl for Hollywood stars. In early 1926 Fisher hired Earl under special contract as a consultant to Cadillac. Prior to that, in September, 1925, Fisher Body (annexed as a division of GM in 1918) had acquired the old-line Fleetwood custom coachbuilding firm of Reading, Pennsylvania, and moved its operations to Detroit to do custom bodies for Cadillac chassis and aid in designing production-car bodies. The 1927 LaSalle, Earl's first design for GM was, in Sloan's words, "the first stylist's car to achieve success in mass production." On June 23, 1927, Sloan proposed to the GM executive committee a plan for a new Art and Color Section of fifty persons, to be headed by Earl and funded by the Fisher Body Division. Renamed the Styling Section in the 1930s, its purpose was "to direct general production body design and to conduct research and development programs in special car designs."[20]

Thus, the conception of automobile styling innovated at LeBaron by Dietrich and Hibbard in 1920 came to be institutionalized in the design of production cars at industry leader GM only seven years later. And Earl's Styling Section gave GM a "long lead" in making the styling of automobiles an institutionalized activity carried out by professional designers rather than a haphazard activity of engineers or salesmen as the need for a new model arose. After World War II both Ford and Chrysler emulated GM in forming styling departments, which were staffed largely by personnel trained under Earl at GM. One of these, Eugene Bordinat, who became Ford styling chief in 1961, recalled that when he started at Ford in 1947 its entire styling section had only fifty people including shop personnel and janitorial staff, whereas GM then employed some four hundred-fifty stylists in its various studios. Earl, who ended his career as a GM vice-president, summed up his design approach in 1954: "My primary purpose for twenty-eight years has been to lengthen and lower the American automobile, at times in reality and always at least in appearance. Why? Because my sense of proportion tells me that oblongs are more attractive than squares."[21]

The GM lead in institutionalizing styling notwithstanding, important contributions were made as well at Lincoln by style-conscious Edsel Ford. In 1925 Edsel introduced the "catalogue custom body." By ordering custom bodies in small lots of three to ten, Edsel was able to offer them as options in the Lincoln catalog at prices significantly lower than one-of-a-kind bodies cost; yet, because there was small chance that the owners of the same custom body would ever cross paths, the bodies could be considered individualized. Edsel also pioneered in formalizing the relationship between stylists and automobile manufacturers by luring Ray Dietrich from LeBaron to Detroit in 1925. A new independent firm, Dietrich, Inc., did catalog custom bodywork and acted as a consultant on the styling of Lincoln production cars. Then in 1928, at Edsel's instigation, LeBaron was acquired by the Briggs Manufacturing Company, and a core of LeBaron master craftsmen were brought to Detroit to open a body plant. The LeBaron Bridgeport Plant was closed in 1932, the same year that Dietrich was hired as a special consultant on body design by Walter P. Chrysler.

The movement of independent custom coach builders into the embryonic styling sections of production car manufacturers was completed in the early 1930s. Sloan's wife, for example, impressed by Hibbard and Darrin designs on a trip to Paris, got him to hire Tom Hibbard in Earl's Styling Section at GM. It was a major error, for the Sloans did not know that Dutch Darrin did the car designs, while Hibbard only sold them. Nevertheless, Hibbard was to end his automotive career as the head of design at Ford in the late 1940s.

Carson sees 1933 as marking the end of the true luxury car market in the United States and of the custom coach-building firms. Luxury car sales peaked at about 150,000 units (or 5 percent of total American demand) in 1928 and 1929, then declined sharply to less than 20,000 units in 1933. They further evaporated to a mere 10,000 units in 1937, while the rest of the automobile market experienced a general recovery. Among the chassis makers, Duesenberg, Franklin, Marmon, Peerless, and Pierce-Arrow failed as firms; Cadillac V-16, Chrysler Imperial, and Lincoln sales shrank to nothing; and Packard was forced to develop an integrated line of cheaper models to survive. Only a handful of custom coach builders continued to cater to a dwindling clientele up to the outbreak of World War II, then disappeared. Carson points out that the popular prestige attached in the prosperous 1920s to ownership of a unique coach-built car turned to aspersion with hard times; affluent owners were stoned while driving past breadlines. Most important, the exorbitant cost of the true luxury car became increasingly unjustifiable even to the wealthy as technological differences were erased vis-à-vis much more moderately priced production cars during the 1930s.[22]

In the final analysis, what killed off the custom coach-built car was progress in automotive technology—a combination of Duco lacquer, the closed all-steel body, and aerodynamic and structural streamlining. The technology of the custom coach-built car—so advanced over the production car in the early 1920s—was outmoded by the mid-1930s.

The Ford Model T came only in black after 1914 because only black enamel would dry fast enough for the Ford production schedule. In contrast, the high-gloss, colorful finishes on custom coach-built bodies resulted from brushing on and rubbing down by hand several dozen coats of primer, paint, and varnish, each of which took twenty-four hours to dry. Mass-produced cars of all shades and hues of the rainbow became possible with the introduction of Duco lacquer in the "True Blue" of the 1924 Oakland. Although the body-finishing process was cut by several weeks with far less labor because lacquer could be sprayed on, the custom coach builders did not begin to use it until after 1928 because it lacked the gloss of hand-rubbed varnish and required better preparation of the body panels to hide imperfections. They were forced to switch over to lacquer, however, once it became apparent that the lacquer finishes on production bodies were far more durable than the varnish finishes on their custom bodies.

Up to the 1920s open bodies prevailed, with closed bodies being found on only the more expensive production and custom-bodied cars. Body frames for both production and custom cars were handcrafted from white ash. Side panels were sheet steel on production cars, but on custom bodies they generally were hammered from more expensive aluminum, which lacked the strength of steel but could be more easily fashioned into the curvilinear shapes desired by the custom coach builders.

The construction of production car bodies was revolutionized in the early 1920s, while the custom coach builders stood still technologically. The single most important innovation in automotive technology in the interwar period was the closed steel body. Only 10.3 percent of cars built in the United States were closed in 1919 versus 82.2 percent in 1927. Closed cars used much more plate glass than open cars and required different materials for upholstery. The cost of plate glass was reduced significantly, and its quality improved by a continuous-process technique introduced and perfected by Clarence W. Avery at Ford between 1919 and 1921. Hudson's innovation of simpler, standardized parts and sub-assemblies for car bodies resulted in its introduction of the first inexpensive closed car in 1921.

Edward G. Budd innovated an all-steel body that was introduced in the 1912 Oakland and Hupmobile models and in the 1914 Dodge. Then Dodge in 1923 introduced the first closed sheet-steel body, with wood and waterproof fabric used only on its roof. The closed sheet-steel body was adapted to the Model T in 1925. Cadillac, Chrysler, and Packard also had adopted the closed sheet-steel body by 1928, although as late as 1934 most GM cars still used wood framing with sheet metal on all exterior surfaces except the roof. Steel roofs did not appear on cars until the 1935 model year, when GM introduced its one-piece steel "turret top" and Studebaker came out with an all-steel roof made by Budd.

The all-steel body, notes William J. Abernathy, "promised strength with less weight, greater styling possibilities, and mass production economies." These promises were realized as production techniques impossible for the custom coach builders to implement were improved. Abernathy describes a number of significant developments:

> Because of the greater temperature tolerance of steel, paint could be 'baked' on, thereby permitting a faster finishing process. . . . Box annealing, normalizing, and loose rolling processes developed by the steel industry improved the quality of sheet steel. Automatic welding machines, improvements in sound deadening materials, and the monopiece body, all developed by the Budd Manufacturing Company, led to quieter and stronger steel bodies.[23]

The spread of automatic body assembly was linked closely to the adoption of the closed steel body. Introduced at Budd in 1925, automatic welding came into extensive use in 1928 at the Ford River Rouge plant in Model A production. Automatic welding reduced assembly costs while increasing the quality of the product. According to Abernathy, it "produced strong and neat joints with greater speed and uniformity than previous assembly methods. The assembly consumed less material, and the resulting body was lighter."[24]

Thus, by the late 1920s, aesthetics aside, the bodies on moderately priced production cars were in fact functionally vastly superior to custom coach-built bodies. As Pfau explains, "In limited production or for an individually built body, wood could be shaped more cheaply than steel, the cost of expensive dies is nominal when spread over hundreds of thousands of cars, but prohibitive on a single unit or even a few hundred." He observes that "the widespread adoption of the all-steel body in the thirties . . . hastened the demise of coachbuilding in the U.S., because its welded construction guarded against deterioration and squeaks as effectively as the most expensive custom body."[25]

While the custom coach builders continued to practice visual streamlining, an intuitive artist's conception of curvilinear shapes, the production car manufacturers in the 1930s began to adopt aerodynamic streamlining—design based upon engineering principles and concepts—and to innovate structural streamlining in the form of the unitary welded body. The unitary body did away with the frame as a separate unit onto which the body was grafted; hence, it struck at the very heart of the custom coach builder's craft. By merging the chassis and the body into one unit, the unitary welded body eliminated structural duplication of rigidity to result in a far lighter, stronger car. The integration of aerodynamic and structural with visual streamlining was first achieved in the revolutionary 1934 Chrysler and DeSoto Airflow models. Carson calls the Airflow "Art Moderne's furthest extension of influence in American auto building" but asserts that it was also a "totally engineered car designed from the inside out . . . the first American production car whose shape was fashioned according to scientific rather than aesthetic standards." He goes on to observe that "the Airflow's heterodox [welded unitary] construction required a technology that was, at that time, beyond the custom coach builders, eliminating the possibility of custom-bodied Airflow cars."[26] Other aerodynamic, unitary-bodied production cars of the mid-1930s were the 1936 Lincoln Zephyr and the 1936–37 coffin-hooded Cord 810–812. These revolutionary cars demonstrated that the custom coach-built car was technologically obsolete, but at the time only the Zephyr was a market success.

Aerodynamic automobile design and the unitary welded body were not to come into their own until the mid-1980s, in part because their full implementation depended upon the development of computer-aided design and engineering and in part because functional automobile styling and engineering in the United States finally was necessitated by federal safety, emissions, and energy consumption standards. Between this recent turn to aerodynamic, unitary-bodied cars and the end of the coach-built era in the 1930s, Detroit designers engaged in any orgy of dysfunctional styling, which Gene Bordinat, shortly before his death in 1987, recalled as "the age of schlock and gorp." Ironically, stylists once responsible for some of the finest examples of the coachbuilders' art in the interwar period, led by Harley Earl and his protégé William L. Mitchell at GM, turned out the most grotesque mass-produced cars in automotive history during the 1950s. How and why this happened is another story.

# 12. Alan Hess

## STYLING THE STRIP:
### CAR AND ROADSIDE DESIGN IN THE 1950s

The autos and the roadside buildings of Los Angeles in the 1950s are cut from the same cultural cloth. The era's evolving car-oriented lifestyle hitched car and drive-in together in a functional symbiosis: cars brought people to hamburger stands; hamburger stands gave people reason to cruise. But there was more. Together, the car and the architecture of the car culture constituted a popular aesthetic of kinetics, symbols, structure, forms and experiment, and a new urban space that flowed freely from the driver's seat to the coffee shop counter.

More than basic transportation or simple shelter, cars and architecture were mass media in an era of mass consumerism, and, more than any other media, they were to interpret the postwar world to the general public. Traditional critics were bewildered by the results. But the stylists and architects who were creating the remarkably coherent vocabulary of the strip, from steering wheel to sign, realized the role of symbol and metaphor in the strip—that indigenous American urban form. Symbols became functional as they helped to shape that space.

I recently drove through California's San Joaquin Valley in a 1946 Ford, one of the first models built after World War II. The two-day tour was one of those illuminating encounters with an historical artifact that brings to life the ideas and views of its era. Driver and passengers sit bolt upright on a seat with all the comfort and propriety of a living room couch—a long way from the slouching cockpits car interiors have become. The western landscape unfolds in the streamlined picture frames of the windows. The passenger compartment itself is a teardrop of space.

In concept, this Ford is a 1930s design, a child of the 1934 Chrysler Airflow, the 1936 Lincoln Zephyr, and even Buckminster Fuller's 1933 Dymaxion car. When it first appeared, it was the image of the streamlined car—an aerodynamic shape in which the individual pieces of the machine (hood, fenders, windows, and trunk) were identifiable but subordinated to the unifying flow of aerodynamic lines.

Roadside architecture after the Second World War likewise exhibited the holdover effect of the late Moderne style. A contemporary coffee shop in

**FIGURE 12.1**

*1946 Ford Fordor DeLuxe Sedan. Postwar car styling continued the Streamline Moderne of the 1930s.*

168

**The Car and the City**

Los Angeles, the 1949 Bob's Big Boy in Toluca Lake, designed by Wayne McAllister, represents the 1939 landscape Aldous Huxley was talking about when he wrote that Los Angeles' streets looked "like the pavilions at some endless international exhibition."[1] If it had been built at the 1939 New York World's Fair, this Bob's, with its tall pylon and broad amoeba-shaped canopies, could easily have passed as the exhibition pavilion for some Balkan nation or maybe a minor industry association. But what is significant about this Bob's Big Boy is the attention given to the restaurant's broad curving plate glass window wall. It is a picture window to frame the panorama of the street as entertainment for the diners. It is a natural evolution from the days of the carhop drive-in, when the car itself was the dining room, and it reveals a frank and relaxed attitude about the car culture; cars were not to be hidden.

The other dominant element in the architecture, the sign pylon, emphasizes another link between building and car by giving the building a graphic presence on the strip by day or night. With bold liquid lettering, this billboard sign is a signature like a car's grill, deliberately designed to communicate identity across the broad distances of the commercial strip.

But as functionally inventive as these late Streamline Moderne forms were, their mechanistic imagery had already been rendered obsolete by the time of Hiroshima. New materials, new modes of transportation and communication, and new energy sources were injecting powerful images into the culture. They were too insistent, too tempting to be ignored by architects, stylists—or the public. The impact of transistors, plastics, television, and freeways on everyday life was tangible, and it was bound to be echoed in the architecture and the cars on the landscape. As major media for dispersing the culture's ideas, both car and commercial architecture design had to reflect those changes.

So the 1950s became an era of pluralist experiment with no single accepted style. The designers of the strip and the car became the culture's interpreters, grasping the confusing, accelerating changes in technology, media, society, and urban growth and giving them expression in a vocabulary accessible to the public. The car companies lagged behind architecture because of the long lead time for retooling. Some architects, frustrated that the models on the streets did not match the spirit of their designs, invented appropriately sleek cars for renderings. More than ever before, commercial vernacular design became public art.

A key building in the development of strip space was architect John Lautner's 1947 Henry's Drive-in found in Glendale, California. The visual

**FIGURE 12.2**

*Bob's Big Boy, 1949, Wayne McAllister, architect, Riverside Drive and Alameda, Toluca Lake, California (extant). Postwar architecture, like car styling, at first picked up where Late Streamline Moderne had left off.*

---

170

The Car and the City

**FIGURE 12.3**

*Henry's Drive-in, 1947, John Lautner, architect, Glendate Boulevard at Colorado, Glendale,
California (demolished). Architect John Lautner paved the way for more daring expressions of
structure, indoor-outdoor spaces, and natural materials.*

contrast between this contemporary building and the 1947 models that parked beneath its canopy was as great as between Le Corbusier's 1921 Villa Stein at Garches and the auto he rhetorically parked in front of it for publication photos. Of course, Le Corbusier meant for us to see the two as cut from the same cloth, but the similarities are largely lost today. The car, typical of the times, looks merely old-fashioned, while the building still looks adventurous.

Lautner's building also pointed to the future, while the cars pointed to the past. The 1940s cars were rounded, solid forms. The drive-in had jagged lines and hovering cantilevers. These lines spoke of an entirely new aesthetic symbolizing an entirely new age. It was an aesthetic of movement, power, technology, space, and especially articulation. Gone were the single, all-encompassing form of the teardrop or the stuccoed abstractions of the Bob's Big Boy. In their place, an array of angles and planes vied for dominance.

A page from a 1955 General Motors promotional booklet, titled "Styling: The Look of Things" showed a universe of floating Platonic volumes and squiggly lines—the primordial soup of 1950s design.[2] It was the stylist's or architect's job to harness more than compose them. The same gravity-defying geometries show up in architecture and cars.

At Henry's, a broad V-shaped roof jutted out toward the corner like a hood ornament. Concrete walls angled up out of the asphalt earth. Brick planes, casually positioned, indicated inside and out. Lautner used a palette of stucco, concrete, brick, and metal, trimmed with neon tubing. The nature of the structure and materials was carefully articulated; at one point a stucco roof falls just short of a concrete wall to flaunt its cantilever structure.

Soon car stylists took up the theme of structural articulation as well, both in fact and metaphor. Authentic cantilever roofs actually were attempted in some dream cars, but symbolic cantilevers were common in production models by the end of the decade. By then cars had clearly caught up with buildings. A 1959 Chevy or Mercury station wagon parked in front of Ship's Coffee Shop on Wilshire Boulevard could match the architecture's catapulting cantilevers and glassy walls. Stretching apparently from the rear seat pillar all the way to the rear gate, station wagon roofs echoed architectural experiments in antigravity. The appearance was strengthened by the placement of the wagon's rear door pillar—set in from the corner. The glass of the rear panel turned the corner, leaving glass where you would expect to see a support. The chromed pillar, reflecting the sky, just disappeared. The entire sheet metal roof read as one jutting plane from front to back.

It was an aesthetic based on experiment, exploring the frontiers of structure and material. It was an aesthetic of lightness, centrifugal forms, movement, and inclusion. The palette was varied, the textures multiple; one representative carwash sign on Fresno's main strip, Blackstone Boulevard, contained two different typefaces (script and serif), three different forms (square, circle, and line), and three materials (neon, metal, and plastic). For centuries columns and arches reflected the fact that gravity had held buildings together. Streamline Moderne's curves seemed glued together by ballistic forces. But no known energy source held the disparate elements of these new designs together. They inferred a binding energy beyond mere gravity. Streamlining's subordination of the parts to the whole was replaced by the articulation of separate but equal elements.

Space was also to be transformed as profoundly as structure by the car and roadside modernism. Lautner's Henry's had taken the integration of interior and exterior space a step further than McAllister's Bob's Big Boy by uniting the dining areas and the strip itself into one continuous car culture space. Here on a commercial corner, Lautner created an outdoor dining patio, buffered from the parking lot by planters and shaded from the sun by perforated metal sheets setting on expanded metal trusses. The same overhead structure flowed inside to link it to the outside. Large plate glass windows from floor to ceiling kept out the heat and noise but never obstructed the sense that the indoors and out were one continuous space.

The New Spaciousness allowed vision to flow from dashboard and windshield to the coffee shop table in one sweep. In architecture, Los Angeles' Biff's of the early 1950s by architect Douglas Honnold went even farther than Henry's in refining this spatial relationship. At Biff's your car sat like a tethered horse directly over your shoulder as you ate at the counter. Under the guidance of Honnold, a sophisticated architect, the idea became an integrated, conscious part of Biff's design. The plate glass went from floor to ceiling as in-fill for the minimal exposed I-beam structure. The car was not to be hidden or ignored; it was a veritable piece of the architecture. And its moving, changing, glinting, evanescent presence was to be integrated and played up in these buildings—the neon strips of Biff's reflected in the curves and moldings of the cars.

The mobile car and the immobile building had slowly been woven into one seamless landscape. Bob's Big Boy gave you a picture window of the strip; Henry's gave you a patio on the strip; Biff's brought the car almost smack into the middle of the restaurant.

The car itself and the way people used it made this new concept of space practical and even inevitable. People ate, watched movies, banked, and often shopped in the car. Architects and businesspeople responded to that fact. But still it took car stylists a few years to catch up with architecture in expressing the connection visually. The destruction of the barrier between inside and out had been stylists' goal for years; it seemed like every other dream car in the 1950s, from the Lincoln Futura to the General Motors Firebirds, had a bubble roof. But production glass manufacturing was not up to the challenge at the start of the 1950s, so advances were incremental as stylists inched toward their goal.

First, windshields, traditionally divided in two, had become one sheet of glass. Still, most car interiors were safely framed in a cage of roof pillars. But step by step, car greenhouses—the passenger compartment above the doors—grew more airy and spacious, as stylists experimented with the possibilities of glass. More and more, the car was banishing obstructions and weaving the passenger into the environment as architecture had. As the driver's field of vision was increased, so was the symbolic inference of these glassy greenhouses, just a stone's throw from the untrammeled freedom of a convertible.

With its enormous resources and staff, General Motors introduced the extravagant but problematic innovation of wraparound windshields in the mid-1950s. They distorted vision at the edges but had the strategic effect of making GM cars look more advanced than their competitors. It was the highly popular aesthetic of experiment.

By 1959 windshields had grown enormous brows and GM's four-door hardtops offered truly panoramic views in all directions. Their rear windows were amazing glass sculptures. The point was made. Car and architecture shared a common spatial concept. The car culture had created a unified environment from driver's seat to counter seat. As drivers metamorphosed into pedestrians and back again, the same concepts of space, symbol, and technology enveloped them.

Form was affected as much as space and structure, as stylists and architects tested the boundaries of manufacturing techniques and imagery. Some of the earlier examples had been fairly chaste. The stripped-down simplicity of Biff's was paralleled in auto styling by the 1949 Ford, which both culminated and broke away from the course of streamlining; while it pulled fenders, hood, and body into one smooth form, its square sides broke the tyranny of the teardrop curve. But for an energetic era bent on testing

chromed side spears, the images of jet propulsion shaped cars. Mid-decade cars, when each bump was still expensive, relied on modest impressions and chrome lines and two-tone colors to conjure the image of lowness and speed.

But if imagination still outran technology, technology was closing the gap. By the decade's end, improvements in sheet metal stampings allowed the entire car to be refigured in the image of the rocket. Remarkable curvilinear impressions were possible in models like the 1959 gull-wing Chevy and boomerang tail-lights of the 1959 Mercury. The 1959 Chryslers transmuted hood and trunk sheet metal into a soft blanket lapping over the fenders.

True, these shapes often flaunted innovation for its own sake. The GM catalog took the sheet metal medium even further, mixing technological phantasms with the sensual topography of the human body. The fiberglass curves of a 1959 Corvette, for example, were virtually human, nearly the line between shoulder bone and the back. Most GM cars of the period had anthropomorphic grills, with glowering eyebrows on the Cadillacs and air scoops full of clenched teeth.

The extravagance and variety of the Le Sabre's automotive progeny led to the canonical criticism of 1950s cars as chrome-plated dinosaurs. "It is inappropriate when jets or rockets inspire the shape of an automobile," complained industrial designer Niels Diffrient as late as 1983. "The 1959 Cadillac Coupe de Ville shows the misapplication of the functional forms of jet planes for aesthetic effect."[3] This being the 1950s, he might have added that jets were inappropriate inspiration for buildings, too. Melvin Zeitvogel festooned his sign for a San Diego Buick dealer with blazing comets, while Douglas Honnold drew inspiration from a rocket plane for his 1949 Tiny Naylor's in Hollywood.

The inconvenient fact was that Le Corbusier had enjoyed drawing lessons from airplanes as much as Harley Earl, GM's vice-president for styling, did. The only difference was the lesson drawn. For Le Corbusier and the high-art critics, aeronautics taught that an appropriate form should result *only* from a response to the physical forces imposed on the machine. But for Harley Earl the spare hard-edged minimalism of the International Style was not the only way to interpret machine imagery. Machines also telegraphed the romance of speed and the optimism of flight.

Chrysler's tailfins reflected this image best. Under styling chief Virgil Exner's guidance, their graceful lines and vivid details turned steel into a story. Chromed nozzles spat red plastic flame, the ritual fire of the space age.

**FIGURE 12.5**

*Falcon Restaurant, 1956, Armét and Davis, architects, Hawthorne, California (project). Ninety-mile-an-hour roofs and wraparound glass brought the progressive ideals and up-to-date technology of modern architecture to the popular audience.*

As stylized as the purifying flames of Buddhist art, the nozzles themselves were asymmetrical, carved away to the outside of the car, a line of propulsion twisting away from the direction of the fin.

Each piece of molded chrome was a narrative with a beginning, a middle, and an end told in line, form, and symbol. The journey of a chrome strip from front to back could be breathtaking, maintaining its organic character, but adapting and changing like a chameleon to the task at hand. A grinning chrome grill swept around to become a spear that ricocheted off a point in space to blossom into a doorhandle before tapering off into a contrail of ruby red plastic as the car slipped down the road. These cars were narratives about connections, lines of force, speed, separate but equal materials, and the transformation of energy into movement.

While Edgar Kaufmann, Jr., of the Museum of Modern Art lamented the compromises that the marketplace placed on pure functional design, GM's Harley Earl and Chrysler's Virgil Exner did not—neither did Wayne McAllister, Douglas Honnold, nor Melvin Zeitvogel.[4] Far from disdaining the limits of mass culture or commercial production, they used all the economic, engineering, corporate, and marketing constraints of the mass market to produce designs that could permit a poetic conceit in the landscape: the transformation of a jet into an automobile, a rocket port into a restaurant.

Critics of car styling and roadside design missed two major factors: addressing a pluralist society, car culture design succeeded because it used images familiar to its audience; and the consistent sculptural logic of the best of these designs showed a creativity that could equal or surpass much of the industrial and product design by better publicized designers of the period.

Roadside architecture and auto styling brought to the mass public a realization of space that placed the driver in the middle of a technologically integrated environment, a sense of structural expression, a pluralist aesthetic of experiment, an aesthetic of light playing on an object moving in space, a sure hand in designing with symbols, and the populating of the streets of the country with aesthetic objects. The significance of the car lies not in its elegance as a machine. The significance of the roadside landscape is not how well it meets the standards of high art and design. Socially and aesthetically, both are mass phenomena. In the 1950s the landscape of the car culture realized a new landscape that incorporated the forces of the new era.

# PART 4
## THE AUTOMOBILE
## AND LOS ANGELES—
## A SPECIAL RELATIONSHIP

# INTRODUCTION TO PART 4

Los Angeles often has been depicted as a city devoted to the automobile with its symbols of the freeway, the convertible, and the drive-in. How true or false is this image? Reexamining conventional explanations of the relationship between the car and the city, the five chapters in this section offer new interpretations that challenge old clichés, by emphasizing Los Angeles' similarities with other cities rather than its uniqueness.

Urban historian, Mark Foster, reviewing the recent historical literature on the city, argues that the automobile's importance in shaping the region has been overemphasized. He suggests that the popularity of this explanation of Los Angeles' urban development was partially caused by the research agenda of urban historians that focused, perhaps too narrowly, on the urban impact of technological advances. Other significant forces were neglected, particularly cultural factors, such as the compelling images of the city produced by Hollywood. In spite of this oversight, urbanization in Los Angeles was far from unique, and the sim-

ilarities with other American cities of the same period outweigh the differences. Rather than being exceptional, the city's dependence on real estate speculation, early decentralization, and ready acceptance of large-scale highway plans were typical, also occurring in areas as diverse as Detroit and Phoenix. To overcome the limitations of these interpretations, urban historians of Los Angeles need to adopt comparative and pluralist approaches.

Urban historian, Scott Bottles, examining the causes of Los Angeles' enthusiastic acceptance of the automobile, finds neither a technological imperative nor a conspiracy by automakers, but a democratic mass movement. Fed up with inefficient, expensive, and poorly planned street railways, built primarily for real estate speculation, citizens turned to the automobile for flexible and convenient transportation. They also organized themselves politically to reform the streetcar situation and, when this failed, to fight for an efficient street system and adequate parking.

Urban planner Rebecca Morales highlights a little-known aspect of

Los Angeles—its continuing role as an automobile manufacturing center. Morales sees the city as an example of a broader phenomenon. The changing nature of auto production has created distinct industrial landscapes. Fordism, the system of large-scale, assembly-line mass production maintained by mass consumption produced a characteristic landscape of large factories surrounded by tracts of housing owned by workers. Los Angeles, with nine auto assembly plants, followed this model, colonizing huge areas of the city from Long Beach to Van Nuys. Complex economic and social changes have altered this pattern, completely transforming the industry. Today, with a single large plant remaining in the city, auto production largely has been reorganized as worldwide flexible production. In this system, Los Angeles plays a specialized role, producing craft and specialty vehicles for limited markets and serving as a center for advanced design, research, and development. These small-scale and highly concentrated activities require a small number of highly skilled workers. The spatial contours of this system have not yet emerged.

Margaret Crawford, an architectural historian, expands the concept of Disneyland into a speculative description of a future Los Angeles, in which the entire city is repackaged into an endless variety of theme environments. These fantasy settings, whose themes range across space and time, reduce their meanings to entertainment for essentially commercial purposes. Crawford argues that the automobile has encouraged simulated realities by allowing Angelenos to shut out sensory impressions of the city around them. From the car the world can be perceived and understood simply as a series of two-dimensional images, similar to those on television. The avoidance of urban reality allows the selective consumption of theatricalized activities in stimulating environments. Without automobiles, the city's increasing immigrant and homeless populations lead public and pedestrian urban lives whose realities challenge and confront the spread of fantasy environments.

In the final chapter in this part, social scientist Raymond Novaco describes the relationship between the automobile and aggressive behavior, such as the recent rash of freeway shootings in Los Angeles. He theorizes that most drivers are inhibited by their socialization from driving their autos in threatening, dangerous, or aggressive ways but *that multiple disinhibitory influences are at work that lead some drivers to commit such aggressive acts as gesturing at others, accelerating in a threatening manner, or even engaging in freeway shootings. Novaco looks at the characteristics of drivers and traffic situations that might be most associated with aggressive behavior.*

# 13. Mark S. Foster

## THE ROLE OF THE AUTOMOBILE IN SHAPING A UNIQUE CITY:
### ANOTHER LOOK

Having made modest contributions over the past two decades to the debate about the role of the automobile in the urbanization of the United States, and Los Angeles in particular, here I will review recent literature concerning urbanization and automobility at the national and local levels. I also might introduce a discordant note by suggesting that analysts of urban form have overemphasized the automobile as a shaping force in the region and the uniqueness of development in southern California.

Academicians, historians included, succumb to fads more often than we care to admit. Certainly, some historical approaches and topics are fashionable for brief periods and receive concentrated attention for several years before intellectual pacesetters move on to something else. The pattern clearly is discernible at the national level. Local historians often reveal more independent thought, but, sooner or later, most are influenced by national intellectual fashions.

So it is with urban historians and chroniclers of Los Angeles. Yet, in some cases, historians responded slowly to clear calls for intellectual "action." In his seminal 1940 essay, "The City in American History," Arthur M. Schlesinger urged historians to reassess their Turnerian bias and consider the city's role as a shaping force in American civilization. The response by historians was listless. The 1940s and 1950s marked publication of dutiful urban biographies, but not until the early 1960s, following an influential essay by Eric Lampard, did American historians begin examining systematically the urbanization *process*. In the meantime, practitioners in many other academic disciplines had long since passed them by. In the mid-1960s urban history sprang to life. George Mowry, Sam Bass Warner, Jr., Blake McKelvey, Roy Lubove, and other leaders offered exciting new agendas for reexamining the emergence of a national urban culture.[1]

Those analyzing the urbanization process dealt with concepts that historians had never directly raised, let alone seriously explored. They quickly made up for lost time, and by the 1970s and 1980s at least one, and often several, historians had assessed the urban impact of dozens of technological advances. Historians also reassessed the impact upon urbanization by immigrants, political machines, and many other interest groups. In their haste to assess all forces influencing the urban landscape, some coverage has been quite thin. While many of the scores of monographs make important contributions to our understanding of urbanization, some scholars treat their topics in a vacuum, almost as if they were independent of other influences. In a 1981 review essay, "Urban History: Retrospect and Prospect," Michael H. Ebner concluded that "urban historians should be pluralists—in method, substance, ideology, and taste—instead of fastening upon oversimplified and needlessly narrow resolutions to obviously complex research problems."[2] This excellent suggestion retains relevance today for urban historians in general and those examining the emergence of the Southland.

Transportation as a shaping force in urban America attracted considerable attention from historians. Before 1960 there was already a large body of literature on transportation's "external" impact on urban growth: the role of improved roads, canals, steam-powered vessels, and railroads. In the 1960s historians examined how transportation transformed cities internally, from the inside out. Sam Bass Warner, Jr., George R. Taylor, George Smerk, and many others focused on the street railway's key role in encouraging decentralization in the late nineteenth century. In the 1970s, Clay McShane, Joel A. Tarr, Charles Cheape, and others stressed the tensions street railway companies experienced concerning their private function as profitable investments and the public's demand for service. Many street railway company founders were interested in little more than quick profits in land subdivision and speculation. Public officials, with valuable franchises to award, were often interested more in bribes and patronage than in solving transportation puzzles. In many cities, streetcar patrons were seemingly the only ones sincerely interested in affordable, efficient urban transportation. Even these citizens seldom considered issues beyond those involving their personal mobility and the integrity of their neighborhoods. Consequently, they possessed little clout. Inarticulate and disorganized at least until the early twentieth century, they were usually relegated to the end of the line in the decision-making process.[3]

Trolley and automobile buffs long ago documented the presence of these two devices on the streets of America's cities, but not until the 1960s and 1970s did historians systematically focus on the automobile's role as a shaping force in American society in general and the city in particular. John B. Rae and James J. Flink were leaders in analyzing the automobile's broad cultural impact.[4] By the early 1970s urban historians began examining the automobile's role in physically transforming the American city. Sam Bass Warner, Jr., offered a provocative analysis in *The Urban Wilderness* in 1972. Paul Barrett, Blaine A. Brownell, Mark S. Foster, Glen E. Holt, Howard L. Preston, and others have documented the automobile's dominance of urban transportation as the twentieth century progressed. A unifying theme in these works was that automobility was a conscious, "democratic" choice by both the general public and policymakers. The "triumph" of the automobile was neither an accident nor a conspiracy.[5]

Los Angeles has fascinated students of urbanization, mass transit, and the automobile. Spencer Crump, Robert M. Fogelson, Marc A. Weiss, and others have correctly observed that real estate speculation, topography, the preferences of early settlers, interurban railways, and other influences spread out Los Angeles even before the automobile arrived. When the automobile appeared in the Southland, however, its impact was immediate and dramatic; its force was evident by the end of the First World War. After World War II, Los Angeles' urban development of large-scale freeway systems portended future metropolitan development patterns in the nation at large. By the mid-1950s the Southland also attracted considerable negative publicity associated with automobile-related problems. The most obvious was the nickname "Smogville." One outstanding sign of the times was graffito reading "I shot an arrow into the air, and it stuck."[6]

National urban transportation policy has evolved in conflict over the past two decades. Twenty years ago critics of the automobile insisted that combinations of publicly funded mass transit responses not only could, but *must*, solve urban mass transit needs. Recent experiences with Washington's Metro system, San Francisco's Bay Area Rapid Transit (BART), plus the continuing decline and rot of bus systems in many cities, have diluted the optimism of many of the most enthusiastic supporters of public transportation. By the late 1980s cold reality has set in; not only is "efficient" mass transit enormously expensive, but it is a fiendishly difficult concept to "sell" to the American public. As Scott Bottles observes in *Los Angeles and the Automobile*, "it would take astronomical gasoline prices, horrendous traffic congestion, or government fiat to force most people out of their automobiles. . . . It is unrealistic to expect anything else in a society that celebrates individual choice and free-market economics."[7] Although Bottles' research focuses on Los Angeles, his assessment is relevant to most other metropolitan regions too.

One need only look at the contemporary metropolitan landscape within a one-hundred-mile radius of City Hall in Los Angeles to be convinced of the crucial role of the automobile in shaping the Southland. Nevertheless, I must ask if we—historians, planners, architects, and public policy analysts—have overemphasized the automobile's role in shaping the region. In his exploration of the development of California, *Inventing the Dream*, which stresses the emergence of the southern half of the state in the late nineteenth and early twentieth century, Kevin Starr allows that some shaping forces were related to technology. Specifically, he cites railroads, the tapping of water sources and cheap energy, interurban railways, and, naturally, the automobile. But other influences were essentially nontechnological and equally significant: the size and layouts of the Spanish ranchos, nineteenth-century agribusiness (particularly citrus and vineyards), and the climate.[8] These insights are not new; dozens of historians of the Southland have helped to develop them.

But Starr's conceptualization of the region in terms of American dreams seems, in some respects, far removed from the more mundane, tangible issues historians and other observers usually associate with urbanization. *Inventing the Dream* provides insights that indirectly might help us reassess the way we look at this process. Scholars have been fascinated with boosterism as a major contributor to urban growth, and Los Angeles historians invariably credit the rise of the movie industry as a major force in the region's development. Starr connects the two, noting that local street scenes filmed in countless Mack Sennett comedies between 1913 and 1916 provided subtle, free publicity of priceless value: "as it flickered before middle America in darkened movie halls . . . Los Angeles was being announced subliminally . . . as a new American place with its own ambience and visual signature, and Americans did emigrate there in droves."[9]

In numerous chapters Starr uncovers long-forgotten or ignored cultural forces in southern California. He identifies hundreds of individuals and dozens of developments affecting Los Angeles' growth, few of which had anything to do with automobiles. He suggests indirectly that, even if Los Angeles is half covered with asphalt, it has not been that way always. Starr argues that in many ways southern California helped Americans define their dreams. While focusing on very different topics, Starr expanded upon a big idea Gerald D. Nash introduced fifteen years ago: in the twentieth century, the West cast off its economic, intellectual, and social colonial dependency on the East and took over economic and, to a degree, cultural leadership. Starr would push back the beginning of the Southland's major contributions to the national culture well into the nineteenth century.[10]

However original or provocative Starr's conceptual framework and supporting vignettes, I take issue with one crucial unifying theme. After reading *Inventing the Dream*, one almost senses that there was virtually nothing *ordinary* about the evolution of the Southland. His voluptuous imagery suggests that almost everything was unusual and larger than life. David Hackett Fischer has accused historians of hundreds of egregious fallacies, including uniqueness. In contrast to his venomous castigation of the logical inconsistencies of many of the "great" historians, Fischer is surprisingly gentle and nonspecific in his brief discussion of historians' analysis of unique situations. Yet historians of Los Angeles regularly describe urbanization of the region as unique, and the list includes those discussing mass transit and automobility. Planner Gordon Whitnall might have set the tone in establishing this idea of exceptionalism in Los Angeles' response to the automobile, observing in 1927: "Instead of the automobile conforming itself to the limitations of the cities, the cities began to conform themselves to the necessities and services of the automobile. That is the BIG thing that has been happening here in the Southland. . . . So prevalent is the use of the automobile that it might almost be said that Southern Californians have added wheels to their anatomy." Even Reyner Banham, in his important work *Los Angeles: The Architecture of Four Ecologies*, succumbs to this temptation: "no city has ever been produced by such an extraordinary mixture of geography, climate, economics, demography, mechanics and culture: nor is it likely that even a remotely similar mixture will ever occur again."[11]

Historians of urbanization and transportation have exaggerated Los Angeles' "special" character. Admittedly, by the early twentieth century the Southland boasted the nation's largest interurban railway network in terms of miles of routes. Compared to "crowded," densely settled eastern cities like New York, Boston, Philadelphia, and Chicago, population density in Los Angeles was, and is, remarkably low. And Southland denizens manifested an unusual propensity to buy automobiles from the time Henry Ford began producing low-priced Model Ts in large numbers. Unfortunately, many historians contrasted Los Angeles to cities at the other end of the spectrum of many quantifiable variables. Somehow, evidence appears more dramatic and arguments more convincing when the comparisons are more extreme.

After World War II some observers saw Los Angeles as an archetype of the late-twentieth-century city. In retrospect, this assessment appears to have been borne out. Many cities, particularly in the Sunbelt, now rival Los Angeles in degree of regional sprawl. Except for foliage, temperature, and humidity, it is often difficult to know if one is in Los Angeles, Houston, Phoenix, or . . . Jacksonville. As Peter O. Muller confirmed in his recent work, *Contemporary Suburban America*, sprawl, whether planned or not, is ubiquitous.[12] Recent explorations by demographers and public policy analysts have focused far more attention on cultural and ethnic diversity in Sunbelt cities than upon uniqueness in their patterns of decentralization. In the late twentieth century the integration of millions of immigrants from Latin America and Asia into Sunbelt metropolitan regions appears to be a far more important social, economic, and political issue than decentralization.

Still, urban critics persist in exaggerating the Southland's uniqueness. I believe that academicians, historians included, have fallen into this same trap. When discussing Los Angeles in the 1880s, 1920s, or 1940s, many historians celebrated its "one of a kind" character. While giving just due to the region's special features, I suggest that many of the differences are more superficial than real. Los Angeles experienced a phenomenal land boom in the 1880s, made all the more dramatic by rate wars between railroads vying to bring in new prospects for real estate subdivisions. Yet as John W. Reps suggested in his monumental work, *Cities of the American West*, dozens of other western urban areas experienced speculative real estate booms matching that in Los Angeles in everything but size.[13] My point is that the parallels might be more interesting—and significant—than the contrasts. When conducting research a decade ago for the book *From Streetcar to Superhighway*, which explores urban responses to the automobile in a dozen cities scattered about the country, I was startled at the similarities in responses of local decision makers to transportation needs. I was all the more surprised because I, too, began research under the assumption that Los Angeles' response was unique.[14]

Yet when local decision makers first considered mass transit responses to increasing central business district congestion, they looked first to models considered—and in some cases adopted—by eastern cities. Even when they rejected elevated lines and subway systems similar to those built in eastern cities, their street widening and highway programs in many ways mirrored those adopted in Detroit, New York, and other cities. The Major Traffic Street Plan approved in Los Angeles in 1924 was quite ordinary, very similar to street improvement designs in many American cities. In fact, public officials and civic leaders in Detroit presented a startlingly advanced rapid transit and superhighway plan in 1923 that anticipated many features of Los Angeles' fabled "freeway" systems two decades later. Detroit's plan included multi-lane, limited access highways with numerous viaducts and underpasses and "segregation" of local and "through" traffic. Admittedly, Detroit's plan never left the drawing board, but, by the time the Arroyo Seco (Pasadena) Freeway opened in 1940, the principles and basic concepts were widely known. Although Los Angeles achieved fame for its "advanced" concepts in responding to the demands of the automobile, the Westchester Parkway System in metropolitan New York was largely in place by the mid-1930s. The technical advances of Robert Moses' masterpiece predated virtually every design feature on the Arroyo Seco Freeway.[15] To be sure, Moses sold his parkway system partly on the grounds that it would provide leisure time "escape" for automobile-owning urbanites. In contrast, freeway designers in Los Angeles frankly emphasized their practicality for moving large numbers of automobiles carrying working commuters.

Answering the question of why Los Angeles achieved fame for its freeways is not quite as simple as one might expect. By the 1960s, of course, the system had expanded to massive proportions, with hundreds of miles of multi-lane superhighway. Yet, even then, the Interstate Highway Act of 1956 had permitted other cities to design urban superhighway networks very similar to Los Angeles' system. Perhaps one answer is that when the Automobile Club of Southern California presented its freeway plan in 1937, readers laid their eyes upon what proved to be a blueprint for superhighway development in the region over the next fifty years. By adopting and following this proposal, decision makers in Los Angeles partially avoided the problems experienced by their counterparts in many other American cities in the 1940s and 1950s, who had experimented with "compromise" solutions.[16] Public officials in many cities tried to accommodate both through traffic and local traffic on point-to-point highways. They segregated cross traffic on some sections but allowed it on others and prohibited adjacent strip commercial development in some sections but not in others. The result in many cities was a hodgepodge of poorly coordinated, inefficient, even dangerous streets and highways. By moving from very ordinary urban streets to modern superhighways very quickly, Los Angeles planners enhanced their image as harbingers of the future.

I do not deny that Los Angeles is different; other cities might build competing Disneylands, but there is only one Hollywood. Local historians could pick out dozens of features that make the city unique. But, as a comparative urban historian, I believe that some analysts of Los Angeles' urbanization have failed to see the forest for the trees. Maybe the Southland really *is* a dreamland, as Starr suggests. The star-struck, vacationers, retirees, cult followers, and other dreamers were attracted to the Southland, but the vast majority of Angelenos were—and still are—working folks living ordinary lives; they have generally the same tastes as other Americans. They watch the same TV shows as residents of Kansas City; fifty years ago they listened to many of the same radio performances.

What has all of this to do with the automobile in Los Angeles? There are no direct connections, but the parallels are clear. The automobile helped shape Los Angeles, but so did many other powerful forces. Metropolitan Los Angeles is different from metropolitan Kansas City or Philadelphia, but perhaps the similarities remain more striking than the differences.

# 14. Scott Bottles

# MASS POLITICS AND THE ADOPTION OF THE AUTOMOBILE IN LOS ANGELES

In 1974 an obscure legislative analyst appeared before a senate subcommittee arguing that the automobile industry had destroyed public transportation during the 1940s. Although few people today remember Bradford Snell's name, his attack on General Motors captured the public's imagination. Snell claimed that GM along with other automobile-related manufacturers plotted during the 1940s to purchase streetcar companies throughout the United States. After gaining control of these local traction companies, the conspirators replaced the trolleys with buses. The inefficiencies of the motor coaches, Snell asserted, subsequently forced millions of rail users into their cars. Snell concluded that GM, Ford, and Chrysler had reshaped "American ground transportation to serve corporate wants instead of social needs." The experience of Los Angeles, he argued, typified the conspirators' methods.[1]

Although Snell's presentation was riddled with factual errors and faulty logic, newspapers throughout the country reported his argument without commenting on some of his more ludicrous assertions.[2] The newspapers lent credence to Snell's argument, which since has become lodged firmly in the public consciousness. The historical record, however, simply does not support his interpretation. GM and various other industrial concerns invested in National City Lines (NCL), which purchased several urban railways including the Los Angeles Railway Company (LARY). But NCL did not attempt to destroy rapid transit. Rather, it attempted to sustain mass transportation by replacing antiquated and obsolete streetcar systems with modern buses. Urban planners and transit officials by this time fully realized that streetcars, with their rigid, fixed rails running down the middle of the road, could not maneuver in traffic. Four years prior to the sale of the railway to NCL, LARY's management had decided to replace nearly all of its streetcars with buses. Only the intervention of World War II and the lack of financial resources had prevented the implementation of this plan.

The streetcar industry by this time had experienced twenty-five years of economic decline. NCL therefore offered a sorely needed infusion of capital

Adapted from *Los Angeles and the Automobile* (Berkeley: University of California Press, 1987).

into a dying industry. GM's interest in this enterprise stemmed from its hope that NCL would save the mass-transportation industry and thereby create a market for its buses. The federal government later brought NCL to trial not for destroying the trolleys, but rather for the violation of various antitrust laws. It was GM's attempt to monopolize the production and sale of buses that bothered the government. Furthermore, there is little evidence that NCL's actions had much effect on mass-transit ridership in Los Angeles or elsewhere. Per capita ridership on Los Angeles' two major rail systems had steadily declined since the 1920s. Even more striking is the fact that, fifteen years before the sale of LARY, one out of every three people in Los Angeles owned an automobile. By 1941, 62 percent of those entering the Los Angeles central business district did so in automobiles. In suburban areas such as Westwood and Pomona, the ratio of automobile users to streetcar riders exceeded four to one. Clearly, the rise of the automobile as the dominant means of urban transportation occurred many years prior to the creation of NCL.

The real irony of the conspiracy theory is that it portrays the traction companies as virtuous, responsible public utilities trying to fight off the evil designs of the automobile manufacturers. In reality the situation was just the opposite. Angelenos adopted the automobile in protest against the inefficient and seemingly corrupt railway companies. Southern California residents during the first three decades of the twentieth century constantly complained about the quality of rail transit. From the public's point of view, the railways sought to benefit at its expense by deliberately running too few cars, refusing to build vital crosstown lines, bribing public officials, and abusing their franchises. Frustrated by inadequate service and the city government's inability to improve the situation, Angelenos turned to the automobile en masse. What began as an individualistic response against a monopolistic public utility soon became a democratic mass movement to improve the city's transportation system.

Near the end of the nineteenth century Angelenos, like most Americans, looked to the streetcars to solve pressing urban problems. Cities during the 1800s were notoriously unhealthy. Lacking efficient transportation, cities found themselves restricted to a radius of about two miles, which was the distance most people could walk in half an hour. As cities swelled throughout the century, they became exceedingly dense, straining their ability to provide adequate sewers, waste disposal, and drinking water. Indeed, the life expectancy of a person living in the countryside during the nineteenth century was significantly higher than that of a city dweller. People who worked in the city therefore embraced the electric streetcar because it promised to lower densities by allowing urban residents to purchase single-family dwellings in suburbs well removed from the crowded central business district.

The honeymoon with streetcars, however, was short-lived largely because they simply were not profitable. The cost of railway construction was so high that the companies could not cover their expenses. In fact, many operators used the streetcars mainly as a means of opening up their suburban real estate holdings to development. Henry Huntington, for instance, owned separate railway and land companies. His railways, the Pacific Electric (PE) and LARY, returned him little or no income prior to 1911, while his land company reportedly booked huge profits from the sale of residential lots on what was previously agricultural land. After developing a substantial portion of his real estate holdings, Huntington sold the PE to the Southern Pacific Railroad, which lost an average of $1,300,000 per year on the railway between 1913 and 1929. Thereafter, the subsidiary lost more than $3,000,000 per year until World War II, with its rubber and fuel shortages, briefly revived the company's operations.[3]

Public antagonism toward the railways surfaced as early as the first decade of the twentieth century. Local newspapers and politicians frequently charged that traction companies freely abused their franchises. "The City has been granting these franchises for years," complained one reformer. "They have been continuously, willfully and persistently violated to the great injury of the City and the people." Indeed, the PE hauled freight across lines granted solely for passenger use, bribed public officials, refused to pave the roadway between their rails, as required by their franchises, laid tracks on streets before obtaining the city's approval, and discriminated against certain regions of the city.

Nor were the railways particularly well planned. Rather than develop efficient, rational transportation systems, the LARY and PE sought to connect Huntington's subdivisions with the Los Angeles central business district. The companies realized that only those lines entering the city could attract enough riders to make them self-sufficient. This policy, however, frustrated residents because the lack of crosstown lines made it difficult to move between suburbs. As early as 1911, a progressive reform journal described Los Angeles' railway system as a "series of radiations from the city's center, lengthened from one real estate tract to another without the slightest consideration of the city's symmetrical and economic development."[4]

The most frequent complaint leveled at the railways concerned the crowded streetcar conditions. People believed that anyone riding a trolley should receive a seat. Yet during the morning and afternoon rush hours, many were forced to stand. A Los Angeles judge reported that "on almost every line in the city the cars running, both morning and evening, are so crowded that a large proportion of the passengers, many of them women, are compelled to stand crowded together. . . . There is no better excuse for this condition than the desire of the company to make more money." The *Examiner* found streetcar conditions in the downtown area "little short of disgraceful."[5] The crowded streetcars inspired impassioned rhetoric. Reforming newspaper editors were particularly vociferous, including those of the *Los Angeles Record*, who wrote:

> Inside the air was a pestilence; it was heavy with disease and the emanations from many bodies. Anyone leaving this working mass, anyone coming into it . . . forced the people into still closer, still more indecent, still more immoral contact. A bishop embraced a stout grandmother, a tender girl touched limbs with a city sport, refined women's faces burned with shame and indignation—but there was no relief. Was all this in an oriental prison? Was it in some hall devoted to the pleasures of the habitues of vice? Was it a place of punishment for the wicked? No gentle reader, it was only the result of public stupidity and apathy. It was in a Los Angeles street car on the 9th day of December, in the year of grace 1912; also on any other old day you are a mind to board a city street car between the hours of 5 and 7 in the afternoon.[6]

The general outcry against the railways reflected a larger disenchantment with the city's public utilities. Concerned citizens realized that the public utility companies offered services that had long since become necessities of urban life. But because the utilities held partial or complete monopolies, individual consumers could do little to protect themselves from exploitation. The time had come, argued many Angelenos, for the municipal authorities to exert greater control over the problems arising from the recent growth of the city.

Despite the fragmented nature of the Progressive movement, a slate of middle-class reformers managed to seize control of the Los Angeles City

Council in 1909. One of the new council's first legislative acts was to create a board of public utilities to regulate the city's gas, telephone, electric, and railway companies. Shortly thereafter, the board set out to investigate the public's complaints about the railways. In 1911, several years before the automobile came into general use, the board found the transit situation chaotic and argued that "the congestion of street car traffic in the business district at rush hour is indefensible." A consultant retained by the board claimed that "even a partial list of these defects makes a formidable catalogue of possibilities for improvements."[7]

Unfortunately, the board could do little to improve the situation. Any lasting solution would require the expenditure of large sums of money to build new lines and to divert streetcars from the streets to private rights-of-way. After 1910 it had become apparent that the electric railway industry throughout the country was unprofitable, making it nearly impossible for Los Angeles' traction companies to raise the money needed for the construction of subways near the central business district. Given this situation, the board could do little to improve the situation. Angelenos therefore began to seek alternative means of transport following World War I.

Although Angelenos toyed with such innovations as jitneys and buses, the real challenge to the railways came from privately owned automobiles. By 1918 significant numbers of Angelenos had begun to use their automobiles for their daily transportation needs. "Traffic congestion in Los Angeles," warned the Department of Engineering at the end of the year, "is relatively more intense than in any other city commensurate with its size."[8] People turned to their automobiles because of their frustration with poor railway service and the failure of the reform government to improve the situation. The average citizen could protest the bad rail service and take reform measures into their own hands by utilizing their cars. The automobile became in fact a symbol of democratic and progressive technology.

The frustration with the railways exploded onto the scene during 1920 during Los Angeles' first parking crisis. During the latter part of 1919, the state Railroad Commission and the city's Board of Public Utilities issued a joint report concerning LARY. The report noted that, although LARY needed to make alterations to its basic service, it could only do so effectively if the city gave it "relief from the intolerable conditions brought about by automobile traffic." The two commissions therefore urged the city council to ban automobile parking in the city center as a way to eliminate most automobile traffic.[9]

Although the proposed ban received some support from delivery companies and the traction companies themselves, most downtown businessmen vehemently opposed the measure. The *Los Angeles Times* accused the City Council of negligence. The proposed legislation, it argued, was an overreaction to the situation because it would "have very much the effect of a wet blanket cast over the business district of the city." Many business people agreed that such an ordinance would drive business out of the dominant Los Angeles central business district into outlying areas. "If this ordinance goes through," one businessman complained, "Los Angeles might as well wave goodbye to all out-of-town trade. People will not come to this city to shop if they are prohibited from using their automobiles."[10]

Resentment toward the railways also surfaced during the early stages of the crisis. P. H. Greer, a prominent Los Angeles businessman, believed that the no-parking plan had "apparently been offered by the railways and swallowed whole by the City Council." What the Railroad Commission and city government did not understand was that the general public had already adopted the automobile. The private car offered flexibility and convenience. It also offered the individual consumer an alternative to the much maligned railways. "The street railway system of our city is and has been for a long period in a very unsatisfactory condition, failing to give prompt and sufficient service," argued a resolution sent to the City Council. One angry citizen saw no reason why the city should attempt to protect the monopoly held by the traction companies over public transportation. "When a public utility ceases to be a convenience to the people," he wrote, "its usefulness is at an end and should not be allowed to burden the public with its mismanagement."[11]

That was the polite way of saying that one did not like the rail service. Another citizen at the time was a bit more direct when he asked the Venice Town Council, "is it not about time you took steps to ascertain just why the Pacific Electric gets by with the putrid brand of transportation they are dishing out? Is there no relief for the hundreds of citizens of this community who are forced to pay high fares to be handled like cattle?" But perhaps the most telling remark made during the whole crisis came from a suburban commuter who lamented that, "if the ordinance is adopted, my machine will be of no use for business purposes. I'll be a straphanger forever." The automobile, in short, had become a symbol of democratic technology by freeing the citizenry from the shackles of the monopolistic railways.[12]

Despite the vehement protests of the business community, the City Council succumbed to the Railroad Commission's demands for a total ban on parking in the central business district between the hours of 11:00 A.M. and 6:15 P.M. The ordinance went into effect on April 10, 1920. The Railroad Commission and the Board of Public Utilities were delighted with the results, as traffic moved 50 percent better than before the ban. Motorists and businessmen, however, were not as sanguine. Within a week prominent business organizations called a meeting to protest the legislation. "We were willing to give the ordinance a fair trial," said one commercial leader. "The actual test has shown that the ordinance has been disastrous [sic] to business, which is the life of our city." The downtown retail district, which at the time accounted for more than 75 percent of all retail sales within Los Angeles County, reported that business had dropped off by 25 percent to 50 percent within a week of the ban having been put into effect. A bank in the city center reported that forty customers in one day alone had moved their accounts to suburban institutions. One businessman argued that the ban would bankrupt half of the city's businesses within three years.[13]

Within a week hundreds of automobiles paraded through the streets of downtown Los Angeles in protest over the ban. Gilbert Woodill of the Car Dealers' Association asserted that "the day when the automobile was a 'pleasure car' . . . is long since past. The motor car is just as much a necessity to business as the street car." Restricting automobile usage was the same as "cutting the throat of business," he continued. The only good thing about the ban was that it pointed out "the extent to which the automobile has become a part of our everyday life." "The vast majority of the people," Woodill concluded, "have felt that the business pulse of Southern California throbbed in unison with the purring motors of its automobiles."[14]

The City Council knew when to retreat and quickly established a forty-five-minute parking limit on the downtown streets from 10:00 A.M. to 4 P.M., with a complete ban on parking from 4 P.M. to 6:15 P.M. This modification presumably allowed people to shop in Los Angeles until the rush hour. Commuters, on the other hand, had to find garage space in which to store their cars during the workday. Property owners responded in droves by tearing down obsolete buildings and putting up parking lots. The parking ban had lasted exactly nineteen days.

The parking crisis was only the first in a long series of incidents in which various interest groups came together to take control of their transportation system. Angelenos, however, soon discovered that their victory over the City Council in the parking crisis was short lived, because the city's narrow and discontinuous streets could not accommodate large numbers of cars. Any attempt to address these problems floundered in the city bureaucracy. Various civic and business leaders consequently organized the Los Angeles Traffic Commission to study the issue. The new body not only used its own funds to commission a plan to rebuild the city's street system, it soon became a major political force within the region. Working with property owners and the city government during 1924, the Traffic Commission managed to get its Major Traffic Street Plan approved as the official program for widening and opening major thoroughfares.

Construction of the street improvements, however, required the cooperation of literally thousands of homeowners. The city government at that time did not have the resources nor legal right to widen and open up roads in the city. Rather, property owners living on each of the streets mentioned in the Major Traffic Street Plan had to petition the city for the improvements. The city engineering department would subsequently design the improvements, hire a contractor, form an assessment district, and then float a bond issue to pay for the work. Property owners in the assessment district would service and retire the bonds through annual assessment payments. Consequently, the homeowners on each of these thoroughfares had to agree to tax themselves in order to rebuild the street system in accordance with the master plan. Despite the awkwardness of this arrangement, homeowners flooded the engineering department with requests for improvements.

Not only did the Traffic Commission aid these property owners with their petitions to the city government, it also convinced the electorate at large to pass several bond issues to help pay for about 10 percent to 20 percent of the costs associated with these improvements. Two years later voters approved a temporary property tax to continue the process of street improvements at an election in which every other bond issue on the ballot was defeated. The *Los Angeles Times* observed that citizens had agreed that "more streets must be paved, many of them widened, a number of scores of new streets must be opened to connect with other highways . . . if Los Angeles was to continue to go ahead at full speed toward achieving its destiny."[15]

The public had turned to the automobile because it felt the streetcar industry had failed in its promise to open up the suburbs to development. The automobile, people thought, could complete the job of lowering urban densities, therefore creating the ideal, low-density metropolis. "We in Los Angeles," wrote a prominent Angeleno during the 1930s, "realize the value of sunshine, of space and of individual homes as against crowded housing conditions and tenements without proper provision for light, air, yards, lawns, trees, shrubs, flowers and individual home units."[16] The key to this suburban utopia was an efficient street system and inexpensive automobiles. Angelenos, then, had created a new kind of public transportation as a substitute for the streetcars. The public provided the streets, and the individual brought along his or her own car.[17]

Although Angelenos embraced the automobile, planners and politicians did not ignore mass transit. There were several serious proposals during the 1930s, 1940s, and 1950s to build either subways or elevated transit systems. The proposals did not amount to much because of the expense involved. "Modern rapid transit construction," noted a leading expert in 1930, "is so expensive to construct that private capital cannot possibly bear the burden with any hope of securing an adequate return from the fares to be collected for transportation." In other words, neither the PE nor LARY could afford to build a modern transit system without substantial operating subsidies.[18]

At the time the public opposed subsidies for several reasons. First, the PE and LARY were privately held companies with a history of poor service and even worse public relations. "What have the Pacific Electric and Los Angeles Railways ever done for the people of Los Angeles that the property owners should contribute over a hundred million dollars in the building of subways where the only benefit would be to enable the local traction companies to enjoy a saving in operation each year of hundreds of thousands of dollars[?]" argued one critic. Nor was the public interested in purchasing railways that were losing millions of dollars each year. At the time it appeared that the automobile offered a more efficient and cheaper method of transportation. Automobile users and suburban property owners could finance the construction of a new street system by either paying user taxes or creating special assessment districts. Motorists, of course, provided their own cars and fuel. What could be more democratic than a self-sufficient transportation system? Miller McClintock, an eminent urban planner from Harvard University, captured this mood very nicely when he wrote: "Shall we subsidize, at great and continuing expense to the public treasury, rapid transit rail facilities affording comparatively low-grade and unprofitable mass transportation? Or shall we, out of public funds made available by the generous contributions of street users themselves, provide adequate, safe, efficient, and modern traffic facilities so that automobile users will provide their own transportation of a high character at their own operating costs?"[19] The answer in 1937 seemed obvious.

The adoption of the automobile provides us with insights not only about urban transportation systems but about the nature of mass politics during the early part of the century. Several historians have argued that the Progressive reform movement was a sham because so much of the period's legislation, including the creation of regulatory bodies, was actually supported by and a benefit to large corporations.[20] Although this argument has some validity, it ignores the democratic thrust behind many urban reforms. Although the corporation remained the dominant economic force in America, it could not always forestall legislation that it opposed. Angelenos turned to their automobiles out of frustration with the monopolistic railway companies. What began as a series of individualistic actions soon became a mass movement out of necessity. Certainly, the parking crisis pointed out the need for motorists to band together to protect their right to use the streets. In that instance, automobile owners forced the City Council to reconsider its ban on parking despite the vehement protests of the California Railroad Commission and the Los Angeles Board of Public Utilities.

It is not coincidental that the latter two bodies were creations of the Progressive reform movement. Both of these commissions were essentially conservative in nature. Their attempts to protect LARY from the competition of the automobile failed miserably. No matter how much influence the railways wielded with the regulators, they could not prevent Angelenos from seeking alternatives to the streetcars. But it took events such as the parking crisis to show the motorists that, collectively, they constituted a formidable political force.

Soon afterward, Angelenos used their newly discovered influence and power to reconstruct the city's street system in a further attempt to free themselves from the control of the traction companies. The railway companies in turn quickly discovered that there was little they could do to prevent this mass movement despite their influence within the state and city governments.

**15.** Rebecca Morales

# PLACE AND AUTO MANUFACTURE
# IN THE POST-FORDIST ERA

## FROM FORDISM TO POST-FORDISM

The imprint of automobile manufacture on urban life and urban form in the United States today reflects an economy in transition. The nation is coming to the end of an industrial era based on mass production known as "Fordism" and is entering another defined by principles of flexible production called "Post-Fordism." Evidence of a transformation rooted in methods of production and patterns of consumption is apparent throughout all aspects of the economy and society. The change is particularly revealing in Los Angeles, a city whose ascendance mirrors the rise of Post-Fordism. To illustrate how the process of change has affected the built environment of the city, this chapter examines the role of automobile manufacture in Los Angeles from Fordism to Post-Fordism and compares it to systems of flexible production visible in Japan, a country that was among the first to bring the concept to light. Despite distinctly different ties to the industry over time, Los Angeles has remained an important regional center during both periods.

The terms *Fordism* and *Post-Fordism* refer to broad economic and social relationships. Fordism was defined by stable markets sustained by large production runs of goods produced for mass consumers. In the United States, Fordism spanned the period from the 1920s to the 1970s. Since then the U.S. economy has become more open to international competition, resulting in smaller market shares and more unstable demand. The increased market uncertainty required that manufacturers shift to more responsive production methods. Greater flexibility in the less predictable market was obtained through advanced manufacturing systems, technology, and labor jointly applied to smaller runs of more specialized products. Firms were also reorganized to make rapid market adjustments manageable. Functions that were part of large, integrated firms have, in some instances, been spun off, a process that is called "vertical disintegration." With a larger number of smaller production units linked in the manufacture of a car, proximity has increased in importance, resulting in the creation of spatially identifiable industrial districts. Yet other economic activities that are more market-oriented, such as research and design, have broken away from central headquarters to be closer to centers of popular taste. Perhaps the most striking examples of emerging systems of flexible production are evident in Japan. Since the transformation, the spatial expression of automobile production in the United States has taken new definition and in some ways approximates that of Japan. In many respects, Los Angeles effectively illustrates the difference between old and new forms of industrialization.

The fifty years of Fordism marked a unique period in U.S. history characterized by the mass production and consumption of consumer durable goods. As its name implies, important influences of Fordism came from the auto industry and its products during this period. Industrial concepts popularized by Henry Ford, such as the moving assembly line (1913) and use of standardized and interchangeable parts, were widely adopted in other sectors. They became the basis for large-scale manufacture, which, in turn, required a massive industrial work force. With the support of social institutions aimed at income redistribution and employment stability, coupled with forms of wage determination that tied wage increases to rises in productivity, working-class consumers became the engine of the economy. Jointly, the relationship between large-scale production and broad-based consumption defined Fordism.

During the height of Fordism in the 1950s, subsidies to homeownership, road-building, and gasoline usage, along with macroeconomic trends toward income convergence, brought the purchase of many domestic goods within reach of middle-income families. Nearly one half of the world's manufactured goods and 75 percent of the world's cars were produced by U.S. manufacturers in 1950. Car ownership became a symbol of personal and social mobility, while the extent of ownership became synonymous with the prosperity of industrial society. With access to large and stable consumer markets, the U.S. automobile industry was unparalleled in high-volume manufacture. Annual quantities of 250,000 to 500,000 units were common for U.S. producers. This volume was unheard of elsewhere. Within urban America the system of mass production and mass consumption found spatial expression in the built environment through its roads, residential communities, and industrial landscape—a physical heritage that changed with the demise of Fordism.

### THE LEGACY OF AUTO PRODUCTION IN THE UNITED STATES

Car manufacture was originally a craft undertaken by many individualists. At the turn of the century, producers making cars by hand were scattered across the country from New England to southern California.[1] Regional definition began to occur after Michigan carmakers adopted methods of mass car man-ufacture.[2] These incipient large-volume carmakers bought out less efficient craft producers, a process that is referred to as "horizontal integration," which resulted in concentration in the industry. Of eighty-eight assemblers nationwide in 1921, only ten remained by 1933. Through the purchase of independent component manufacturers, or vertical integration, the large car-makers controlled access to parts producers as well as access to product and process technology.[3] The remaining craft manufacturers were eventually squeezed out of the market. With the shift from craft to mass car manufac-ture, car production was defined as design and development, the fabrication of key components, the assembly process, and the distribution of cars all undertaken or controlled by large, vertically integrated firms.

By 1911 mass car producers were establishing branch plants around the United States. Each branch plant tended to assemble the full model range. Thus, with every model change, the entire system shut down. Only after World War II, when auto demand was at an unprecedented high, plants were converted to achieve economies of scale through the production of only one or two models. Engine plants, previously situated close to assembly facilities for manufacture of the entire range of engine models, also began specializing, thereby diminishing the need for proximity to any particular assembly plant.[4] As the industry matured, the assembly process and manufacture of major parts became increasingly specialized and spatially separated. The assembly function took place in branch plants close to final markets, as did the manufac-ture of minor mechanical parts used in both the original equipment and after markets.

Engine plants, as well as those making stampings and other major parts, were located at strategic locations central to the industry as a whole, such as the Midwest. Management and research and development staffs were generally headquartered in Detroit. The model of industrial location among these large, vertically integrated mass production firms was one of dispersal and de-agglomeration. During the 1950s Los Angeles grew to become the most important of these dispersed branch plant sites in the United States and the largest site of auto manufacture in the world after Detroit.

Critical to this model of industrialization was a competitive relationship that developed between suppliers and automakers. To a large extent, techni-cal and design decisions remained within the domain of automakers. They communicated with suppliers on a strictly contractual basis. The competitive spirit improved efficiency when production runs were long and predictable

**FIGURE 15.1**

*Location of Ford Plants in the United States, 1953.*

and parts requirements were standardized. Buying parts from more than one supplier and parallel production from different sites represented further competitive measures designed to minimize costs. Jointly, these practices discouraged innovation. They also hampered cooperation between automakers and suppliers as well as the creation of modular systems and built-up components.[5]

Consequently, disassembled parts would come to an assembly plant in batches and would be held in inventory until time for incorporation into the final product. Thus, branch plant sites consisted of large, single-story buildings that housed the subassembly and final assembly process. Surrounding these buildings were expansive lots for holding inventory. As a metropolis coming to terms with its manufacturing capacity during the height of Fordism, the growth of Los Angeles after the Second World War illustrates how this concept of industrialization was reflected in the built environment.

### LOS ANGELES AS A FORD CITY

Subsequent to World War II, Los Angeles emerged as a major manufacturing center, albeit one that functioned largely as a branch plant site. Within four years of the war's end, there were seven automakers in Los Angeles with an annual capacity of approximately 650,000 cars. The Los Angeles car industry in 1950 was making thirteen different models, more than Detroit, and was second to Detroit in the manufacture of automobiles worldwide.

Carmakers sprawled across the city straddling the railroad and clustered near related industrial development. The first to open a branch plant was Ford Motor Company in 1912. Initially, Ford located downtown along with numerous local craft producers. In 1927 the company moved to Long Beach to take advantage of the port as a point of trans-shipment linking sea and rail transportation. Another Long Beach facility was Kaiser-Frazer. Beginning in 1946, its manufacturing operations were contained in an unused portion of the Douglas Aircraft plant, but this shared site arrangement proved to be only nominally successful. When Douglas expanded in 1950, Kaiser's operations were forced to close.[6] Nash Motors, another car manufacturer to locate in an aircraft building, was situated in El Segundo near the Los Angeles Airport, on a site vacated by North American Aviation.

For most car manufacturers, however, the preferred location was along the main rail line that traversed the city from the port, through downtown, and across the San Fernando Valley. Following this path were Willys-Overland (1928), Chrysler (1928), and Lincoln-Mercury Ford (1947), which all

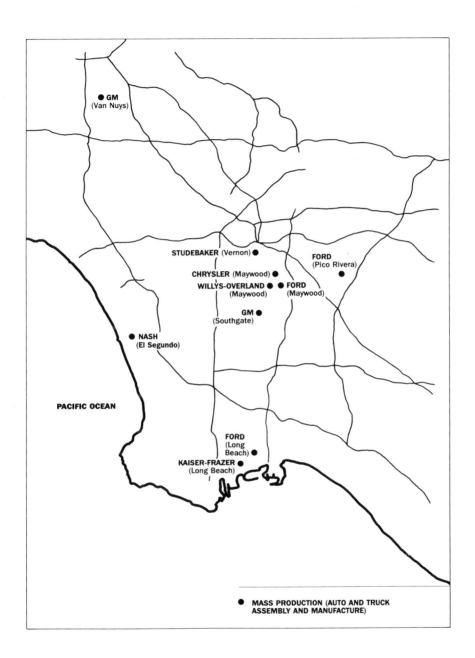

**FIGURE 15.2**

*Location of automakers in Los Angeles, 1985.*

---

*Place and Auto Manufacture*

opened plants in Maywood. Studebaker located a plant nearby in Vernon (1936), and General Motors (Buick-Oldsmobile-Pontiac) did so in neighboring South Gate (1936). The last to open was GM Van Nuys (1947), which sought a less-congested location than that of the central manufacturing district rimming the southeastern portion of the city.

As the plants grew and expanded, they became ringed by other industrial users and working-class residential neighborhoods. Vast portions of the city were devoted to manufacturing activities that were primarily assembly in nature and that used a largely unskilled or semi-skilled work force. The skills required for product design, tool and die manufacture, and sophisticated parts fabrication lay elsewhere, or they were lost in the region when craft production was superseded. Thus, the city grew on the basis of its blue-collar work force, which consumed as well as manufactured the product of their labor, and the urban landscape became a reflection of Fordist economic relationships.

## THE BREAKDOWN OF FORDISM

While it appeared to be a stable industrial structure, in fact by the 1960s the vulnerability of the United States was beginning to show. In 1968 the European Economic Community instituted a policy of free internal trade, which, coupled with a 17.6 percent external tariff, resulted in greater market integration. The role of European producers in the U.S. economy grew to more than 10 percent of the market, creating a balance-of-payments problem by 1968. The dollar was allowed to devalue and the gold standard was dropped in 1971 both efforts toward improving trade relations and investment conditions. But the 1973 and 1979 Organization of Petroleum Exporting Countries (OPEC) oil shocks raised the price of oil fourfold, thereby triggering a series of deep recessions.

With their smaller, more fuel efficient cars, Japan rose to second after the United States in the production of autos and first in passenger car exports by 1975. Small cars had become the choice of new car buyers, and imports rose to nearly 19 percent of the U.S. market in 1977. By 1981 U.S. producers accounted for only 21 percent of world auto production in contrast to the Japanese contribution of 30 percent. Furthermore, the U.S. market was becoming saturated and fragmented.

Drawing from the automobile experience provides only one example repeated across a wide range of consumer durable goods. While in 1950 only one fourth of U.S. residents owned a car, by 1977 the figure was one half, and

| INDUSTRY | % | WHITE | BLACK | MEXICAN |
|---|---|---|---|---|
| Agriculture, Mining | **3.6** | 2.8 | .6 | 10.5 |
| Construction | **8.2** | 8.1 | 7.7 | 11.0 |
| Manufacturing | **25.9** | 25.5 | 16.7 | 40.2 |
| Nondurable Goods | **15.1** | 15.5 | 7.6 | 17.3 |
| Durable Goods | **10.8** | 10.0 | 9.1 | 22.9 |
| Trans., Comm. and Public Utilities | **7.2** | 7.3 | 7.9 | 6.4 |
| Wholesale and Retail Trade | **23.4** | 24.3 | 16.1 | 18.6 |
| Services | **31.7** | 32.0 | 46.6 | 13.2 |
| Finance, Ins., Real Estate | **4.8** | 5.3 | 4.5 | 1.3 |
| Business Services | **3.6** | 3.8 | 3.3 | 1.6 |
| Personal Services | **7.0** | 5.4 | 25.8 | 5.8 |
| Entertainment | **2.8** | 3.1 | 1.7 | 0.7 |
| Professional Services | **8.5** | 9.3 | 7.5 | 2.3 |
| Public Administration | **5.0** | 5.1 | 8.3 | 1.5 |

**TABLE 15.1**

Los Angeles SMSA Industrial Distribution by Race or Ethnic Group, 1950, in Percentage
SOURCE: PUBLIC USE MICRO SAMPLE, U.S. CENSUS, 1950.

---

*Place and Auto Manufacture*

| OCCUPATION | % | WHITE | BLACK | MEXICAN |
|---|---|---|---|---|
| White Collar | **43.6** | 54.4 | 16.1 | 19.1 |
| Managers | **13.6** | 15.3 | 2.5 | 5.1 |
| Professional/Technical | **10.4** | 11.9 | 3.1 | 1.7 |
| Clerical | **14.6** | 15.9 | 7.7 | 7.4 |
| Sales | **10.1** | 11.2 | 2.8 | 4.9 |
| Blue Collar | **40.2** | 36.4 | 43.6 | 57.0 |
| Craft | **14.5** | 15.4 | 8.5 | 11.9 |
| Operatives | **18.4** | 16.4 | 21.5 | 36.1 |
| Laborers | **7.3** | 4.6 | 13.5 | 27.0 |
| Service | **11.2** | 9.4 | 40.3 | 5.9 |

**TABLE 15.2**

Los Angeles SMSA Occupational Distribution by Race or Ethnic Group, 1950, in Percentage
SOURCE: PUBLIC USE MICRO SAMPLE, U.S. CENSUS, 1950.

**The Car and the City**

| INDUSTRY | % | WHITE | BLACK | MEXICAN |
|---|---|---|---|---|
| Agriculture, Mining | **1.3** | 1.0 | .6 | 2.3 |
| Construction | **4.5** | 5.0 | 2.8 | 4.9 |
| Manufacturing | **24.8** | 20.6 | 24.3 | 41.2 |
| Nondurable Goods | **8.1** | 5.7 | 5.0 | 16.3 |
| Durable Goods | **16.7** | 14.9 | 13.7 | 24.9 |
| Trans., Comm. and Public Utilities | **6.8** | 6.8 | 10.8 | 5.1 |
| Wholesale and Retail Trade | **20.7** | 21.8 | 16.9 | 20.1 |
| Services | **41.8** | 44.9 | 50.2 | 26.5 |
| Finance, Ins., Real Estate | **7.1** | 8.1 | 6.9 | 3.5 |
| Business Services | **6.0** | 6.5 | 6.1 | 4.7 |
| Personal Services | **3.3** | 2.5 | 3.7 | 4.0 |
| Entertainment | **2.9** | 4.0 | 1.7 | 1.2 |
| Professional Services | **19.2** | 20.7 | 24.7 | 10.9 |
| Public Administration | **3.3** | 3.1 | 7.1 | 2.2 |

**TABLE 15.3**

Los Angeles SMSA Industrial Distribution by Race or Ethnic Group, 1980, in Percentage
SOURCE: PUBLIC USE MICRO SAMPLE, U.S. CENSUS, 1980.

| OCCUPATION | % | WHITE | BLACK | MEXICAN |
|---|---|---|---|---|
| White Collar | **59.9** | 70.5 | 54.6 | 31.3 |
| Managers | **11.4** | 14.9 | 6.8 | 4.3 |
| Professional/Technical | **17.4** | 21.9 | 13.8 | 5.3 |
| Clerical | **22.0** | 22.6 | 27.4 | 16.7 |
| Sales | **9.0** | 11.0 | 6.6 | 4.9 |
| Blue Collar | **28.0** | 20.0 | 27.0 | 53.8 |
| Craft | **9.4** | 8.7 | 7.2 | 13.0 |
| Operatives | **13.3** | 7.9 | 13.8 | 29.7 |
| Laborers | **5.3** | 3.4 | 6.0 | 11.1 |
| Service | **12.2** | 9.5 | 18.4 | 15.0 |

**TABLE 15.4**

Los Angeles SMSA Occupational Distribution by Race or Ethnic Group, 1980, in Percentage
SOURCE: PUBLIC USE MICRO SAMPLE, U.S. CENSUS, 1980.

it continued to rise. Because the U.S. market was extremely crowded, product differentiation became ever more significant. This meant that producers had to increase their product lines or retool to address market volatility at a time when profits were at an historic low.

Unable to meet the international challenge, domestic plants across the United States closed. Within Los Angeles the effect of imports on the local car market was particularly evident. From a 26 percent share of the market in 1968, imports rose to 41 percent in 1971.[7] In the face of heightened foreign competition and as a result of changes in rail rates, all but one of the Los Angeles carmakers shut down. The rail rate changes now made it economically viable to ship cars west from eastern locations.

To remain competitive, U.S. automakers were forced to bring a greater number of low-volume models to market. (By one account, in 1996 less than half of U.S. car production will consist of models exceeding 150,000 units. The fastest growing segment will consist of models produced in annual volumes of 25,000 to 50,000.)[8] In light of the changing market structure, automakers began to reorganize. The changes made by the auto industry have been so significant that, according to industry analyst Martin Anderson, they may have constituted the largest shift in technological, human, and capital resources in U.S. industrial history.[9] With these changes, the industry has attempted to transform itself from one that is dependent on high-volume production to one that is competitive through low production runs.

### THE EMERGING POST-FORDIST INDUSTRIAL LANDSCAPE

In contrast to the United States, Japanese producers developed along very different dimensions, due to their narrower market segments and the Japanese socioeconomic system. Japanese society places much of the responsibility for social welfare in the hands of the private sector. The distinction between U.S. and Japanese manufacturers and the resulting geographic distribution of production is illustrated clearly by the Toyota Motor Corporation.

To compete successfully in the domestic and later world markets against U.S. transnational corporations, Toyota began by manufacturing for entry-level consumers in 1933. From the 1930s to the 1950s the company developed by using or copying state-of-the-art designs of parts taken eclectically from U.S. manufacturers.[10] Designs were constantly modified by Japanese engineers, who, as a result, developed critical design skills. In recognition that many mistakes would be made during the first years of operation, the company chose to limit the size of production runs. Consequently, multipurpose machinery was preferred over specialized equipment. Single-function machines used by large-volume producers required less expensive, less skilled labor and were cost effective during long production runs. They were less economical, however, under highly variable conditions.

Since a lack of suppliers constituted another potentially serious obstacle, the company opened a specialty steel factory and worked closely with Japanese component firms. By the end of World War II, Toyota was bringing cars to market that not only used the most advanced technology but that could be produced in relatively small lots very cost-effectively. Furthermore, it had the ability to change the design of engines, stampings, and other critical parts easily and inexpensively.

Initially, the firm was located in Koromo, outside of Nagoya. Later, the town changed its name to Toyota City when the company opened a second assembly plant in 1959. Koromo was the core of the production system that extended to neighboring Kariya City, Nagoya, and Tokyo. By 1980 there were eleven facilities operating at Toyota City engaged in assembly, engine, chassis, transmission, and other parts manufacture as well as casting and the fabrication of machinery, dies, and molds. In 1985, 83 percent of employment and 95 percent of the value of shipped goods were in auto or auto-related industries.[11]

A system of tiering among component manufacturers coupled with the practice of just-in-time inventory sourcing was instituted. It minimized scrappage, improved quality, and lowered inventory. Toyota's ten subsidiaries comprised the first-tier contractors who subcontracted with two hundred twenty second-tier providers. In turn, this second tier subcontracted with thirty thousand third-tier firms. The first-tier contractors are responsible for bringing pretested modules to the assembly on an as-needed basis.

Within this hierarchy, the higher up the value-added chain, the larger the firms and business profits and the more privileged the conditions of work. Approximately one-third of the work force is attached to core firms and is assured of lifetime employment. Those working with suppliers and subcontractors tend to be part-time or temporary, non-unionized, and female. Jointly, this multilayered collection of operating units producing in close proximity and linked in the manufacture of a final product has led to the creation of a geographically defined production system. As an illustration of the extensive interaction among firms and out-sourcing, even assembly currently is contracted out. While Toyota produces high-volume cars in its own plants, the

Kanto Auto Works, once an auto body supplier to the firm, now produces small-lot specialty cars. Flexibility is introduced into the system in the way technology is shared between the assembler and suppliers. It is also formed through the use of flexible manufacturing systems and by the creation of hierarchical specialization among firms with different productive capacities. The industrial complex that has been created in Toyota City is the antithesis of the large firm, branch plant system that was the tradition in the United States. Despite differences in social norms, a variation on this model is being recreated in the United States today. While at first its development was inadvertent, it has become widely accepted as part of the industry's corporate policy.

One of the first signs that mass production methods in the United States were no longer competitive came as large carmakers began sub-contracting out more of their productive activities. Through out-sourcing, firms lowered the high cost of market uncertainty by transferring risks to supplier companies. This practice led not only to an increase in component subcontracting but also to the contracting out of research and design functions. With a redefinition of subcontracting relations, there has been a rise of modular component manufacture, coupled with greater contract assembly. In contract assembly, the complete assembly of small-lot production is taken over by leading suppliers, and prototype manufacture is done by affiliate companies.

In addition, U.S. automakers are adopting policies of just-in-time inventory sourcing in varying degrees. As a result, with the closure of most branch plants, 60 percent of all assembly plants are within a two hundred mile radius or four-hour truck drive of Detroit. And due to the falling dollar, among other reasons, the United States is again considered a competitive site for auto manufacture. Whereas only forty-three assembly plants were operating in 1980, that figure increased to forty-nine in 1985 and is still growing.

The spatial aspect of U.S. car manufacture has changed in significant ways with the adoption of methods of flexible production. The branch plant system has been replaced by a system in which industrial activities share greater geographic proximity due to increased out-sourcing. This change has created a regional reconcentration of production within the Midwest. It takes its definition as a broad industrial district in which economic activities once retained by assemblers are externalized to the community and other firms. Among the activities that are becoming increasingly independent of large automakers are research and development, financing, labor education and

● STAMPING PLANTS

□ ASSEMBLY PLANTS OF U.S. MANUFACTURERS

▲ ASSEMBLY PLANTS OF FOREIGN MANUFACTURERS

**FIGURE 15.3**

*Location of major auto plants in the United States, 1985.*

deployment, and marketing, along with component manufacture. In contrast to the branch plant industrial landscape of the 1950s, the sense of place in the Post-Fordist era is taking a more regional focus. Consequently, peripheral locations, such as Los Angeles, have become tenuous sites for continued assembly by large-scale producers. But as the case of Los Angeles illustrates, peripheral locations nonetheless continue to have a significant role in auto manufacture.

## LOS ANGELES AS A PLACE FOR AUTO MANUFACTURE

The Post-Fordist era is distinguished by the fragmentation of consumer markets, the breakdown of large integrated firms, and a resurgence of specialty producers. In contrast to mass production, manufacture for small market segments by specialty producers often requires highly skilled labor, emphasis on research and development, and investment in advanced technology. Because of the need to interact with other firms, production tends to be more agglomerated and regionally concentrated. In this way, car manufacture of the 1980s is significantly different from prior years. Despite the loss of most large-scale auto assembly in Los Angeles, there are three ways in which the city remains important to the industry. The aspects of production are, reflected in turn, in the industrial landscape; in brief, the city now serves as a waning producer of mass cars, an emerging producer of specialty cars, and a burgeoning site for marketing research and development.

Mirroring trends in the Midwest, the sole remaining large auto plant in Los Angeles, GM Van Nuys, is beginning to adopt policies of just-in-time inventory sourcing. This policy includes encouraging suppliers to locate in the immediate vicinity. The company also is considering adding a stamping plant to the existing site. These measures, along with the adoption of cooperative forms of labor relations, indicate that it is possible for isolated plants to engage in auto assembly and parts fabrication. Nonetheless, the opportunities are limited, and, even at these locations, the tendency is for agglomerated production.

Southern California also continues to flourish as a site of car conversion and customizing. Among factors that encourage this continued importance to the auto industry are the world-renowned auto design school, Art Center College of Design in Pasadena, the relative proximity to Asia, and access to the deep-water port. Los Angeles is also a favored location for specialized producers on contract with Japanese or Korean manufacturers for making

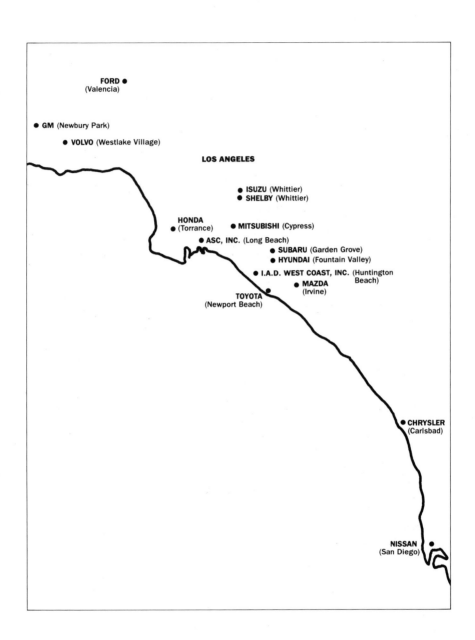

**FIGURE 15.4**

*Location of Advanced Concept Centers in southern California, 1989.*

**The Car and the City**

convertibles or other modified cars. Consequently, several emerging specialty producers have located in the region.

Finally, at present all the major Japanese and U.S. automakers as well as one European and several niche producers have located advanced concept centers in southern California. They recognize the region as a nationwide leader in market trends. These advanced concept centers undertake research on changing demographic and buying patterns and translate them into vehicles of the future. This unusual activity is found in only a few places worldwide and requires access to a skilled labor force to function correctly. These centers are located at sites that attract engineers and researchers who work in aerospace and other high-tech industries rather than the older assembly sites of the 1950s. What this illustrates is that not all car production activities are necessarily tied to the current trend toward reconcentration in the Midwest. Large carmakers have been externalizing certain critical functions associated with car manufacture, such as design and marketing. As a result, new regions devoted to keeping a pulse on fast-breaking trends are taking definition. The thriving concept centers of Los Angeles are proof that functions such as design and marketing can be spatially separate from component fabrication and car assembly.

With these changes southern California is becoming a specialized center for research and development and small-lot production. For these activities to become even more prominent, the region would have to be cognizant of its role in providing support activities. This support must include the education of highly trained personnel. Equally important is the awareness of benefits to the industry that come from interaction with other industries requiring investment in constant innovation, such as aerospace and electronics. If the role of small-scale production continues to expand in this industry, it is conceivable that the region will see this function grow in the future. Consequently, despite the apparent loss of branch plant activities of the past, the prospects for continued ties to the auto industry appear not only strong in the new industrial period but more anchored within the region.

Seen as a whole, the Post-Fordist era nearly reverses earlier patterns. Rather than assembly being scattered to market locations, it is concentrated near a central core, while research and development has become more spatially mobile. In this respect, Los Angeles suggests the importance of regional markets in redefining the shape of the industry and illustrates how the concept of place has changed in the process.

# 16. Margaret Crawford

## THE FIFTH ECOLOGY:
### FANTASY, THE AUTOMOBILE, AND LOS ANGELES

With the opening of Disneyland in 1955, an environmental paradigm emerged that was to haunt the ecological, cultural, and psychological landscapes of southern California. By organizing his amusement park around thematic zones based on fictional environments, Walt Disney replaced the squalid ambience of the carnival with conceptual models of American mythology at two-thirds scale. Main Street equals small-town America, Frontierland, the myth of the western frontier, and Tomorrowland, the corporate and technological promise of the future. These myths were packaged to be consumed, which quickly made Disneyland the most visited attraction in southern California.

In spite of its incredible success, Disneyland itself was only good for an afternoon, not for life; physically, it was too limited and its technology too evident to be directly adopted as a model for environmental planning. At the same time, its reduction of a complex and debatable reality to a single, agreed-upon theme—a theme that could be both cliché and archetype—suggested that environmental reality could be replaced by a focused thematic unreality at a larger scale.

This possibility offered a way out of the ecological impasse facing Los Angeles in the late 1950s. Although the city had long generated fantasy commercial architecture, such as Tail o' the Pup, a hot dog stand shaped like a hot dog, or the Brown Derby, a restaurant built as a hat, based on limited images, these buildings existed as isolated elements in a larger environment dominated by powerful geographic features. In the early 1960s Reyner Banham classified Los Angeles into four ecologies: three natural systems, the beach, the foothills, and the basin, connected by autopia, an artificial network of roads and freeways.[1] Fantasy architecture, confined to a setting of palm trees, orange groves, and snow-capped mountains, had no room to expand.

By introducing the concept of the theme environment, Disneyland allowed a new system of land use to emerge, liberated from the physical setting of the city and based on a landscape of the imagination. Like Disney's "lands," theme environments consist of controllable settings designed to convey a unified image. Based on a carefully selected set of themes presented with a consistency and coherence not found in everyday life, they offer a reduced

**FIGURE 16.1**

"The Stack"—four-level intersection of the Hollywood, Harbor, and Pasadena freeways, Los Angeles.

***

*The Fifth Ecology*

experience of a more complex reality, whether historical, geographic, or cultural. Themes, drawn from anywhere in time and space, are unlimited, but their presentation is restricted to communicating nostalgia and comfort. Whether based on fictional texts like Tom Sawyer's Island or on historical locations like New Orleans Square, these spaces have been drained of ambiguity and contradiction, their meanings reduced to entertainment.

This concept had significant social implications. In addition to providing thematic arenas for consumption, Disneyland transformed public space itself into a commodity. Charles Moore noted that although Disneyland introduced public space into the "private floating world of Southern California . . . you have to pay for the public life."[2] The public realm, described by Hannah Arendt as an area where people define their own identity and awareness of others' identities through participation in ritual and civic life, was replaced by a place where human needs for public experiences are shaped by fundamentally commercial purposes. In spite of its window dressing, which is derived from reassuring visions of other times and places, Disney's artificial version of public life is totally divorced from any traditional social, religious, or cultural context.[3] Here, the individual defines himself through consumption choices.

The multiplication of similarly packaged environments testifies to the accuracy of Disney's insights. "Consumerist" architecture, its principles based on behavioral manipulation through communicable imagery, primarily characterizes building types directed toward leisure activities.[4] Offsetting the rationalist standardization imposed by the workplace, its fantasy fuels the need for entertainment and escape in other areas of life. Most widely applied to consumption environments such as shopping malls, stores, and restaurants, and often to hotel and resort architecture, thematic approaches are increasingly appearing in residential architecture. The extra level of metaphor provided by theme images, such as clapboard villages or Spanish haciendas, gives otherwise indistinguishable housing and condominium developments a marketing edge over less communicative projects.[5]

Existing buildings, particularly those with historical associations, can be easily repackaged into theme environments, as the transformation of several city blocks into New York's South Street Seaport "festival marketplace" indicates. A large area of the town of Monterey, California, has been thematically unified with the widespread application of motifs inspired by John Steinbeck's novel, *Cannery Row*, turning the real Cannery Row into a parody of itself.[6] The ultimate expansion of Disneyland beyond the confines of the theme park into daily life is illustrated by Disney Corporation's own

**FIGURE 16.2**

*Map of Disneyland's Tomorrowland.*

225

*The Fifth Ecology*

Studio Backlot project in Burbank, a complex containing a shopping mall, entertainment center, hotel, and theme park, all based on a completely fictional premise.

The theme of a movie backlot provides a mental structure that allows the infusion of fantasy and spectacle into every aspect of the building. The nature of the cinematic medium, inherently fragmented, justifies the juxtaposition of disparate attractions, such as a steakhouse in a boat that appears to be teetering on the edge of a waterfall, a seafood restaurant where diners would have the illusion of eating underwater, and a nightclub hosted by holographic images of celebrities of the past. Hotel rooms would replicate famous movie sets, with employees dressed as film characters. Even the parking lot, covered by a huge sheet of water, would become "the Burbank Ocean."[7] The megastructure requires only the addition of housing to become an inhabitable fantasy, a complete world in itself.

More than simply extreme examples of kitsch, these environments represent a broader cultural tendency toward the domination of fantasy images, which has significant cultural implications. Theme environments can be seen as particularly visible examples of a hyperrealism increasingly present in contemporary life. As defined by the poststructuralist philosopher, Jean Baudrillard, hyperreality is a condition in which "simulation" effaces and replaces reality.[8] Hyperreal representation produces an imitation that becomes more real than reality itself. One effect of the hyperreal is to impoverish reality. An actual small town can never be as perfect as Main Street in Disneyland, just as Fifth Avenue will never be as clean or well organized as a shopping mall.[9]

Theme environments are not unique to Southern California. Boxcars made into train restaurants and newly built New England fishing villages that are actually shopping malls have become a staple of the American commercial landscape. They are perhaps most evident in recently developed Sunbelt cities, without historic infrastructure or hierarchical organization. Only in their point of origin, however—Southern California, with its constant stream of immigrants, absence of conventionally perceivable history, and lack of urban self-definition—have they become a dominant realm of spatial and social experience. As in Hollywood films, also clearly a significant cultural influence in the local acceptance of theme environments, fiction vanquishes the real.

The means for achieving the dominion of the hyperreal was the subsumption of the region's three natural ecologies by the fourth, autopia. The triumph of the automobile and its necessary road network allowed another, latent, ecology to emerge, the ecology of fantasy. Fifteen years later Banham's original taxonomy, still tied to natural processes, is no longer valid. The automobile severed the links between Los Angeles' culture and its natural setting. This development resolved the increasing contradiction between the automobile and the basin's natural limitations, which produced environmental damage from smog, ruptures of urban pattern, and destruction of landscape features. In the new ecology of fantasy the car is no longer an ecological villain but a means of liberation, providing access to an unlimited and constantly changing set of theme environments.

The automobile connects individual circuits of theme environments, a coherent conceptual grid overlaid on the real economic and topographic surface of the city. Driving from one theme environment to another, the endless, nondescript blocks of the city disappear. Robbed of conceptual validity, they become neutral filler between a set of points that construct a coherent thematic reality, physically discontinuous but conceptually integrated. Thus, although individual themes have coherence, serial themes only can become dominant in a setting of disjointed context.

More than just transport from one fragment to the next, the automobile functions as a medium, transforming our experience of the landscape we are traveling through. In the car we move through the city without disturbing it or it disturbing us. Like television, another individualized medium, the automobile distances us from the world outside our sealed capsule while restructuring and abstracting it. The world, through a television screen or a windshield, becomes two-dimensional, and substance is reduced to the level of image, a strictly visual event that does not invite participation.

Unlike the pedestrian, whose fully utilized senses require buildings providing a full range of stimuli, the driver's senses are numbed by the metal jacket of the car. Thus architecture, intended to be perceived slowly through touch, smell, and hearing, has been replaced by facades perceived completely with the sense of vision. Moving too fast to smell, sealed off from sounds by air conditioning, radio, and tape decks, and with touch limited to the steering wheel, the automobile's perceptual limitations have distanced the driver from a traditional sense of reality, dematerializing the world beyond the windshield.[10]

Moving through space in an automobile is also a televisual experience, a succession of quick cuts and rapidly edited fragments unified by the medium of the automobile. Baudrillard has observed that increasingly fluid and auto-

*The Fifth Ecology*

**FIGURE 16.3**

*Los Angeles through the windshield.*

---

**The Car and the City**

mated vehicles produce fluid and automated space in which we let ourselves go, tuning into them like we tune into a television set. Driving promotes a flattening effect, erasing the fragmentation of time and space and homogenizing everything to the absolute present. It allows the continuous bombardment of people, places and things, once driven past, to be forgotten quickly. Driving erases memory.[11]

The physical environment reinforces these perceptual changes. Roadside architecture, identified primarily from the car, has undergone a similar transformation. Marc Treib and Philip Langdon have charted the shift away from the lively individualism of early commercial strips to today's bland "television roads" composed of standardized franchise outlets.[12] Similar economic and marketing forces have fragmented the city into single-use enclaves, accessible only by automobile. Without apparent logic, collections of disparate themes and functions face each other across roads and parking lots. Our unquestioning acceptance of this landscape of juxtaposition owes much to Disneyland's radical compression of themes remote in space and time.

Looking from nineteenth-century New Orleans across an African jungle and into the future has accustomed us to a fragmented vision of a discontinuous environment. At Disneyland discrete worlds collide with an ease previously achieved only in the most speculative science fiction. Spatial proximity breaks down accepted boundaries between near and far, past and future, and reality and fantasy. The abrupt shifts of time and space and the equation of fiction and fact present in Disneyland also resemble the perceptual model presented by television. Changing realities appears to be as effortless as changing channels.

To convince its users, the theme environment must sever all perceptual connections with its automobilized origins and setting. The theme environment's ability to communicate depends on its isolation from the realities of the necessities of its daily life. As the counterpoint to the automobile's diffuse, reduced experiences, encapsulated pedestrian spaces offer intensity and increased stimulation. In order to entertain, shopping, eating, and relaxing have become highly theatricalized. Spectacle has begun even to penetrate daily activities such as food shopping. West Hollywood supermarkets sell sushi from a bamboo structure with costumed Japanese chefs expertly trimming raw fish and emphasize fresh produce by displaying it on hay-laden carts with clerks dressed in overalls.

To maintain the illusions, valet parking has become a central element in the ecology of fantasy. Now offered by supermarkets, art galleries, and de-

**FIGURE 16.4**
*Valet parkers on Melrose Avenue, Los Angeles.*

partment stores as well as restaurants, valet parking reduces the need to physically interact with the social reality of the city to the six feet of sidewalk between the car door and the entrance, which allows an existence consisting totally of theme environments to become conceivable. So far, this degree of selectivity over one's surroundings made possible by avoiding city streets and urban reality is unique to Los Angeles. Unlike the structural layers of Fritz Lang's film, *Metropolis*, which separates the workers from the owner's skyscraper city, the automobile permits a synchronic organization in which, without physical barriers, consumers of theme environments are equally well protected from the unwelcome realities of class and ethnic differences.

An increasingly pluralistic and eclectic selection of themes has emerged. Mass consumers are limited to itineraries of shopping malls, chain restaurants, and purpose-built tourist attractions, but Los Angeles also has generated permutations of increasingly specialized and sophisticated theme circuits. The apparent profusion of choice follows the logic of marketing, which dictates constant novelty aimed at specific market segments. New themes rely on more abstract imagery; punk, new wave, and heavy metal themes are obvious. Art themes, utilizing constructivism, minimalism, or graffiti art, depend on less-accessible codes. Self-consciously hermetic high-art architecture, with its unique stylistic vocabularies, has been subsumed into a readily identifiable, therefore marketable, product.[13] Even recent immigrant groups, such as Koreans and Japanese, have created distinctive theme environments along Olympic Boulevard and in Little Tokyo, with images derived from Buddhist temples and zen gardens now used for restaurants, hotels, and shopping centers. In a city of endless atomization, infinite individual ecologies are available.

The consumption of fantasy themes is not available to everyone. The homeless, present in increasing numbers in the city, are both physically and economically excluded. Put on the streets by the shutdown of mental hospitals, the disappearance of family assistance programs, and the contraction of blue-collar industries, they must claim whatever marginal territory is available for living space: cars, sidewalks, and vacant lots. Rather than consuming prepackaged environments, they are forced to produce their own. They improvise provisional shelters from whatever materials are at hand and gather into temporary communities for safety and to obtain services. Their spontaneous creation of living environments from virtually nothing implicitly questions the calculated construction of the theme environment. Even seen from a passing car, it is difficult to reduce the density of despair in Skid Row to a purely visual image.

More and more, irreducible realities intrude on the neutrality of the street, making it difficult to maintain an uninterrupted circuit of theme environments. "Street people," no longer confined to downtown, panhandle in many areas of the city. Unemployed immigrants sell oranges and peanuts at stoplights and gather at designated corners for the "shape-up"—of an informal labor market—to announce their availability for any kind of manual work. When they do find employment, it is often as the service workers, waiters, busboys, and valet parkers on whom theme environments depend. The presence of these silent observers, implies another, as yet unrealized, ecology, presently submerged but likely to become dominant given the fact that, according to demographic projections, immigrants will constitute over 40 percent of Los Angeles' population by the year 2000.

In a city devoted to the search for increasingly esoteric individual themes, immigrant groups establish community against great odds. Inheriting the physical city of pre-Disneyland Los Angeles, they lead urban lives familiar to the inhabitants of many cities: walking through crowded downtown streets, using public transportation, and gathering in public parks. All over the city, newcomers have reclaimed public places such as streets, parks, and markets, transforming them into functioning social space. Spanish-speaking Broadway, between Third and Eighth streets, offers the most concentrated street life in the city, with pedestrians far outnumbering vehicles. Olvera Street, Los Angeles' original civic plaza, turned into an ersatz tourist attraction in the 1940s, has come full circle to be used once again as a public square and paseo. The authentic intensity of these pedestrian experiences recalls traditional urban ecologies and points out the hollowness of their recreation inside theme environments. This forms a major barrier to the total incursion of the ecology of fantasy.

What will be the result of the inevitable collision of these disparate ecologies? One possibility is suggested by the science fiction film *Bladerunner* (regarded by many as an accurate projection of Los Angeles' future) in which everyone who can afford to has moved "off-world", leaving the city to its Third world inhabitants. Off-world is not yet available, but outlying, privately developed new towns (such as Mission Viejo or Westlake Village, whose physical and social coherence are maintained by deed restrictions and security guards) address the same needs. Another scenario is the expansion of theme environments to include "melting-pot" content, with non–Spanish-speaking, second-generation Chicanos happily dining in Hispanic-theme restaurants.

Less likely, given the constraints of consumer economics and class and ethnic division, is the possibility of synthesis. One can still imagine, however, a future in which environments that do not orchestrate escape from daily life might include an awareness of multiple realities. We cannot expect the individual automobile to disappear or for Los Angeles' dispersed fragments to come together, but we still can hope that the theme circuits we endlessly create might become inclusive rather than exclusive, expansive rather than reductive, and that the principle of mobility might be used to cross boundaries rather than to construct them.

# 17. Raymond W. Novaco

## AUTOMOBILE DRIVING AND AGGRESSIVE BEHAVIOR

The roadway assaults that have occurred in recent years raise questions about anger and aggression and their relationship to driving. Our everyday discussions about driving experiences incorporate considerable lore about aggression on the road, yet the subject has been neglected academically. Broadly speaking, aggressive behavior on roadways is understood in simplistic terms, such as defective personalities, "copycat" behavior, or traffic stress. Although such ideas have some plausibility, they are overly simplified accounts for incidents that vary considerably in their form and causes.

Contemporary manifestations of roadway assaults have galvanized several themes in the literature on the psychology of aggression, and this chapter will examine them with regard to automobile driving. Territoriality, frustration, modeling influences, and sustained arousal are conditions that heighten the probability of aggression and are very much part of driving.

Although assaultive behavior and other forms of aggression on the road have many causes and dissimilarities, a range of aggressive behaviors on roadways can be understood in terms of factors or conditions that disinhibit aggressive behavior. That is, aggressive behavior is restrained by inhibitory controls within the individual and society. Personal and social control mechanisms, however, are weakened by various factors that operate in the context of driving. Physiological and emotional arousal, the anonymity of highways, the opportunity to escape, and the promulgation of scripts of "road warrior" behavior by cinematic and mass-media sources can override the personal and societal forces that otherwise inhibit and regulate aggressive behavior.

The weakening of controls of aggression is a matter pertaining to urban violence generally, and automobile driving is just one arena. Violence on roadways involves particular "activating" and "releasing" mechanisms, and the growing problem of traffic congestion in urban areas can add to the violence risk. Before addressing those contextual matters, there are symbolic aspects of the car itself that are linked with aggression. In a variety of ways,

Preparation of this chapter was supported by the Drivetime Foundation, The Institute of Transportation Studies (Irvine), and the Public Policy Research Organization at the University of California, Irvine.

the very image of the car has been cast with aggressive features, and this symbolization of the car is congruent with some aggression-engendering conditions of the roadway.

### ELEMENTS OF AGGRESSION IN THE AUTOMOBILE'S SYMBOLIZATION

Far from being a contemporary phenomenon, aggressiveness has been fused with driving at least since chariots careened around the Circus Maximus in ancient Rome, generating clouds of dust and choruses of roars among the spectators.[1] The association of aggression with automobile driving, however, has been a recurrent element in the symbolization of the car. Car names, advertising themes, design features, and engineered capacities often have cast an image of the car in aggressive terms. It is not incidental that cars have been called Chargers, Cougars, Jaguars, Stingrays, Thunderbirds, Cutlasses, Firebirds, and Challengers. Such names fit themes of power and excitement packaged by Madison Avenue, so as to induce significant segments of the buying public to get behind the wheel of the latest ego-enhancing product. Aggressiveness blends with automobile excitement and the sense of self-efficacy.

Dominance is the core concept of the high-performance automotive machine. The car is frequently an instrument of competitiveness in various forms of ritualized dueling, from hot-rod drag racing to frenetic scampers through freeway traffic by hurried drivers jockeying for lane position. The car or truck can be a means of asserting dominance, and sometimes they are transformed from vehicles to weapons in the hands of enraged drivers. The hood ornament, now passé, might well have been a metaphor for a gun sight. The car is an instrument of the assertion of power, as many people have observed, such as Norbert Schmidt-Relenberg, who described the behavior of Mercedes drivers on the autobahn in terms of "power trials."[2]

The car is also a territorial entity, a highly personalized space, sensitized to crowding, jarring, and marring. Especially in circumstances that are otherwise arousing (such as driving under conditions of time urgency, ambient discomfort, and travel impedance), being in a car is to inhabit a microenvironment that can be easily geared for frustration and anger. The car is an extension of a personal space zone, the encroachment of which can elicit an aggressive response. New-car owners can be found to be exceedingly vigilant about preserving their car's pristine condition, and some maintain this obsession well past the vehicle's freshly minted days. Even the slightest damage to it can provoke strong antagonistic responses.

These are aggressive themes in the symbolization of the automobile, but they do not correspond to violence. Marketing images, arousal, ritualized competition, and territoriality do not automatically convert to assaultive, harmful behavior. Human aggressiveness is not foreign to automobile driving, but violence is a significantly different matter than competitive acceleration, impatience with traffic, and irritability about parking lot dents. Hence, the association between driving and aggression must be mapped in a differentiated way.[3]

This chapter will discuss a number of long-standing themes in the psychology of aggression literature that pertain to automobile driving. The topical areas from research on aggression include territoriality, frustration, and environmental cues. Before elaborating on these psychological themes, I will discuss the highly publicized road aggression episode that prompted my interest in the topic and examine some common misconceptions about its causes.

### THE CALIFORNIA FREEWAY SHOOTING EPISODES

When the wave of freeway shootings erupted in California in the summer of 1987, it raised concerns about anger and aggression and their relationship to driving. Communities became alarmed about an allegedly new threat of violence in California that signaled the further decay of the social fabric. Many people saw the shootings as a by-product of the snarl of traffic congestion that has become an increasingly bothersome feature of the southern California landscape and metropolitan areas nationwide. The potential influence of the mass media as inducers of copycat behavior was discussed, and resemblances to gang-related drive-by shootings were also noted. Some observers glibly viewed the spree of freeway shootings as a passing fad, while others saw the episode as indicative of the miserable condition of congested roads.

During the summer of 1987 freeway shootings became a daily news item in California, and the publicity spread nationally and internationally. Between mid-June and the end of August, 1987, there were approximately seventy shootings and one serious stabbing on southern California roads reported in the newspapers. Based on newspaper accounts, there were over one hundred shootings reported throughout the state. The incidents were distributed across days of the week, with no particular pattern for time of day, although most of the shootings occurred during the afternoon or in the evening before midnight. Most of the incidents occurred on freeways, but about 25 percent took place on surface streets. The victims were predominantly males; the assailants were all males, with female companions in a few cases. This domain of male exclusivity was maintained until March 5, 1988, when a female passenger in a red Hyundai punctuated her driver's obscene hand gestures by blasting a car of teenagers, which had passed them previously.

The vehicles used in the shootings varied considerably; shots were fired from cars, trucks, and motorcycles, although pickup trucks were involved disproportionately. Most freeway shootings were perpetrated by solo drivers, although at times there were three or four assailants. Indeed, this form of roadway aggression is to be distinguished from gang-related incidents known as drive-by shootings.

Once the wave of shootings passed, the common tendency was to view what happened as a vanishing aberration. Driving on freeways is ingrained in our lifestyles, so we are commonly in the environments where the highly publicized assaults have taken place. The apparent randomness of the shootings certainly heightened the alarm. Yet, few of us want to think that our communities have become so uncivilized that we must worry about being bushwhacked on the way to work. The shootings were less random, however, than commonly believed. The majority of incidents involved some prior dispute or conflict about road privilege, based on victims' accounts, which are likely to be underestimates of prior provocation. Death and serious injury victims were often passengers, which should give drivers pause in becoming ensnared in a dispute about road space. Far from being an aberration, the conditions that facilitate road violence remain, and this manifestation of aggression was more than an episodic occurrence idiosyncratic to California.

Sequential outbreaks of roadway shootings have occurred periodically in other metropolitan areas, and aggression on highways happens more frequently than is recognized generally or officially. Before the California episode there was a spree of freeway shootings in Houston in 1982. At that time there was a large influx of newcomers to that city, and its freeways were very congested. There were twelve traffic-related homicides, and another thirteen happened over the next five years. Those were homicides—shootings were generally much more numerous. Following the 1987 California episode, there was that fall a similar freeway shooting contagion in St. Louis, involving twenty-two confirmed shootings between the end of October through December. Also in Detroit about a dozen roadway shootings occurred during the year after those in California. The wave of shootings in southern California, therefore, was not at all unique.

The road assault incidents had dissimilarities and many causes. Why the assaults occurred and why they "stopped" remain interesting puzzles, although the answer to the latter question has a twist—they have not stopped. Roadway assaults taking the form of shootings, throwings, and brandishings that are not gang-related have not abated at all; what has diminished is the thematic presence in the news media. From data tabulated by the California Highway Patrol (CHP), "freeway violence" has increased from 1988 to 1989. After a rise and decline in the first half of 1988, for example, the CHP tabulations indicate 114 and 98 incidents in the months July and August of 1988 and then show a steady rise to 250 and 325 for June and July of 1989. The latter figure was an all-time high, according to Commander Susan Cowen-Scott.[4] This respected police agency certainly does not consider aggressive behavior on roadways to be a passing fad, although it is fortuitous (from a contagion standpoint) that it has lost its topical value for making the news.

In considering why the freeway shootings occurred, this particular form of assault must be viewed in the larger context of societal violence and in relation to other forms of aggression in automobile driving. Several explanations having colloquial appeal must be recognized as oversimplifications that fail to address multiple pathways of causation. Attempts to account for freeway shootings as being due to "wackos," copycats, or even traffic stress are too narrow and go astray.

Personality pathology is certainly a relevant factor in road shooting incidents, and it is likely that some of those who did the shootings would have engaged in some other form of aggression, if this particular script had not been salient. A case in point is that of Albert C. Morgan, who was convicted of shooting Paul Gary Nussbaum on the freeway approaching the Costa Mesa Fairgrounds on July 18, 1987. Nussbaum is now paralyzed from the neck down. Morgan was sentenced to ten years imprisonment. During the trial several significant facts emerged. When captured, Morgan had ammunition in both pockets (four bullets in one and five in the other). He was drinking heavily prior to the shooting, and, four hours after the shooting, he had a blood alcohol level of 0.1. His past history had notable aggressive features, including a prior roadway assault in which he fought with another driver.

Certainly, in this case there is a conspicuous aggression-proneness factor operating.

The expression "a man drives as he lives" is a theme that was pursued by a number of British researchers in the 1960s and 1970s, who investigated the relationship between aggressiveness as a personality trait and motoring offenses as well as accident liability. This research was partly inspired by an early study by W. A. Tillman and G. E. Hobbs on accident proneness.[5] The point to be made is that aggressive behavior has many causes, some of which are personal dispositions and some situational. When aggression occurs on the road, we must examine the roadway context as containing some of the determinants, especially when patterns of aggression occur across individuals.

Personality factors are only part of the picture. Someone such as Albert Morgan likely would be violent off the road as well as on it. But traffic circumstances, the freeway shooting script, alcohol consumption, and the availability of his weapon surely boosted his aggression potential on that Saturday afternoon when he was stuck in a traffic jam, had a prior altercation with someone in a blue truck, and then leaned across the car, in front of his wife's face, to shoot Gary Nussbaum.

In contrast to being perpetrated by "pathological" types, some of the shootings might have involved ordinary people undergoing periods of stress who lost control of their impulses. They might have used a weapon for attack that they were carrying for defense, despite the illegality. Alternatively, the victims might have expressed annoyance with words or gestures but then provoked a more aggressive counterresponse. More tragically, the victim might not have been the person who initially provoked the assailant. The escalation process need not be confined to the original players. Various disinhibitory processes and cues for aggression can catalyze an angry emotional state into harm-doing behavior. When people get very angry, they often do not consider the consequences of their actions, and they do not pick targets very carefully.

Another common explanation for the freeway shootings is that they are copycat incidents. There is some credence to this theory, as modeling effects are among the most well-documented phenomena in psychological research on aggression.[6] The copycat explanation, however, plausibly accounts for only part of what happened. Most of the incidents involved some dispute or altercation, so it was not a matter of sensation seekers merely duplicating a newscast, movie scene, or newspaper story. Millions of drivers were exposed to multimedia coverage, yet only about one hundred did the shooting. Imitative behavior and modeling influences are certainly part of the diffusion, or spread, of road aggression throughout some geographic area linked by the media, but the effects are more than copycat phenomena. The escalation of many incidents from disputes to assaults, and the fact that assaults that begin in cars sometimes culminate outside of cars, render the copycat idea as pseudo-explanation. Some examples from the "roadside confrontation" category will illustrate this point.

Roadside confrontations refer to traffic disputes that have been extended outside the vehicle. Following a dispute about road space or privilege, one driver might force another off the road or simply be in a position to impede the other's movement, setting the stage for confrontation. During the California 1987 summer episode, there was a stabbing in Newport Beach that left a man in critical condition after two men who were on a motor scooter began to scuffle with two men who had been in a Corvette. In January, 1988, an irate motorist got out of his car to confront another motorist, a pregnant woman. He pushed her against the freeway railing, punched her, and tried to throw her over the railing but was deterred by six passing motorists, who received humanitarian awards for their efforts. In the Detroit episode, which occurred in late 1988 and early 1989, there were two roadside confrontations that were extensions of freeway disputes and that resulted in serious injuries, one of them fatal. The man who died was pursued off the interstate after he and his companions made obscene gestures. He died from kicks to the head and neck. In the other case, a driver was forced off the road and was badly slashed with a knife. These events surely indicate that there is more involved than copying previously publicized shootings.

An example that illustrates the limitations of the copycat and the pathological personality views is the case of Arthur Salomon, a Wall Street investment banker. This prominent fifty-two-year-old, seemingly model citizen, shot an unarmed college student on June 19, 1987, in a road dispute on the Hutchinson River Parkway.[7] The conflict began over the right to pass on the freeway. It escalated to verbal exchanges on the side of the road and ended with the shooting of the young man by Salomon as the victim was walking back to his car, saying that he had the license number of Salomon's Mercedes. Salomon was reported to be under strain at the time. Although he was known to be stubborn, he was also well known for his generosity.[8] Apparently, the model citizen became ensnared in a road dispute, which escalated and resulted in his using a gun for attack that normally he carried for protection. I doubt that he, his family, nor his associates were inclined to account for his behavior in terms of a thrill-seeking wacko fad, copycat behavior, or an anti-social personality.

Finally, viewing the road shooting episode as a product of traffic stress is also misguided. The California summer incidents were distributed evenly across days of the week with no distinct pattern for time of day. The shootings were not done by rush-hour commuters stuck in traffic jams. A traffic jam is a rather unlikely place for a road shooting, presuming that the person doing the shooting wishes to escape. It is precisely the anonymity and escape potential of freeways that provides for disinhibition. Albert Morgan, however, was in a traffic jam when he shot Gary Nussbaum, and he was quickly apprehended at the Orange County Fairgrounds. Morgan was the exception, but he also had several other disinhibitory processes operating—that is, readiness of gun and ammunition, alcohol consumption, and arousal from a prior altercation.

Traffic conditions are not irrelevant. Some years ago Daniel Stokols and I did several studies on commuter stress, which applied naturalistic field research to the effects of automobile commuting.[9] As psychologists, we were concerned with long-term exposure to traffic congestion, chronic health and behavior effects, individuals who were most at risk, and conditions of the home and job environment that influenced the stress of commuting. We found that continued exposure to traffic congestion elevates resting blood pressure, increases negative mood states, lowers tolerance for frustration, and can lead to more impatient driving habits. More recently, we have found additional negative effects on physical health, work absences, and mood at home in the evening.[10] Physiological arousal, irritability, and impatience, however, are qualitatively different from assaultive behavior. These internal states can activate aggression, but aggression is a significantly different matter because it requires an override of inhibitions about harm-doing. Traffic conditions might affect our mood and produce other stress consequences, but many other factors operate in producing flagrant assaultive behavior.

The convenient explanations for freeway shootings are oversimplified; the violent incidents were heterogenous and multicausal. Moreover, freeway shootings are only one type of aggression that occurs on roadways. They are a relatively uncommon form, perhaps exceeded in novelty only by the veritable highway robbery spree that occurred in South Florida in 1985 when over one hundred motorists were ambushed and robbed on Interstate 95 between Fort Lauderdale and Miami. Other violent behaviors, in addition to shootings and robbery, involve the use of the vehicle as a weapon. That form has received some scholarly attention; there is a study of vehicular homicide cases in Columbus, Ohio, by Raymond Michalowski and the British *Criminal Law Review* by J.R. Spencer.[11]

The more common forms of aggression on roadways are the not-so-violent variety, such as verbal nastiness, threat displays, and various antagonistic driving behaviors. The community surveys that I have conducted indicate that these behaviors are more prevalent than generally or officially recognized. Presented here are a set of themes in the psychology of aggression literature that pertain to automobile driving. These long-standing themes are territoriality, frustration, and environmental cues for aggression.

### THEMES IN THE PSYCHOLOGY OF AGGRESSION RELATED TO DRIVING

Psychological research on aggressive behavior is voluminous; hence, this presentation is only a cursory discussion of some primary topical areas that are related to driving. Roadway conditions that are conducive to aggressive behavior are discussed in light of these psychological themes about which there is considerable consensus among aggression researchers.

#### Territoriality

The territoriality theme was mentioned earlier in conjunction with the symbolization of the car. Aggression has been linked with territorial defense among numerous species of animals in ethological research.[12] While there is little quarrel about the fact that aggression occurs in the defense of space among animals and humans, the assertion of an "instinct" mechanism is another matter, and such claims have been strongly rebutted by so many research scientists that it is no longer an issue. Yet, the idea of a territorial instinct has appeared in the road aggression literature, notably in the monograph by Francis Anthony Whitlock, who examined the association between road deaths and general mortality statistics in twenty-six countries.[13] Whitlock's proposition was that road violence is an aspect of social violence in general, and he explained aggression on the road in terms of instinctive drive and territoriality. He hypothesized that the inclination of young men to be aggressive on the road was due to their lack of real estate ownership and the transfer of aggressive instinct to the automobile. His ideas prompted Joel Richman's interview study with Manchester, England, traffic wardens concerning "errant motorists," which had disconfirming results for Whitlock's ideas.[14]

There is no need to bind ideas about territorial defense with the notion of aggressive instinct in order to account for aggressive behavior on the road. The automobile can be understood as territory, in terms of both property to be defended and as a personal space zone not to be encroached. The automobile is a highly personalized property, and aggression can be elicited by the perceived need to defend it. Peter E. Marsh and Peter Collett wrote colorfully about the car as a special territory with personal space zones, the invasion of which provokes anger and aggression.[15]

Finally the territorial behavior of gangs, exhibited in drive-by shootings, reflects both economic and security aspects of the defense of turf. Such shootings also have symbolic causal dimensions. In southern California, drive-by shootings are perpetrated almost exclusively by Latino gangs, although there are many Black and Asian gangs. The prototype was established by predominantly Italian mobsters in New York and Chicago in the 1920s. Such shootings are often acts of retaliation executed on rival turf; hence, they are much more than territorial defense, which in this regional context occurs when, for example, someone wearing the wrong "colors" in a particular neighborhood is shot from a passing car. In the past few years there has been a distinct increase in this form of roadway aggression.

### Frustration and Arousal

The relationship between frustration and aggression is the oldest theme in the psychology of aggression. It has its ancestry in the writings of Sigmund Freud, but it was born as a research topic with the publication of the famous monograph *Frustration and Aggression*, by John Dollard, Leonard W. Doob, Neil E. Miller, D. Hobart Mowrer, and Robert R. Sears, and it appeared prominently in studies in the 1950s and 1960s.[16] Aggression was viewed as always being a consequence of frustration. The instigation to aggression was held to be a function of a number of aspects of the frustration, including the degree of interference, the importance of the goal, and the number of frustrations. Dollard and his coauthors, developed elaborate propositions about the frustration-aggression relationship, including matters concerning displacement, inhibition, and catharsis. The theory received a major reformulation by Leonard Berkowitz, who argued that anger and interpretation were important mediators.[17] Later, aggression theorists, notably Albert Bandura, moved away from the term *frustration*, which had become an omnibus concept, and looked more extensively at varieties of aversive instigators and the arousal states that they produced that heightened aggressive responding.[18]

An interrelated idea is the "interruption" concept, which pertains to the blocking or delaying of an organized response sequence, the effect of which is to activate arousal and emotion.

Roadways in metropolitan areas are replete with frustrations and interruptions, the essence of traffic jams, as well as properties of various traffic control devices. Commuters learn to adapt to these aversive conditions in a variety of ways, cognitively and behaviorally, so the potentially frustrating nature of such conditions indeed is determined by the driver's appraisal of them. Nevertheless, someone who has otherwise adapted to existing levels of travel constraints might be sensitized momentarily, on a particular day, to traffic frustrations or be already agitated by preceding events (at home or work) such that his or her capacity to cope is weakened.

Traffic congestion has become a conspicuous and bothersome feature of the urban landscape. In our research on commuting stress mentioned earlier, traffic congestion is understood as a stressor in terms of the concept of impedance, a behavioral constraint on movement and goal attainment. The frustrative and arousal-inducing properties of travel constraints are assumed to be stressful. We have operationalized impedance as a physical or objective dimension in terms of the distance and time parameters of commuting. We have also examined impedance as a perceptual or subjective dimension in terms of perceived aspects of travel constraints. Both the physical and the perceived dimensions of impedance have been found to impair personal well-being, job satisfaction, and quality of home life, and we have developed an ecological model for understanding these effects of commuting stress.[19]

The existing transportation environment in southern California is predisposing to aggressive behavior because of increased impedance conditions. In the 1988 Orange County Survey, a telephone interview sampling of one thousand residents, only 5 percent of those surveyed reported being satisfied with existing freeway conditions, down from 8 percent in 1987 and 32 percent in 1982. Nearly 50 percent of residents considered traffic congestion to be the county's most important problem.[20] Traffic congestion, based on California Department of Transportation (CALTRANS) measurements, has increased by a factor of fifty in Orange County and had increased in Los Angeles County by 12 to 15 percent per two-year interval since 1979. The national picture is also one of increased congestion. A 1989 report from the General Accounting Office states that the metropolitan-wide problem of traffic congestion has become more severe, showing major increases in average daily traffic volume for U.S. urban interstate roads from 1980 to 1987, calculated in terms of volume/capacity ratios. The thwartings associated with increased traffic raise the probability of hostility and aggression on the road.

Frustration and stress due to traffic conditions are by no means automatically generative of aggressive behavior, but they do present predisposing conditions. The research that Daniel Stokols and I have conducted with regard to chronic exposure to traffic congestion has found significant increases in baseline blood pressure, lowering of frustration tolerance, increases in negative mood, and aggressive driving habits to be associated with exposure to high-impedance commuting. Such conditions present risks for violent behavior, especially when aggression-inhibiting influences are reduced.

### Environmental Cues

Field studies on human aggression have often been concerned with stimuli in the environment that elicit aggressive behavior. Berkowitz used the term *aggressive cues* to refer to these stimuli that enhance the likelihood that someone who is aroused (typically, by anger) will attack an available target.[21] He attaches great importance to such cues when examining impulsive acts of aggression.[22] A person who is aroused to aggression still might be able to restrain him- or herself, but efforts to control this arousal can be short-circuited by aggressive cues in the situation—for example, insulting words that prompt fighting, the availability of weapons, the presence of other people who reward aggression, or the modeling of aggressive behavior by others.

In the road aggression literature there is a small set of studies on horn honking that seemed to have been inspired by a combination of the frustration-aggression research tradition and Berkowitz's work on aggressive cues. These studies began with Anthony Doob and Alan Gross and are best exemplified in the field experiments by Charles Turner, John Layton, and Lynn Simons.[23] Although there are difficulties with the use of horn honking as a criterion measure for aggression, as it has been used, there would be little quarrel with understanding it as a cue for aggression in a context of thwarting or frustration.

Relatively little is known about the prevalence of hostile reactions among drivers. An early, pioneering study done by Meyer Parry in a London borough found that 15 percent of the males and 11 percent of the females stated that; "At times, I felt that I could gladly kill another driver."[24] That statement was endorsed by 12 percent of the males and 18 percent of the females in a Salt Lake City sample surveyed by Turner, Layton, and Simons in preparation for their experimental studies. On a more behavioral level, Parry found that 27 percent of the males and 12 percent of the females had given chase to another driver who had annoyed them.[25] The results for Turner et al. on this item were 12 percent for men and 4 percent for women. Marsh and Collett report that a study in Scotland found that 25 percent of the drivers in the seventeen to thirty-five years of age group admitted chasing drivers who had offended them.[26] My own surveys with two university student samples and two community samples in southern California have found the percentages to be over 40 percent for males in each sample and from 11 percent to 21 percent for the females sampled. Many other provocative behaviors, such as throwing objects, shouting or yelling, deliberately riding someone's bumper, and making obscene gestures, were reported to occur with worrisome frequency. For example, 6 percent of the university sample and 9 percent of the community sample reported making obscene gestures on a weekly basis.

The carrying of weapons in the automobile presents another cue for aggression. A prospective freeway shooter might be someone who is otherwise law-abiding and has a gun in his or her car for protection that is then used for attack. Although experimental studies of the "weapons effect" in the aggressive cue literature have failed to replicate initial findings of Berkowitz and Anthony LePage, the ethical limitations of research on human subjects restrict a suitable test of the hypothesis.[27] It is surely plausible that the presence of weapons intensifies ideas of attack, and the prevalence of guns is not on the decline. A *Los Angeles Times* newspaper poll of 2,032 southern California residents found that 5 percent of drivers carry a gun in their car, a number higher than the 2.9 percent of my community samples of 412 Orange County drivers in a self-report survey.[28]

To the extent that drivers engage in provoking behavior and carry weapons in their vehicles, there is a troublesome potential for roadway aggression to amplify. Some drivers might be quite inclined to persevere in a quarrel, and an antagonistic exchange between drivers can escalate to harmdoing consequences. Indeed, it is surely a mistake, especially during a community contagion of road shootings, to become ensnared in a road dispute. To do so is to engage in an ego-oriented script that potentially has a very bad ending.

## SUMMARY

Aggressive behavior has had a recurrent association with automobile driving, as reflected in our symbolization of cars and trucks, as well as being linked to psychological experiences on congested roadways. Dramatic occurrences of violence, such as the 1987 California freeway shooting episode, might be seen as idiosyncratic events. Instead, such occurrences need to be understood in a historical and phenomenological context. Freeway shootings are only one type of aggression occurring on roadways and are in no way unique to California. Overly simplified views of the California summer contagion as being due to pathological personalities, copy cats, and traffic stress have been shown to be pseudo-explanations.

Although research on human aggression has neglected the roadway context as a field of investigation, there are several major themes in the psychology of aggression literature that offer hypotheses for analysis, such as territoriality, frustration, and environmental cues. A number of surveys and field experiments can be found in the existing literature that are either based on these themes or are convergent with them.

While it would be an exaggeration to say that antagonism and aggression are a routine part of automobile driving, various lines of evidence indicate that such behavior is not uncommon among American and British drivers. The stereotyped form of road aggression known as drive-by shootings is in need of a thorough analysis of its historical, cultural, and subcultural underpinnings. Since aggression on roadways exists in many forms and since conditions that are predisposing to such aggression are not diminishing, the topic merits concerted attention.

# PART 5
## REFLECTIONS, INTERPRETATIONS, ANTICIPATIONS

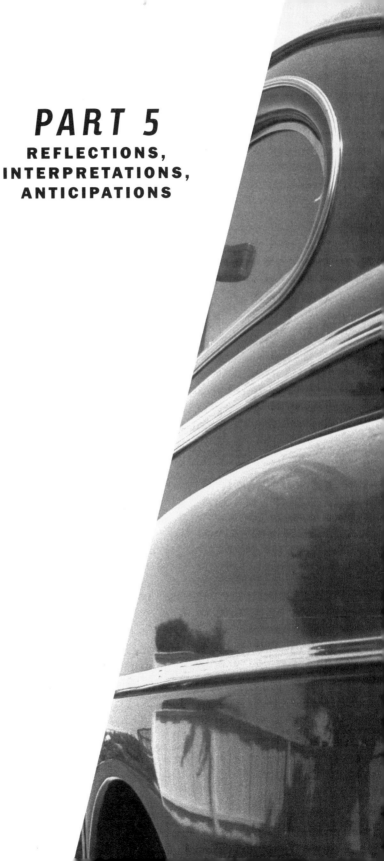

# INTRODUCTION TO PART 5

The final part consists of three chapters that interpret the place of the automobile in daily urban life and look toward the future. In the first chapter of the section, architect Barton Myers, acknowledging the dominance of the automobile, proposes an urban design strategy that uses the car as a positive element in creating exciting and livable cities. Using Los Angeles as an example, Myers advocates "episodic urban congestion," creating a series of zones all over the city in which intensive activity can occur. Rather than separating the pedestrian from the automobile, as both developments like Century City and artificial environments like Disneyland have done, this solution emphasizes their coexistence. To strengthen the role of the street as a public realm, it must be accessible by car and foot, provide a diverse set of activities, and allow architectural changes to take place over time. Projects from Myers' office offer specific examples of how physical design can foster public life.

The second chapter in this section, by urban planner Melvin Web-ber, was presented as the keynote address at the Car and the City Symposium from which this book emerged. Futurist Marvin Adelson contributes the final chapter, which is, in a sense, a response to the previous presentations and discussions in this volume. While Webber and Adelson agree on a number of critical points, they disagree with respect to some central issues. Both note that traffic and transportation in the modern American city have recently evolved in response to several overarching trends about which there is relatively little planners can do but react. The decline of manufacturing and heavy industry and the rise of the services and information processing in their place have a profound decentralizing effect on our cities. The entry of large numbers of women into the work force and the suburbanization of employment have caused a shift of economic activity and traffic congestion from downtown areas to suburban office centers.

Webber predicts a future landscape of relatively uniform, low- to medium-density residential and *commercial areas, punctuated by occasional urban villages of higher density and the older central cities that predate recent economic shifts. In this environment Webber is clear—the automobile is the preferred mode of transportation, not because of an irrational attachment to it, but because it serves our needs better than any other mode of travel yet devised. Webber believes that traffic congestion will be influenced by market conditions— congested areas will become less attractive for development than uncongested ones, and congestion will thus be self-regulating. He is more concerned about the fact that a transportation system dominated by the auto will be inequitable. Those too young, too old, too handicapped, and too poor to rely on autos will be left immobile, and, in the auto-oriented metropolis, immobility is a clear economic and social disadvantage. To Webber, our most pressing problem is not to relieve congestion but to provide public transit for those who must depend upon it. He concludes that the type of public transport that we need in the emerging metropolis is one that mimics the automobile in its characteristic of ubiquity, responsiveness to individuals, and relative low cost. He also concludes that the empty seats in the millions of cars that are in daily use are resources upon which we must capitalize.*

*Adelson recognizes the validity of Webber's view that the automobile will remain central to life in the American metropolis, but he also recognizes the high costs imposed by social decisions to keep it that way. He is frustrated by our dependence on the auto and the congestion, energy dependence, and air pollution it engenders. Like Webber, Adelson asks what characteristics would be associated with transit alternatives. He concludes that many urban institutions—companies, hospitals, schools, and theaters— should and can use vans, buses, and other vehicles to pick up and deliver their customers, patients, and employees. Thus, Adelson advocates a kind of decentralization of responsibility for group transportation. He also sees greater spatial integration of home and work activities emerging in the future, enabling larger numbers of people to telecommute. Adelson predicts that for some the solution will be to accept long trips but to use travel times more productively. By developing work-oriented vans for commuting, for example, we will talk on the telephone and produce memos while en route from place to place.*

*Taken together, the chapters in part 5 provide a lively, sometimes serious, sometimes caricature vision of the future. Like the other chapters in this volume, they are not definitive but are rich in interpretation and suggestive about the directions of future relationships between the car and the city.*

Barton Myers
with John Dale

## DESIGNING IN CAR-ORIENTED CITIES:
### AN ARGUMENT FOR EPISODIC URBAN CONGESTION

For decades, car-oriented cities have been the nemesis of planners and urban designers. They defy all attempts to redefine them as vital urban environments. This chapter makes a case for fostering the use of the car as a positive component that can contribute to the health of the city. "Episodic urban congestion," where cars and people mingle to create richer and more intense places, should be encouraged in our cities.

Like critic Paul Goldberger, who once called for "new common sense" in urban design, I believe we need a new approach to urban development—an approach that builds upon the existing fabric of the city. This approach is meant as an alternative to the clearing away of the old to make way for the new without regard to history, context, neighborhood, or the particularity of each situation.

In 1978 my Toronto office conducted an analysis of urban design that was later entitled "Vacant Lottery" and was published in *Design Quarterly*. The article was a reaction to the North American syndrome of the proliferation of vacant lots and the discontinuity of scale threatening to sap the life out of our urban streets. It presented a number of alternate strategies for increasing densities while preserving the surviving urban fabric, thus filling in the holes again.[1] We searched for ways to mitigate the effects of the unicentered city with its overdeveloped core and underdeveloped periphery by promoting more evenly distributed growth and fostering a respect for particular contexts, physical as well as social. A "multicentered" approach to the design of cities can encourage growth without overburdening the infrastructure in one small portion of an urban area, increase densities without sacrificing neighborhoods, and promote alternate transportation systems without sacrificing personal mobility.

Los Angeles is a multicentered city by simple virtue of being many cities that have grown together. Its constituent municipalities, however, tend to be unicentered in form. Typically, there is an imbalance between high-density cores and the sprawling residential districts interconnecting them. The cores tend to be highly specialized, and the activity they generate tends to be circumscribed within a limited, particularized schedule. The surrounding low-density districts are less specialized, but they lack the overlapping uses and intensity of development necessary to create a lively public realm. The form of Los Angeles needs to be redefined.

Our city has evolved from a car owner's paradise to an increasingly congested and compromised megalopolis. The suburban sprawl of Los Angeles with its low-density, suburban, single-family housing maximizes vehicular travel for all aspects of daily life. We drive to work, the market, the child care center, the movie theater, and the mall. Once such travel was problematic only during the proverbial "rush hour," but during the last few years this hour has extended itself into a three-hour stretch at the beginning and end of each day. The rush-hour period is experienced even on the weekend. We are threatened with a blanket of congestion covering the entire city.

Angelenos have reached a watershed in which, as urban dwellers, we are forced to adapt to, rather than be accommodated by, an increasingly strained infrastructure. Without dwelling on the historical factors that have made Los Angeles what it is today, it is easy to see that a city dependent upon the automobile and its necessary support system—its freeway network—will survive in its present form only with difficulty.[2]

While the increase in vehicular congestion in Los Angeles threatens to bring the city to a standstill, *pedestrian congestion*—the kind of lively, sidewalk activity that supports a real sense of urbanity—has increased only minimally in isolated districts of the city. This definition of pedestrian congestion is not merely a matter of quantity (that is, numbers of people); it is also very much a matter of diverse activities integrating the car, pedestrian, and street. An approach to urban planning that distributes the activities of the city more evenly mitigates the amount of time spent "getting there" and increases the amount of time "being there." Through a process of urban consolidation, we can create episodic congestion throughout the city—distinctive places of high use and intense activity that occur on a regular basis within the urban fabric rather than being concentrated in one or two major high-density cores.

Ideally, one effect of such nodes of congestion would be an increased use of public transportation. Even without a significant increase in mass-transit options, a more even distribution of working, residential, and recreational environments throughout the city would decrease significantly the length and number of trips required by the automobile. In Los Angeles, where we are unwilling to forgo the freedom associated with our cars, we nevertheless need to plan for the effective integration of the automobile with public transportation so that both can be used to get us to pedestrian areas.

Los Angeles provides us with some successful examples of episodic urban congestion. The most intense nodes of street life in this city, however, tend to be highly controlled environments in which the car and the pedestrian are deliberately kept separate. The most extreme and artificial instances of this manufactured street life are in amusement parks like Disneyland and Universal Studios. Along Main Street in Disneyland, cars are replaced by trolleys, and priority is given to foot traffic, marching bands, and staged spectacles. The buildings along the street are scaled and populated to reinforce the definition and activity of the street.

A less artificial example of this kind of experience is found at Venice Beach, where the boardwalk is entirely given over to strollers, roller skaters, and street performers. In this case the beach provides a natural draw and the continuous row of stalls, shops, and cafés lining the opposite side of the walkway provides a protective, supportive, and intensely used edge. It is clear that scale, continuity, and overlap of activities are all key ingredients to the success of such an urban setting.

There are also a few examples of healthy activity in which the car and the pedestrian are well integrated. Rodeo Drive in Beverly Hills, Broadway in downtown Los Angeles, Hollywood Boulevard, and Westwood Village are examples of episodic congestion. Each of these areas tends to support a specific activity—shopping along Broadway and Rodeo Drive, entertainment along Hollywood Boulevard and in Westwood Village—but all employ similar principles that contribute to their success. Like Venice Beach and Disneyland, the activities in these areas occur largely at grade level—including parking—and the scale of buildings is predominantly small. Where the density of development is higher, the first stories of buildings are given over to a variety of pedestrian-related activities like shops, restaurants, and cinemas. Each place creates and supports a series of events that contribute to the urban experience. In addition, each place has created its own distinctive flavor, reflecting a particular context or neighborhood. These examples offer pertinent guidelines for the development of other places of episodic urban congestion.

The following strategies assume the present form of Los Angeles as their starting point. Rather than starting from scratch, we can play upon the

**FIGURE 18.1**

*Venice, California—the Boardwalk. The beach provides a natural draw and the continuous row of stalls, shops, and cafés lining the opposite side of the walkway provides a protective, supportive, and intensely used edge.*

*Designing in Car-Oriented Cities*

best of what this city represents and search for ways to intensify and improve its urban qualities.

### CELEBRATE THE STREET EDGE

Our streets should be thought of as positive urban spaces, outdoor rooms to dwell in, not just as the leftover, residual spaces of a privatized world. Each new building therefore should be thought of as an opportunity to enhance the public realm. Some very traditional devices can be used to enhance and celebrate the street edge. Arcades can define and protect a comfortable pedestrian zone and articulate the transition from indoors to outdoors. Towers and special entry portals can indicate landmark locations within the grid of the city and help orient the pedestrian. Special paving patterns and curb treatments can articulate zones where cars and people merge and where important points of arrival are located. The importance of how we arrive by car needs to be given special consideration in cities where the automobile is a dominant aspect of urban life.

In southern California, the significance of the street edge and arrival by car has not always been ignored. Bertram Goodhue's plan for the 1915 Panama-California Exposition in San Diego's Balboa Park suggests rich possibilities for the coexistence of people and cars. Both motorists and pedestrians arrive across a ravine on a handsome viaduct, pass through an arch into an intimate paved courtyard dominated by a domed exhibition hall, and follow an arcaded avenue before reaching parking lots, gardens and galleries. The Spanish Baroque architecture and landscape produce a surprisingly compelling environment, one that makes a dramatic and effective statement about arrival.

Every landscape intervention should likewise be conscious of the opportunity to reinforce the spatial continuity of the street. Dense shade trees and, in the Southwest, lofty palms can be used to articulate and reinforce major public spaces. In our metropolis some of the most moving streetscapes are the residential enclaves of Beverly Hills where trees have been planted to give elegance and rhythm to the boulevards. Grand avenues of lofty palm trees alternate with more intimate ones lined with jacarandas, which produce brilliant lavender blossoms in the spring. The trees distinguish one street from another and provide a sense of orientation within what would otherwise be an undifferentiated neighborhood. They effectively scale the street, both from the viewpoint of the motorist and the pedestrian. Landscape is a vital and powerful element in the urban experience; it should play a greater role as we continue to redevelop the city.

## PRESERVE AND ENCOURAGE SMALL-BLOCK DEVELOPMENT

The superblock is the scourge of a vital urban environment. It encourages the proliferation of large, single-use enclaves with highly restricted public access. Activity tends to be internalized, inevitably at the expense of surrounding streets and districts. The modern prototype for commercial development provides office towers, food courts, and stores within a single structure: an isolated, self-contained world contributing little to the rest of the city.

The best urban prototypes have dense city grids and relatively small blocks. In schemes of this nature no single development becomes too self-contained, as the point of reference always reverts to the street and the public realm. The street is constantly reinforced as the vital interface between a multitude of activities. By preserving the scale of smaller blocks and encouraging small-scale, incremental development, building densities can be kept in check, diversity of use can be maintained, and the street can retain its primacy as active public space.

One of the most successful examples of this theory in action is the central business district of Portland, Oregon. The city's rich urban setting is structured on a dense grid of streets. Three key factors contribute to its vitality. First, Portland is very aware of the importance of its streets. The downtown area has a highly developed network of transit malls, broad sidewalks, and handsome street furniture that both celebrate the importance of the public realm and accommodate pedestrians, buses, trolleys, and cars together comfortably. Second, Portland has successfully preserved its small urban blocks and controlled the scale of new development within the existing downtown grid. This effort has meant that the usual bulldozing of whole districts has not taken place, and much of the older fabric of the city has been preserved and renewed. Third, because of the scale and density of the urban fabric, its compact layout and abundance of public amenities, a diversity of institutional, business, entertainment, and retail functions coexist in close proximity.

Reduction of an existing network of streets and lanes tends to funnel vehicular traffic into fewer, larger arteries that increasingly become separators rather than connectors of human activity. Preserving the traditional city grid and distributing development over a larger area enables the existing infrastructure to accommodate traffic effectively and efficiently. Where larger blocks of land have been consolidated for urban redevelopment, it is incumbent on architects, urban designers, and planners to safeguard passages and rights-of-way that acknowledge the structure and scale of the surrounding city.

### ZONE FOR MIXED-USE DEVELOPMENT

The North American habit of segregating zoning uses should be abandoned in favor of the conscious integration of mixed uses and activities. Conventional zoning practices that separate functions over different parts of the city have contributed to mindless sprawl. Presently, Los Angeles is a collection of highly specialized nodes rather than a series of diverse district centers. Westwood Village and downtown Hollywood function more as entertainment districts than neighborhood shopping centers, in spite of dense residential development nearby. It is rare to find districts where people can shop and work within walking distance or a short bus ride from their homes. The resulting overdependence on the private car and the freeway system is inevitable.

The negative aspect of exclusive zoning is the duplication of support systems. In Los Angeles this duplication of services translates into more surface parking lots and garages. Every mini-mall needs its own convenient dedicated parking; the boulevards of the city are being eroded consistently by the familiar configuration of single-story rows of shops, buffered from the street by a sea of cars.

While such zoning practices have begun to shift and large-scale developments involve increasingly complex programs, much more needs to be done to encourage the effective blending of diverse activities. If housing can be combined with offices, shops, and institutions, more people will be able to work and live in the same district, and less space will have to be devoted to the storage of cars. If large-scale development can be programmed for diversity and given a fine-grained texture of complementary uses, more streets will gain a healthy twenty-four-hour population. Zoning for mixed uses implies zoning for healthy congestion in an active public realm.

Mixed-use development has been a fact of life in Toronto's central core for several decades. The Yorkville district is a particularly successful example of how mixed-use zoning can revitalize a neighborhood. Once a working-class district of quiet, narrow streets, Yorkville became an enclave for the counterculture in the 1960s, emerging in the 1970s as a popular shopping area with specialty shops, restaurants, and bars. The transformation of the neighborhood into a commercial district also encouraged the redevelopment of adjacent arteries with hotels, high-rise condominiums, and office space arteries. New developments continue to reinforce the mixed-use character of the area and expand its twenty-four-hour resident population.

There are tentative signs that such patterns can exist in car-oriented cities such as Los Angeles, too. A new mixed-use project by Kamnitzer and Cotton in Beverly Hills—including parking, retail, and senior citizen housing—is a hopeful example.

### PRESERVE AND CONSOLIDATE THE EXISTING URBAN FABRIC
### WITH NEW DEVELOPMENT

Living cities are the physical embodiment of our collective memories. As cities grow and evolve over time, centers of activity shift or intensify, neighborhoods grow old and mature, and traditional institutions are juxtaposed with new ones. The layering of new city fabric on top of the old enables us to measure the changes taking place in the city and renew our connections to it. Where change is gradual and incremental, the networks of a city are often strengthened and enriched; where change is cataclysmic—that is, when the existing fabric and its networks are completely swept away for new large-scale development—the life and energy of a particular district can be damaged seriously. It is difficult to foster a sense of attachment to a place when it is constantly being transformed. We need familiar landmarks to serve as anchors in periods of transition.

Where the existing physical fabric of the city is sound and useful, it should be preserved and adapted to new uses. New development is most often effective when it complements existing buildings. As urban designers and architects, we have a responsibility to respond to established contexts and to enrich and foster their consolidation.

Such layering has taken place successfully in both Toronto and Portland. In the Los Angeles area, Old Town Pasadena is a more recent experiment. The area is reversing the trend of shopping malls and attempting to reinforce more traditional urban settings by combining older buildings with new development and preserving the streetscape. While it is too early to judge its success, it seems to be succeeding. In each case redevelopment has involved the incremental transformation of a relatively "complete" fabric of existing older buildings with a distinct character of their own, while living and working patterns have evolved gradually with a minimum of disruption.

When Century City was converted from studio lots to large avenues of gleaming skyscrapers, the goal was the separation of the car and the pedestrian. As parts of downtown Los Angeles have undergone redevelopment, they have followed the same model: the streets are multilane arteries for relatively high-speed traffic; pedestrians are accommodated high above the street by overhead bridges; and offices and hotels provide raised courtyards, internal plazas, and mid-block walkways safely removed from the motorists' view. Ostensibly, the model functions successfully, but its effect on life in the public realm is deadening.

It is possible to foster the coexistence of pedestrians and cars in appropriate settings. Some of the richest urban settings are precisely the result of this kind of integration. In the Ramblas in Barcelona, Spain, most of the pedestrian traffic is literally in the middle of a boulevard lined with kiosks for selling plants and pets. It is said (and this might be apocryphal) that waiters from adjacent restaurants often dodge the traffic to serve tables in outdoor cafés in the middle of the street. The sharing of streets between vehicular movement and more pedestrian-oriented activities reinforce their role as dynamic settings for public life and human interaction. In Los Angeles such action occurs on an intermittent, ritual basis as voyeurs in cars and their counterparts on the sidewalk become the object of each other's attention. Of course, in this case the local police ultimately ban vehicular traffic altogether in order to "keep things moving along." The question then becomes how to accommodate and normalize such episodic congestion that it is seen not as extraordinary but as an everyday occurrence.

My own civic projects have drawn from many of these concepts regarding episodic urban congestion. It is crucial that each project responds to its urban context in a way that both enhances the place and enriches its traditions. Four such projects—the completed Portland Performing Arts Center, the Phoenix Municipal Center, the competition for Los Angeles' Bunker Hill ("A Grand Avenue"), and a Master Plan for the proposed expansion of the Los Angeles Music Center—demonstrate my efforts to bring the public realm back to late twentieth-century cities.

**THE STREET AS STAGE: THE PORTLAND PERFORMING ARTS CENTER**

The Portland Performing Arts Center project has all the ingredients for the kind of episodic congestion I believe cities should aspire to. Downtown Portland's success as an urban environment, which has been described above, played a crucial role in the successful implementation of this project.

The primary objective of the program was the revitalization of Portland's theater district and the creation of an urban theater experience similar to the London and New York experiences.[3] Early in the design process we identified the need to promote a lively urban environment. Retail and community needs were viewed as an integral part of the center and as a link to the adjoining city fabric. The street itself became support space connecting various parts of the complex to each other and to the rest of the city.

The program was divided into two phases, the first of which was the restoration of the Paramount Theater, designed by Rapp and Rapp in 1927. In 1984 the Paramount reopened as home to the Oregon Symphony Orchestra. Across Main Street from the existing theater, the program called for two new theaters: the nine hundred–seat Intermediate Theater for touring shows, repertory drama, dance, and chamber music, and a three hundred sixty-seat Showcase Theater for drama productions requiring a flexible audience and stage arrangement.[4] The new theaters were completed in August of 1987.

The new buildings are woven carefully into the existing context through attention to massing, detailing, and materials. At the same time modern technologies are expressed through the stair towers with their soaring walls of glass, sleek steel window frames, and boldly cantilevered balconies. The theater complex, while consciously blending with its neighbors, nevertheless expresses a modern vitality and new confidence in the life of the street.

The stretch of Main Street between the old and new theaters plays a key role in connecting the isolated elements of the project into a cohesive whole. In effect, we have redefined it as part of the theater. While it continues to serve vehicular traffic during normal business hours, it can be closed off with ceremonial gates to become an outdoor stage. This closure allows the street to function as an anteroom to the interior theater lobbies.

The Portland street grid, with its conventional relationship of car to pedestrian, has been preserved, but it has also been designed to be disrupted and transformed. Architecture, in this case, extends beyond the making of buildings or spaces into the arena of event making. Arrival at the theater, in itself, becomes an act of theater. The soaring entry foyer alludes to the classical opera house with its tiered horseshoes of boxes for seating during intermission and a large proscenium-like opening addressing the street. Orig-

**FIGURE 18.2**

*Portland Performing Arts Center, the Broadway and Main Street entrance facade of the new theaters
with entry gateposts for traffic control.*

inally, this large glazed opening was designed as an immense overhead door that could be raised so that the street could literally be a stage to the lobby. In the evening the theatergoer can be dropped off by car in the middle of the street to become an actor who must proceed through the proscenium opening of the lobby to reach the performance hall. The distinction between being inside and outside is broken down in the creation of a ghost stage within a complex of real stages. It is at once the traditional grand lobby and also the "third stage" for informal performances, and café and bar activities.

### A CROSSROADS AS THE "CITY ROOM": THE PHOENIX MUNICIPAL CENTER

The municipal center project underlines my belief in celebrating and animating the street edge, preserving and enhancing small-block development, and providing settings where the car and the pedestrian can coexist in a rich environment.[5] The Master Plan for the Municipal Government Center in Phoenix, Arizona, proposes a rich urban fabric of linked high-density, low-rise buildings, a network of gardens, courts, and lanes, and a new civic plaza. Designed to encourage public access to all government facilities, officials, and services, the central feature of the project is a 300-by-300 foot open-air plaza called the City Room. Symbolizing an open and dynamic democratic society in the Southwest, the City Room provides a major focus for public life, encompassing both everyday activities and special events. As an outdoor public room in a downtown dominated by high rises and parking lots, it is to be the preeminent place of civic assembly and ceremony.

The core of the development includes the new City Council Chamber, the Municipal Courts Building, and two administrative support buildings. Both addressing and enclosing the Civic Plaza, each of these buildings has an arcaded base that provides a shaded walk. Trellises projecting above the cornices shade the upper floors; steel masts cantilevered over the City Room carry giant canvas awnings to provide protection during the months of intense summer heat.

The high-density, low-rise configuration and the intricate network of gallerias, streets, and lanes stem from a wish to preserve and strengthen the existing urban blocks and inhabit the street. The city government becomes a collection of accessible departments housed in many buildings.

The automobile is welcome in this heavily defined heart of the city. Washington Street, bisecting the City Room, is maintained as a major thoroughfare. The street and plaza are paved with sandstone; conventional street

**FIGURE 18.3**

*Portland Performing Arts Center, interior of the entry lobby. With its adjacent oyster bar and a piano pulled out onto the floor, it becomes an extension of the public life of the street throughout the day and evening.*

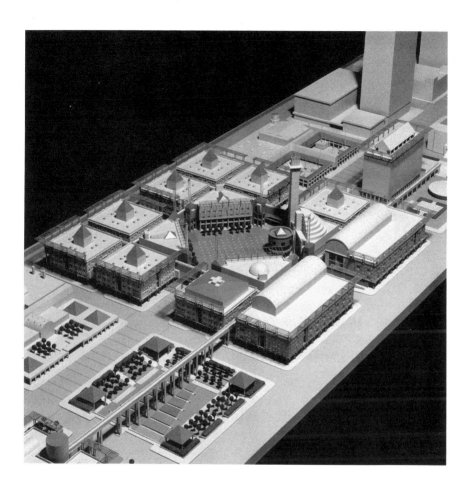

**FIGURE 18.4**

*Phoenix Municipal Center. The core of the development includes the new City Council chambers, the Municipal Courts Building, and two administrative support buildings; all of these buildings address and enclose the Civic Plaza.*

curbs give way to a series of removable bollards. With the bollards in place, pedestrian and vehicular traffic can safely coexist while the continuity of the plaza remains intact; with the bollards removed and Washington closed to traffic, the plaza becomes a ceremonial room capable of accommodating large crowds. In either case, the City Room is a public place, accessible at all times to Phoenix's constituents.

## THE BUNKER HILL COMPETITION: "A GRAND AVENUE" FOR DOWNTOWN LOS ANGELES

The Bunker Hill competition represents a unique opportunity to study ways of converting a prototypical "megablock" development to create a richer, denser environment. A Grand Avenue was the result of a competition held by the Los Angeles Community Redevelopment Agency (CRA) for an eleven-acre site in the downtown Bunker Hill area. The five-million-square-foot project includes office towers, condominium apartments, a hotel, a museum of contemporary art, a people-mover station, entertainment facilities, shops, restaurants, and a restored funicular railway. More than five acres of the total area is devoted to parks, plazas, and promenades.[6]

The design bridges two distinct parts of central Los Angeles: the old downtown area to the east, which has densely built-up streets lined with stores and cinemas, and the new business district to the west, with its widely spaced skyscrapers, spacious plazas, overpasses, and parking structures. The former is crowded with shoppers and sightseers during the day—its streets jammed with trucks, cars and buses; the latter is more spacious and relatively empty, with little evidence of pedestrian activity. The challenge was to create a cohesive district from the two areas, a district that responded architecturally, socially, and economically to the needs of both.

One of our major concerns was the reintroduction of pedestrian traffic into the urban fabric of the newer business district; we also wanted to reinforce a growing residential presence and extend the life of the street beyond the eight-hour working day. Accordingly, we fashioned Grand Avenue into a "boulevard" with all the major functional components of the project—its plazas, arcades, and smaller-scale pedestrian streets—addressing the artery.

The stretch of Grand Avenue bordering the project becomes an "urban room." Special paving extends across sidewalks and the street to slow down traffic and unify the space. The buildings facing Grand Avenue are given generous arcades and special entrance towers to add rhythm and animation to the streetscape. To minimize the barrier of grade separations, all major en-

**FIGURE 18.5**

*Bunker Hill Competition, aerial perspective of Grand Avenue. The street is treated as a boulevard from which all the major functional components of the project—its plazas, arcades, and smaller-scale pedestrian streets—are addressed.*

trances are at grade level; the sidewalks have been widened to accommodate outdoor cafés. Using a rich vocabulary of fountains, trees, and street furniture scaled to pedestrian and vehicular traffic, Lawrence Halprin and Charles Moore created well-defined outdoor rooms. These rooms step down at right angles to Grand Avenue, linking with Olive Street at the foot of the hill. One has been specifically designed to double as an amphitheater. The "Angels Flight" funicular, salvaged from the original neighborhood atop Bunker Hill, is reinstituted as another public link within the city grid.

The parks redefine the megablock of the site into a series of smaller parcels clearly separated by the system of open public spaces. The parcels were divided among the various participating designers on our team to promote architectural diversity.

The completed design maximizes the potential for episodic urban congestion. The program itself provides for a high-density area of mixed use with a strong urban expression at the street level. Every attempt is made to connect into the existing structure of the city. Within the limitations of a mega-project with a single development, an emphasis has been placed on defining smaller, diversified parcels that are suggestive of a more natural, incremental growth process.

Our scheme was not chosen by the CRA.

### THE LOS ANGELES MUSIC CENTER EXPANSION:
### COMPLETING AN URBAN ROOM

Similar to the Bunker Hill project, the Music Center expansion presented the opportunity to create public space in an unfocused downtown area. We were hired by the County of Los Angeles to prepare a Master Plan for three blocks of high-density commercial development on First Street adjacent to the Civic Mall. In conjunction with this development, we were asked to study alternatives for the placement of three new theaters as part of the Music Center expansion program.[7] Subsequently, the CRA requested that we provide urban design guidelines for the area.

The proposed site of the new theaters is to the southwest of the existing Dorothy Chandler Pavilion on Grand Avenue. The site is inherently isolated; the Dorothy Chandler Pavilion actually turns its back on the site to face the Mark Taper Forum. The proposed siting seemed to suggest the creation of two theater centers rather than the strengthening and reinforcing of one. The configuration of the existing Music Center also raised concerns, as the plaza sits a full level above Grand Avenue, completely cut off from the lush

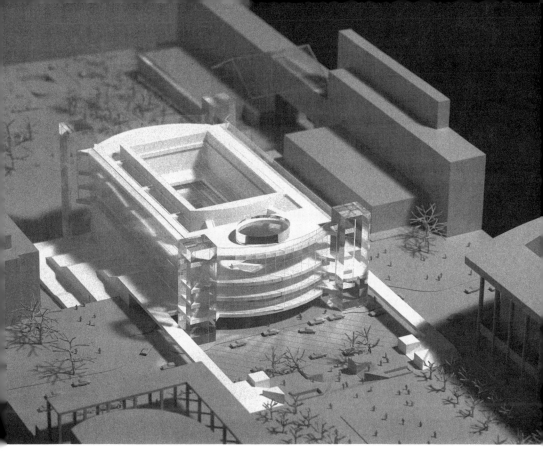

*Los Angeles Music Center Expansion, aerial veiw showing alternative location of a new Concert
Hall on the Civic Center Mall opposite the Music Center's plaza.*

*Designing in Car-Oriented Cities*

green of the Civic Mall beyond. The Civic Mall itself, isolated between the arms of two county buildings, is remarkably underutilized. Here was an opportunity to make sense of existing public spaces and revitalize one of the most important cultural institutions in Los Angeles.

After looking at many alternatives, our favorite solution utilized the proposed theater site for mixed-use commercial development and placed the new theaters at the head of the Civic Mall. While the idea of occupying a park with a new building seems radical and anti-civic, its prime objective was to reinhabit the existing open spaces and reappropriate them as pockets of public life in the city.

In the proposed plan the new theaters occupy the highest elevation of the mall, immediately opposite the plaza of the Music Center. Thus, the plaza is given a greater sense of enclosure. Generous pedestrian bridges, unavoidable in this case because of the change in grade, stretch across Grand Avenue so that all of the lobbies of the adjacent theaters share a common forecourt and elevation.

At street level the pedestrian bridges become porticoes that enclose part of Grand Avenue as an arrival courtyard. Paving, fountains, arcades, and trees unify this space and give it a "roomlike" quality. As the drop-off for all of the theaters, this stretch of the street becomes a grand entrance; in the evening the bustle of arriving cars and alighting patrons creates welcome activity on a normally empty avenue.

The new theaters terrace out into the green landscape of the mall. Flanking, cascading staircases link the Music Center plaza, Grand Avenue, and the park. Cafés, restaurants, and lobbies form a transparent ring around the lower elevations of the theater, encouraging activity to spill out and occupy the open space.

When carefully orchestrated, cultural institutions can be powerful catalysts for the episodic congestion that enriches urban living. If they are developed in isolation, they will remain island objects. The ultimate success of the proposed Music Center will depend, in part, on how well it can be weaved into the surrounding fabric of the city. In the end, our favored site for the expansion was rejected in favor of the original site.

### CONCLUSION

The making of a livable city is an ongoing process requiring bold innovation, a healthy respect for existing successful precedents, and sensitivity toward the existing context. Our own work, especially on the scale of urban design, attempts to take each of these approaches into account. Each new project is seen as an opportunity to build on the lessons of our past experiences and explore our philosophies for the design of cities. The argument for episodic urban congestion rests on the belief that the best cities—and the city Los Angeles can become—foster and maintain exciting, habitable, and intriguing urban spaces that welcome both the pedestrian and the automobile in complex and not altogether predictable encounters.

**19.** Melvin M. Webber

# THE JOYS OF AUTOMOBILITY

All over the world, public officials and informed publics are alarmed about the growing numbers of automobiles. Some see the situation as akin to a conflagration that's out of control, made all the more menacing because automobiles are proving to be such powerful agents of change. To be sure, there is less anxiety in the United States than elsewhere, and less still in the western United States, because the major cities there grew up in the automobile era and have street systems that are much better suited for automobile use.

The real reason for the automobile explosion should be clear, yet the commonplace explanation for the car's popularity is wrong. People everywhere are attracted to cars not because they are lovable nor because they are prestigeful, but because they offer better transport services than does any other mode. Automobiles are chosen because the auto-highway system is the culmination of the long and cumulative process of testing and improving ground transport technology. Or, to state that more flatly, autos are popular because the auto-highway system is the best ground transportation system yet devised. Its superiority lies in its capacity to offer no-wait, no-transfer, door-to-door service. No other transport mode comes close to meeting that standard of service. It is the failure to meet that standard that is troubling mass-transit systems.

In competition with other transport modes in low-density places, the car wins hands down—mostly because travel time from origin to destination is typically shorter than via other modes and because money costs, although not low, are tolerable. Travel times are short because a car available for an individual's exclusive use is immediately accessible—always on call, as it were. Where parking is available at both ends of a trip, as is common in the low-density American metropolis, the car promises door-to-door accessibility. Where traffic flows freely, it promises a high-level of mobility. Money costs are tolerable because auto use is partially subsidized. U.S. motorists are charged a modest gas tax to cover most—but not all—costs of road building, while the heavy costs of congestion and air and noise pollution are not directly charged to the motorists who generate them. It's scarcely any wonder then that, given the car's inherent advantages and the impositions of some of its costs on others, it has become the preferred mode for so many. It seems to be as popular in places like Mexico City where mass auto use has generated levels of congestion and air and noise pollution that nineteenth-century Pittsburgh steelworkers would have found intolerable.

Of course, there are still some for whom discretionary use of a car is still a dream. About 9 percent of U.S. households lack automobiles, and about 10 percent of the driving-age population is not licensed to drive, most of them because they are physically unable to do so. They are either too young, too old, or too disabled. Perhaps a fourth of them are too poor to own cars, even though auto use is underpriced. About half of U.S. families still have only one car, which all family members must share. Thus, even though automobiles are dominant over all other modes of personal transport, we have not yet attained free automobility for everyone.

The central transportation problem lies precisely here. It is not that we have too many cars, but, rather, that everyone does not yet benefit from the equivalent of the automobility enjoyed by those who do have discretionary use of cars. Our central mission is to redress the social inequities thrown up by widespread auto use, and our central task is to invent ways of extending the benefits of auto-*like* transportation to those who are presently carless. The task is made all the more imperative because the automobile has been such a powerful agent of geographic, technologic, and social change. Two of those changes concern me here.

First, the inherent improvements in mobility have combined with inevitable traffic congestion to induce a geographic explosion of metropolitan areas. Second, the auto's popularity has spelled the decline and, in some places, the demise of public transit services. In light of the popularity of suburban locations among families and firms, metropolitan spatial dispersion strikes me as a rather benign consequence of automobility. The loss of public transit services, in contrast, seems to be something of a tragedy. Large numbers of people have been positively hurt by the rise of the auto-highway system because the alternative of public transit service has thereby been eroded.

## THE METROPOLITAN SPATIAL EXPLOSION

The automobile and its analog, the telephone, have shaped both the form of the modern city and the ways we live out our social and economic lives there. When accompanied by a ubiquitous road network of the sort we've built in this country, and especially in the new western and southern metropolitan areas, autos permit direct connection *from everywhere to everywhere*—just the way telephones do. Moreover, because so many people have discretionary use of cars whenever they wish, they enjoy the benefits of random access to people they have dealings with—direct connection from virtually *everyone to everyone*, whatever their geographic locations.

This degree of connectivity by telephones and automobiles is unprecedented, of course. Throughout human history people have had to locate near each other if they were to have frequent dealings, or else they had to suffer delays in making contact. Business firms thus tended to concentrate in business districts where mutual access was greatest. Employees had to locate near jobs sites, lest time and money costs became excessive. The search for cheap connectivity is indeed the only reason cities were ever built. It's only because of the cost of overcoming geographic space that people concentrated in cities in the first place. Were it not for these costs, there would be no cities. Were it not that costs of connectivity decline as densities rise, we would never have built the New Yorks, Londons, Tokyos, or even the Los Angeleses of this world.

These relations between connectivity and density are universal facts of life. For a couple thousand years nearly everyone sought to locate near the center of town, willingly accepting some degree of crowding. But expanding urban populations inevitably meant that most people nevertheless would have to live at considerable distances from the center. Indeed, every town and city has been suburbanizing ever since it was settled, growing ever outward to accommodate more and more inhabitants.

For most cities in eighteenth- and nineteenth-century America, the expansion was slow, limited by the slow speeds of available transportation systems—walking for most, horse-drawn vehicles for some. Later, faster electric trolleys permitted people to live far away and still get to work on time, but not very far away. When automobiles became available in large numbers in the 1920s, new suburban settlements quickly surrounded the old cities. Then it was possible to get to work in the center within a half-hour, even if one lived ten miles out.

During recent decades a series of dramatic technological and institutional changes have coalesced to accelerate that expansion—to trigger a virtual explosion of urban settlements, dispersing their parts into what we used to call the hinterland. Four of these changes have been especially consequential.

First, the conduct of business and industry has been changing. Expanding managerial activities, information processing, and specialized professional services have combined to displace mills and factories with offices as primary workplaces. By now, somewhere between half and two-thirds of all employed persons work in offices. Some of them are involved in managerial and other professional roles that require skilled judgment and frequent intercourse with other specialized persons, and many of these people therefore need to be physically near each other. However, the vast majority today are engaged in routine paper-handling or computer-processing activities that resemble routine production—activities that are much like factory work. People in these jobs don't need to be geographically adjacent to each other. Most can be located anywhere—even in isolated anywheres, even at home.

Second, manufacturing has been declining—from a third of all jobs in the United States at the end of World War II to less than a quarter today. Moreover, many industries that survive are largely freed from sites adjacent to sources of raw materials and power. By now, many manufacturers are more dependent on specialized knowledge than on stuff like ore and coal. Spatially footloose, a growing number of factories are able to follow their workers to wherever the workers prefer to live—an absolute reversal from early patterns.

Third, women have been going to work in ever-increasing numbers. Well over half of the nation's women are working or seeking work outside the home. Nearly two-thirds of married women between the ages of twenty-five and forty-four who are living with their husbands are in the labor force. (Twenty-five years ago only one-third of them were.) Moreover, nearly two-thirds of married women living in conventional nuclear families, complete with husbands and children aged six to seventeen, are now in the labor force.

Fourth, automobiles, airplanes, telephones, and now communication satellites and computer networks have made nearly everywhere immediately accessible to everywhere else, thus vitiating many locational advantages that once attached to certain cities and city centers.

Any one of these changes would have been enough to generate a revolution in urban development. Together, in concert, they are making for new kinds of cities without precedent.

Not long ago most corporations and business service firms clung to the metropolitan center, creating that most visible urban symbol of the century—the high-rise, center-city skyline. In the 1950s and 1960s a few bold firms moved their headquarter offices to outlying places such as Westchester

County, but they were exceptions—at most, portents of things to come. In recent times, however, a great many companies have become aware of those four fundamental changes that had been evolving unobtrusively over the decades, slowly accumulating force enough to provoke a virtual revolution in urban spatial structure.

The fundamental changes have unleashed a cadre of land developers who are now building gigantic office complexes on previously vacant land at the metropolitan edge and beyond. Tens of thousands of office jobs are being relocated out of the central city to each of these sites. Two new sites, well east of San Francisco, are projecting thirty thousand jobs within the decade. Tysons Corner, outside Washington, D.C., already holds over twenty-five thousand jobs. Throughout the country office buildings surrounded by extensive parking areas are sprouting near the single-family housing projects that supply workers to them. Although less visible than the skyscrapers downtown, these office parks are fast becoming successors to the high-rise central business districts and may become prime symbols of the future city. Several will soon contain more office jobs than are now in their metropolitan central business districts—San Francisco and Washington, D.C., among them. By relying on automobile access and by moving jobs out to where job holders live, office parks may be signaling the dissolution of the last force that has been holding the traditional city in place.

That's the big news for cities for the 1990s. The glue that has held them together is dissolving. Even when tens of millions of people were gathered into the large metropolitan areas, they were compelled to cluster around the city center; even the extensive suburbs have had to wrap around the old city and to stay within commuting distance of it. But that requirement is fast disappearing.

Especially in the new cities of the West and South, the compounding effects of the four trends I've noted are permitting a scale of spatial dispersion that was never before possible. With real-time accessibility permitted by automobile, telecommunication, and computer technologies, even the most specialized corporate executives are free to abandon the high-rise city center in favor of the countryside, where many of them prefer to live. Their employees, both male and female, need no longer suffer the discomforts and costs of the long commute into the city center. They too can live and work in the exurbs. Given the average American's manifest preference for a single-family house cum garden, it seems reasonable to expect that the long-term centrifugal move away from the old city center will accelerate, now that even office jobs are leaving.

The signs of the new urban patterns are everywhere. Populations have been expanding in small and middle-sized settlements well outside the old commuting range, even in such seemingly nonurban places as Vermont, the Rockies, the desert of the Southwest, and the foothills of the Sierra Nevada range. Equally striking, many of these migrant companies are engaged in highly specialized activities, just the sorts that require intimate contact with suppliers of diverse business and technical services. They've been able to locate far away from the old-style cities precisely because their employees want to live in those outlying places and because they can stay intimately connected to suppliers and customers through the now-ubiquitous transportation and communication links. Many firms are dispersing their parts to far distant suburbs located in places like Hong Kong, Singapore, and Taipei.

Do these signs suggest that the old cities will disappear? Not, of course, in the short-range future. There's far too much investment in buildings, institutions, and public infrastructure for the old cities to be abandoned, and, besides, the old cities are likely to remain viable in the long-range future as well. But the incremental growth is bound to be largely outside and at much greater distances than ever in the past. Hence, the recent construction boom in central cities may soon end. Tremendous oversupplies of downtown office space already have put a stop to construction in some cities, and others are fast overreaching their markets, too.

And so it seems that the age of the high-density cities might be coming to an end, to be succeeded by a wide array of new settlement types, most developed at low densities, mixing high-rise and low-rise buildings, in environmentally amiable settings, readily accessible to recreational areas, typically in scattered locales with a relatively small population in each, and exhibiting much greater variety in spatial structure than was feasible in the past. Can the trend be stopped? Probably not. The forces propelling it are powerful—the automobile among them—and most are outside anyone's control. Does the new direction portend a loss of the cultural richness long associated with the city and city life? I think not. Current capabilities for travel and communication permit even the most highly dispersed populations to be intimately associated and to enjoy the society's intellectual and material wealth.

Los Angeles has long been the exemplar of the culturally rich metropolis made viable by widespread availability of automobiles, highways, and telephones. As compared to many living in the midst of America's old urban centers, the new exurbanites surely must enjoy comparable opportunities to those in Los Angeles, suggesting that spatial patterns of cities no longer shape the important qualities of peoples' lives.

But it's clear that the quality of exurban life depends on open automobile and telephone channels. The continuing revolution in telecommunications has been expanding channel capacities of telephones at persisting exponential rates—and with constantly lowering costs. In contrast, capacities of the auto-highway system have been falling while costs have been rising.

The automobile's popularity poses a genuine dilemma for us. The car's success has generated its own greatest limitation, for few cities in the world were designed to accommodate automobiles. Most cities were built for pedestrians or, at best, small carts, so, when autos swarm into Florence, Bangkok, Lagos, and Tokyo, there is simply no space for them. Even the new auto-based cities of the American West—even Los Angeles—are proving incapable of accommodating the numbers of cars being amassed there, in part because even enthusiastic highway planners never expected that there would be so many cars.

As one outcome of rising traffic congestion, employers and families are moving farther and farther out into the expanding metropolitan fringe in an effort to escape congestion. The consequences, of course, are to further increase reliance on automobiles, further contribute to the traffic congestion that caused them to seek relief in the first place, and further erode the existing, but marginal, public transit services. What, then, are the social equity consequences of the automobile transportation system?

### PUBLIC TRANSIT ALTERNATIVES

As employment in each metropolitan area expands, slowly in the older center cities and explosively in the suburbs and exurbs, commuters are overloading suburban road systems that were never designed for the numbers of cars they're now having to carry. In another unanticipated switch, suburban and exurban traffic congestion in many places is now more severe than center-city congestion, with little prospect for expanded capacity in sight.

But, even if there were more roads, efforts to counteract rising highway congestion by expanding highway capacity traditionally have yielded only temporary relief. That's because the Law of Highway Congestion assures that traffic volumes will expand to fill the available space—until just-tolerable levels of congestion are again reached. In this country even that temporary remedy is seldom available any longer, because environmentalists and NIMBYs are standing by, ready to file suit to block virtually any capital works project suggested.

And, then, perhaps the most negative and devastating consequence of mass auto use has been the decline of the public transit systems that the car has displaced. All those who do not have discretionary use of motor cars thus thereby lack even the modest levels of mobility their parents and grand-parents knew. With most new jobs locating in the suburbs and exurbs, persons who, because of racial discrimination or low income, are geographically constrained to central-city housing districts thereby lack adequate access to employment. Indeed, all who lack discretionary use of cars are deprived to some degree, and they are deprived because the auto has been so successful.

I suggest that this bare fact poses the central policy imperative that transportation policy planners must face. The task is to create *public* transportation systems capable of approximating the degrees of mobility that uncongested *private* automobiles provide.

Contemporary suburban land-use patterns in western and southern metropolises and in suburbs everywhere are increasingly mixed, densities are low, and, so, origins and destinations of trips are spatially dispersed. To be effective, a public transport system must be able to serve groups of persons having the same origins, destinations, and schedules. Inevitably, and especially in exurban districts, these are small groups of persons. Prospects for *mass* transit systems—that is, for systems using large vehicles—are nil for most trips in the new western and southern metropolises or in suburbs everywhere. Large-vehicle systems, like railways and subways that effectively serve older high-density cities of Europe and the American East, are complete misfits for most travel within suburban areas and within western and southern metropolitan areas.

Instead of new underground railroads of the kind built in the San Francisco Bay Area, Miami, Atlanta, and under construction in Los Angeles, we need to make better use of automobiles, vans, and small buses. Even the standard fifty-passenger bus is often too large for travel within low-density settings. The appropriate modern transit system must employ small vehicles whose operating characteristics match contemporary land-use and travel patterns. Those are either automobiles or vehicles that resemble automobiles.

The joker is that we don't need much more road or rail capacity, because we presently have tremendous excess passenger-carrying capacity going unused within the present auto-highway system. As Wilfred Owen has noted, we now have enough front seats in the nation's automobiles to carry the entire American population at the same time, plus enough back seats to carry everyone from the Soviet Union as well. The trouble is that many of these seats are being driven around empty.

Varieties of suggestions have been offered for encouraging carpooling, including giving free video-tex computers to commuters so that drivers and riders having the same origins, destinations, and schedules can be matched up. On the San Francisco–Oakland Bay Bridge where East Bay carpoolers are rewarded with a free toll and a fifteen- to twenty-minute time saving, commuters collect strangers who queue up at bus stops and BART stations. The result: average car occupancy on the bridge during the morning westbound peak period is 2.1 persons, compared to 1.25 elsewhere—70 percent greater! Other market-like schemes, aimed at filling those empty seats, need to be invented and tested.

In the short term many other proposed ameliorative techniques remain to be exploited for squeezing more cars onto the existing road system. Schemes such as "smart" traffic signals, which count cars moving through a road network and then adjust themselves to maximize traffic flow. Schemes like "flex time" for spreading commuters' cars over more hours of the day. I suspect that the most effective means for getting the auto-highway system to work well in the short run is to increase the number of persons in each car.

Suburban commuters' automobiles are carrying only about 1.25 persons on average. That means that only a fourth of the front passenger seats are being used at any given time—that three-fourths of the front seats and all of the back seats are running around empty. Traffic congestion would disappear, as if by magic, if we could somehow fill just a few of those seats—say, raising the ratio from 1.25 to 1.4 persons per car.

But how do we fill near-empty cars? Clearly, incentives must be sufficiently rewarding as to induce solo drivers voluntarily to share their cars with others. Congestion-free diamond lanes have proved successful in some places. Computer-linked carpools promise to make it easier for drivers and riders to find each other. Jitneys and collective-taxis that use automobiles as public-transit vehicles thus approximate what private autos do best. But the most likely instrument for filling the empty seats is congestion-pricing of roads. Dollar charges that approximate each motorist's contributions to the collective congestion can be justified on sheer equity grounds. But they are also incentives that encourage motorists to share the monetary costs with passengers. Differential prices that vary with levels of congestion and time of day would also encourage commuters to shift their hours of travel, thus reducing congestion levels directly. Road-user charges in the forms of substantially increased fuel taxes and substantial tolls seem to be increasingly acceptable to political leaders, and we may soon see experiments designed to increase car occupancy while simultaneously reducing traffic volumes.

In the near-term, nevertheless, improvements must be made in public transit systems. Any workable public transit system must be compatible with urban land-use patterns that have been shaped by automobiles. If it's to compete with the automobile, a transit system must do so on the automobile's terms. That is to say, it must approximate the door-to-door, no-wait, no-transfer service the auto provides. If public transit can mimic the private car's operating characteristics, there is a decent chance that we can raise bus occupancy enough to make suburban places accessible to each other and provide mobility for people who cannot drive or who do not have discretionary use of personal vehicles. Only auto-like vehicles can do it. Paradoxically, small-vehicle, auto-like systems operate successfully and effectively throughout the third world. We have much to learn from the jeepneys of Manila, the collectivos of Caracas, and the mutatus of Nairobi.

In sum, I contend that there can be no question about the automobile's virtues as an instrument of personal mobility—indeed, as an instrument of personal freedom. People everywhere adopt it because it offers better service than any other transportation system yet available. Despite the high personal and social costs attached to its use as the mass-transportation system in the new western and southern metropolitan areas, and despite the costs of congestion, the consensus holds that it's well worth the price.

The auto—or its successor with comparable traits—is here to stay. We obviously need to do something about its negative environmental effects, and we need to find effective fuel substitutes and other means for stemming its horrendous appetite for petroleum products. Enough has been done on the chemistry and engineering of the automobile to assure that technological possibilities for ameliorating these undesirable side effects are virtually in hand. Prospects for a better battery and for electrified roadways are becoming real, and so too then are prospects for an electric car that generates neither air nor noise pollution. In the long run, but within the life-times of most of us, we might even see a fully automated auto highway system with operating characteristics equivalent to those of both autos and buses. Such a system would vitiate the devilish dichotomy that distinguishes highway and transit systems. Recent developments in electronic sensors and in computers suggest that an automated urban transportation sytem may soon be feasible.

There can be no question either about the auto's contributing role in reshaping the modern city, helping to convert it from a single-centered, high-density concentration to low-density, highly dispersed, and variegated settlements scattered over the landscape. But, as car ownership has spread, mass-transit systems have declined—positively handicapping all who do not have personal cars at their disposal. Obviously, this group includes the rapidly increasing numbers of aged persons, who, by losing their driving skills, are also losing personal mobility.

I am suggesting that the most difficult and most important problem of the automobile is not that it's tied up in traffic jams or that it has been reshaping the modern city. Land-market responses to traffic jams induce people to move to less-congested places in a constantly self-adjusting search for preferred locations. Out of the search process, a new urban spatial structure has been evolving—a structure that seems, in turn, to be workable for the collective society as well as for the individual relocators who are inducing it.

By far the most difficult and most important problem attaches to the automobile's negative effects on social equity—to the loss in mobility it has caused for people who don't have cars. To attack that shortcoming we need, minimally, to develop public transit systems and market-incentive systems that extend auto-like transport services to the carless. Maximally, we need new transportation technology that, through automation, will make cars available to those who do not yet have free use of them. Our central challenge is to invent ways of extending the equivalent of automobility to everyone.

# 20. Marvin Adelson

## THE CAR, THE CITY, AND WHAT WE WANT

J. B. Jackson says that "we have a great lag in our imagination." If we dwell on well-studied, accepted notions, the future drives us; we do not drive it. Designers and planners ought to help imagine a broad range of alternatives, even if, at first, some of them seem flawed, for with ingenuity and work flawed ideas are often correctable and liberating, whereas lags in imagination remain limiting.

Sandra Rosenbloom's notion of our love affair with the car turning into a love-hate marriage is insightful. Divorce seems unthinkable, and the hate side is often kept hidden in public. But, oh, Car, how do I hate thee? Let me count the ways: congestion; drivers behind pressing me while the ones ahead dawdle; the quest for parking; the need to tend the meter; restive passengers; missed opening curtains; threats by stoned, aggressive, or drunk drivers and my reactions to them; drug deals through car windows; mobile vandalism; topless insurance rates; predatory car sales- and service-persons; high blood pressure; lost productivity; *un*quality time spent chauffeuring; houses deformed by garages; coiled dragons of parking structures making precious urban space inaccessible; unreasonable speed limits; cops with quotas of tickets to give; the "pigs" who gridlock intersections and the others who strand me there when the traffic light changes; smog hiding the mountains from my scratchy eyes; oil dependency; and the encroachment of oil wells on landscapes—for starters.

So I *hate* cars, but, like the Listerine junkie with his mouthwash, I use mine twice a day. And I love the feeling I get when roads and vistas are clear and I can just get up and go—no wait for buses or trains, my car in good condition, and the blessed privacy . . . .

Of course, mainly I hate others' cars and how they use them. That I am your "other" and you are mine we need not mention, but that the pathology of the car and the city is largely a social one we must mention because it implies social dimensions to any amelioration strategy. Cars shape our lives, characters, and attitudes, as they shape our cities and ecology, and the present volume is important as an assessment, however preliminary, of what we ought to be looking at. We grow distressed at the car and the city we have—

but what is it that we want, and what can we have? We want the car, that goes without saying; we want the city, or we would be elsewhere and "urbs" would not be growing worldwide. But how might they fit together better?

In many subtle ways the car both follows and leads our tastes and experiences. Low-riders cruise. Off-road vehicles scar the hills and turn avenues into arenas. Freeways become more precious than the communities they dissect and the lives they displace. Cars help spread graffiti. Cars indenture us. Cars are serious business, and we pay a lot for them. We need to realize how they impede work, relationships, community, and even, in the end, mobility. This is the crucial point: cars' benefit-cost ratio is dropping sharply and at an increasing rate.

As we obstruct each other more, pressures and delays increase pathology and other costs. We had better treat the car's role in the city, the economy, the family, and the community not nostalgically, romantically, or rigidly, but clearheadedly, fully recognizing its downside. In that way we can start to consider conceivable alternatives and redesigns. The issue is not car versus no-car but how best to serve each "market segment," each class of demand, keeping in mind the interest we all have in a well-functioning whole.

### IMAGES OF TRANSPORTATION

Our mix of public and private transportation serves many complex purposes. For one, it exchanges people and goods among places. From this point of view, vehicles are corpuscles, and the important issue is the exchange rate of whatever is transported, just like the oxygen and nutrients and waste products that the blood exchanges with the fixed tissues in our bodies. Should any of the rates drop too far, some disability occurs. We have understood the parallel (for example, major streets are called arteries). Fortunately, we have avoided total disability somehow, but we seem on the verge of strangling again—the arteries hardening and the blood pressure rising. I doubt if the condition is terminal just yet, though; our urban system is still partly redesignable. But restoring good health sometimes requires a tougher regimen than we care to implement. It pays to recall that in the contest among cities, as among athletes, the one with the greatest "vital capacity" has an edge.

To increase our vital capacity we might: expand some arteries and add some; improve the behavior or capacity of the corpuscles; reduce their size; improve their efficiency; reduce demand for whatever is being exchanged; relocate or redesign the exchange sites; provide a better flow medium or control system; or find alternative means to mediate the exchanges. No doubt, we will have to explore all of these ways. To get a sense of what we might need to do, remember that cities will be at least as different forty years from now as they are now from what they were forty years ago.

A transportation system is also a way of taking people where they want to go or are wanted and to supply their needs and desires up to changing standards. From this point of view, we must focus on expectations, tastes, trade-offs, decision propensities, prices, incentives, designs, technology, and other factors that influence behavior, preferences, politics, and economics.

One contemporary consequence of cars, for example, are sprawling commercial strips with their Golden-Arch-itecture. Do micro-Vegases add to or detract from urban life? Some architects can live with, and on, them, and they are nourishing and profitable, but do we love them? Are they to be seen as the seeds for growing the kinds of neighborhoods we covet? Will we accept whatever the combined car-and-market system implies?

As we think about alternatives for our urban regions and their transportation arrangements, it pays to examine the associated decisions, both public and private, that might affect them. Creeping incrementalism has its virtues, but it does not suffice at all scales. Planning, too, has its limitations. How are we to make our decisions? The approach we use will depend partly on the language we select for talking about them and the images and concepts we employ in making judgments. It is tempting to oversimplify by choosing a single view and deriving logical conclusions, but all too frequently the result turns out to be illogical on other grounds we failed to consider. When we become too committed to a single way of thinking, we typically find ourselves blocking all available alternatives, because each is certainly undesirable from some—and someone's—point of view.

### VIEWS OF THE CITY: THE LOS ANGELES CASE

We need more work on the images of the city we argue about and pursue. Such images need not refer only to physical arrangements and forms, such as how big downtown should become. How caring or antagonistic, collaborative or competitive, diverse or uniform, and ethical or expedient will we be, should we be? Such issues are important to ponder. They are usually not part of the planner's or designer's job, and editorial writers tend to ignore them, but dialogue about these issues is vital.

New arrangements typically displace former ones only slowly, often creatively blending with them over long periods of transition. Electronic

*The Car, the City, and What We Want*

communication did not displace transportation; they grew and diversified together. Some claim that the telephone helped the automobile develop by allowing people to make appointments, reservations, and other arrangements so they could use cars efficiently.

"Info-tech," often proposed as an alternative to transportation, can connect us up for certain important purposes, but not adequately for all purposes, and increasingly it disconnects us. Many have deplored the social cleavages that are occurring along information lines. Groups seek, acquire, handle, use, and esteem information differently. They have different informational appetites and are targeted to receive different messages. Their thinking thus might diverge drastically, and their mutual attributions could become less and less well grounded.

Our very mobility, together with how work is presently structured, often keeps us apart most of each day, diminishing the local interaction on which important human relationships depend. More care is required in assessing the role of the car in the pattern, but the structure of work is at least as open to redesign.

In some ways we benifit from separation, and therefore we should take care before "remedying" it, just as we benefit from contact across class, cultural, and ethnic lines and must enable it. We might need some isolation, but having it imposed on us or having it happen inadvertently (through congestion and encapsulation, for example) is not a good thing. Thus, both the car, with its present limitations, and telecommuting have a long way to evolve before they respond well to emerging conditions.

Car phones contain the germ of an idea. They are a partial technological fix, as were citizens band radios (CBs) before them, but they are pricey and exclusive. A cheap and flexible signal system between nearby cars would be one helpful step, especially if we developed new modes of courtesy instead of the disconcerting discourtesy that is now rampant. Note the social/technological tie-in.

Transportation both responds to and shapes urban structure. In this volume we see several hypotheses about desirable directions. In Sam Bass Warner's discussion, for example, activity centers are concentrated enough to make public transport between them efficient, and efficient transport reduces barriers between centers. Each center achieves socioeconomic diversity and vitality through affordable housing, job-housing balance, effective use of underutilized human resources, better traffic management, and maintaining flexibility for further options to develop.

Melvin Webber foresees city-regions sprawling across more of the countryside because we do not circumscribe them. He wants to ameliorate the class inequities that past transportation arrangements have exacerbated. He draws upon the mixed-system-with-jitneys that some large third world cities use to exemplify a high-volume, surface-based, public transit system that is irresistibly convenient, safe, cheap, and fast. He expects cars to metamorphose to fit varied purposes. This rich idea deserves imaginative treatment as to how it might play out in an age of appropriately designed vehicles, control and incentive systems, urban forms, and new kinds of services. Of course, the exemplar cities Webber cites had public transit networks before they had many automobiles; his approach might falter in cities where the car came first.

Webber's sprawling regional city in many ways resembles Warner's writ large. It also resembles Christopher B. Leinberger's and Charles Lockwood's "urban villages"; Frank Hotchkiss' "galaxy"; and the "Centers Concept" developed in the early "Alternatives for Los Angeles" planning study as well as its successor concept, "Targeted Growth Areas." Herman Kahn once envisioned a San-San (San Francisco–San Diego) Corridor, a stretch he thought would inevitably build up its own string of centers. For a long while it seemed that he was wrong, but we might be heading that way again. Such a longitudinal array might have quite different characteristics than a more globular one.[1]

Visions such as these grow naturally out of the uncentered Los Angeles region we know, especially as interior growth controls push development outward. If anything about the transportation future is certain, it is that the mix of transportation modes in large places will include many forms of the indispensable, equivocal, but evolvable car, along with plenty of other expedients. During the early middle years of our lives when we are infatuatable by members of the opposite sex, we will also no doubt be infatuatable by cars, but, as we grow older, as individuals and as a population, we might outgrow the unrealistic part of our infatuations and grow more mellow about transportation options, too.

In a market system the car has the advantage that it can be bought and sold, operated or not, individually and ad lib. Our independent choices, often made on short-run needs and preferences, generate an aggregate outcome none of us had in mind, but some far-reaching choices (in both public and private sectors) must also be made, generally by people acting for us. Especially with respect to alternatives to the car, we could benefit from having clearer shared understandings and visions of what future cities might be like. These visions, at various scales, must somehow coincide, while preserving sufficient latitude for variation and adaptation.

How might we envisage our city (the Los Angeles region) in a way that lets us talk about it productively and work to improve it collaboratively? It is, among other things:

1. A *world city*, competing economically and (if Jane Jacobs is right that cities, rather than nations, are the key actors on the world scene) needing to displace imports with domestic production ever more effectively if it and the country it supports are to flourish. If urban planner Harvey Perloff was right on another front, the Los Angeles region will also have to stimulate the arts and generate cultural activity of the very best kinds if it is to attract and retain people a city increasingly must have to produce its wealth and well-being. This proposition means that we all have a stake, not only in manufactures, but in the arts and amenities; not only in our own neighborhoods or special interests, but in the commonwealth, the kind of city we make as a whole—a key idea that seems to have slipped out of focus recently but must be retrieved. And the kind of city we aspire to must fit well with new global realities as well as our personal dreams so that local, parochial preferences, while important, are not all that counts. How well we do all this affects not only us and our visitors, but every American and many others beyond our borders.

2. A *regional city*, home to almost one in every twenty Americans, and responsible for far more than its pro rata share of the nation's product, needing forms of governance that transcend present jurisdictions, needing to vitalize its enormous spread through better transportation and communication, needing to prepare and use all of its human potential in constructive channels, and needing to place the narrow ambitions that developers and residents have often shown into a broader context that rewards us all.

3. An *information-based and "in-formed" city*, more closely interlinked than at present in ways that are capable of (literally) changing our minds as new connections are made and appreciations developed. It is ready to move as other cities might not because it is closely tied to information technologies, industries, and networks.

4. A *combination first and third world city*, embodying diverse values that have not yet been effectively blended anywhere in the world, with new kinds of hopes and antagonisms having to be dealt with in newly humane

ways. (Will we need armored cars if we fail?) How can we use, not abuse, our diversity? Is not a more humane and supportive spirit part of the kind of city we want? What is the role of the car in the pattern?

5. An *expedient city*, responsive to invigoration via technology and immigration, having grown up without much regional planning and with a taste for change, even impulsiveness. Will such expediency generate health and wealth, or will it lead to trouble and rubble? Is the kind of past we have had a model for our kind of future? How can we do what we have to do together so that we can also do what we want to do separately? How does how we get around affect how we interact?

## TRANSPORTATION MIX IN THE BIG PICTURE

To the extent that the car is indispensable, the challenge is to retain or enhance its charm by evolving it, while also displacing it with attractive alternatives whenever they can be found. In addition to the vehicles, modes, and routes in our system, we might consider altering patterns of ownership, incentives, finance, laws, technology, consumer tastes, and fashions. We could come to value the car's use, for example, rather than the thing itself, preferring, our "other car [to be] an Avis," and not such a *rara* one at that. That is, should car renting and leasing become cheap, convenient, and stylish enough, many people might kick the car ownership addiction, settling instead for just one or (as many New Yorkers already do) none at all. A large subsystem of cars based on rental/leasing could help approach social equity through subsidizing some use of cars for those who need subsidies.

Incidentally, in a system based on the purchase of *use*, vehicle fleet services combined with a guaranteed level of maintenance for a fixed price could make cars cheaper and more reliable. It could also change the basis for car insurance that is now sold at retail, and substantially reduce legal costs. Large vehicle maintenance companies could achieve economies that small ones cannot. The incentives they would have to minimize vehicle downtime and operating expense could change the shape of the repair business and, eventually, the way cars are designed.

Some other possibly evocative ways of thinking about the car and life in the city (beyond Metrorail versus buses), based on existing precedents or known technology, include the following.

*Congestion.* The cost of congestion in the Los Angeles region in 1984 ran above seven million dollars per day, over two billion dollars per year, conservatively estimated by the Southern California Association of Governments. Today it is of the order of twelve million dollars per day, or three billion dollars per year, and rising fast. We can afford to do something substantial about keeping this aspect of life from deteriorating further, even if we cannot restore what we thought we loved.

*Service.* The car is an extension of the self—a sort of powerful prosthetic device. In our service-oriented society it is also a vestige of self-service and indentured servitude (to children and other dependents, for example, and to employers) that we value but retain only at growing personal sacrifice. The car used to be—and emotionally remains—a symbol of freedom, but the road is less and less one, and we are all becoming captives to each other's desire to use, or abuse, it. These impositions limit the city's, and the car's, attractiveness and workability. If we could see our needs for mobility as more finely articulated, possibly much more convenient ones than the expedients we know, we might intensify our search for better services.

What might personal transportation services in the information and service age really be like? Even if we could invent them, could they be marketed? Would they take? The usual answer tends to be "no," but there is room for disagreement. Considering how a taste for expensive condominiums in Manhattan, or more to the point, along Wilshire Boulevard in the very Los Angeles whose open space and single-family plot structure was one of its attractions, leaves little doubt that tastes can change when the stakes become high enough—even, or perhaps especially, at the elite end of the continuum.

*Angelcars.* Consider the chauffeur-driven limousine. Imagine one-upping it with the "angelcar," a technologically equipped vanlike vehicle in which one also leaves the driving to someone else but uses the time on board to work or learn or relax, with the help of keyboard and modem, videodisk and monitor, or phone and fax. Working in such a set up would make it matter less how long the trip took, particularly if you were credited for the time by your employer, or could sell your product or develop your service, or learn your lessons. Adding important new features, suppose you could get picked up on demand (within five minutes of your call) by a computer-dispatched and routed vehicle, and transported over a route to your destination that was optimized according to your criteria, meanwhile working or watching television, learning, or visiting a video museum on the way, carrying on a continuing video game with teams in an international league, or even helping your child learn to read the city, in a vehicle that served a few others as well. I would readily abandon self-service, having to keep my eyes on the road even when I am tired, bored, or aching to get something done, if I could afford such options. To begin with, such arrangements would work only for the few, as phone-fax vans do already between Century City and downtown for lawyers, but, once the taste is established, I think it might spread, providing multiple classes of service at different prices for most urban uses.

*Collector-run or collector-subsidized systems.* We ordinarily think of transit as going to and returning from destinations, but, from another point of view, it serves people in coming to and going from places. Large employers, shopping centers, theater districts, convention centers, theme parks, hospitals and health maintenance organizations, hotels, gambling resorts, and many others all have real interest in collecting people and bringing them in. Precedents are many—school buses, hotel pickups at airports, shared shopping trips for retirement communities, school systems, and day camps in cities, among others. Some restaurants in downtown Los Angeles provide parking and take diners to and from nearby theaters.

Hospital collector vehicles could pick up patients, provide check-in, screening, and room assignment before arrival, and signal ahead for special arrangements, if needed. In an increasingly competitive health care environment, such services could help in marketing, and, once restrictions were lifted, any land saved from parking lots as a result could more than pay the costs. Magic Mountain, Disneyland, and the Children's Museum could pick up and deliver groups of kids who otherwise could not come to these places. Chauffeuring in various forms could become the source of many more jobs. But, of course, the insurance companies would have to approve.

Employer-provided merchant-run collector systems, or, alternatively, employer or merchant subsidies for needed, new public transit serving their needs, could replace even more employer- and merchant-provided parking or parking allowances than vanpools already do, provided code requirements for parking, which grew out of an earlier era and its demands, could be modified. So far, this has not happened, but in some form it should eventually become politically feasible. The price for not doing it is becoming excessive, as land values in urban centers and the costs of congestion both skyrocket. Making a few such systems work well would help justify code changes that could enable more of the systems to follow.

It might help to recall that vertical transportation in cities (via elevators and escalators) is provided "free" to riders, provided indirectly through rents by those who occupy high rises or by merchants in department stores and shopping malls. In this sense, collector systems, underwritten from the intended destination, are a familiar expedient, used to lubricate commerce. Can we be as inventive on the level?

*Job/housing balance and intermediate-work buildings.* We talk about the job housing balance—that is, locating housing and jobs closer together—as a way to cut travel between work and home. It means locating workplaces close to where people live and housing near where people work. Such arrangements become more acceptable as work becomes cleaner and quieter and a taste for mixed-use develops. In trying to improve the balance, however, are we underestimating the propensity of people to change jobs and choose living quarters for non–work-related reasons? Without concentrating job types in certain subcenters, or the intermediate-work buildings to be described below, sooner or later any balance achieved might tend to revert to imbalance. Still, there are opportunities to improve the intermix between workplaces and homes, all the way from mixed-use buildings to appealing high-tech industrial parks and planned unit developments.

The shift from zoned construction, a vestige of industrial-age urban practices, to mixed-use clusters enables child care, schools, gyms, meeting rooms, work spaces, living units, social service outlets, shopping, museum, libraries and other information utilities, and dining and other functions to be collocated so as to reduce some trips and increase the local "desirable congestion" Barton Myers advocates.

*Specialized urban centers.* At the moment many "urban villages" resemble each other in most essentials. Some have recognizable uniquenesses, such as Westwood (UCLA) and downtown Los Angeles (financial and cultural). In time, other centers are likely to acquire other special distinctions. Once that happens, we can expect a natural congealing of related activities (companies, proprietary schools, rental housing, and government offices, for example) to accelerate in each vicinity. As a result, the city and region would become increasingly subdifferentiated by function. Such concentrations of types of use can bring attendant secondary, tertiary, and quaternary efficiencies. People then have clear signals about where to locate advantageously, change of employer need not mean too much change in commuting patterns, and traffic can become more efficient, too.

*Specialized college and university campuses.* Such campuses could invigorate these major subcenters, providing ready access to postsecondary and continuing education that are linked to major institutions as appropriate. This notion has been proposed for Kawasaki, Japan, with the idea that businesses and other activities will catalyze around the specialties implanted via the campuses. Thus, for example, one center might focus on health, starting with an existing hospital center, attracting nurse-training institutions, pharmaceutical houses, health spas, and other health-related activities having reason to collocate there. Housing of health-related professionals and other workers would inevitably spring up nearby, generating a natural job-housing balance. The net effect would be to both reduce trips and improve the quality of life.

*New marketing approaches.* Newer approaches to product marketing are likely to reduce consumer trips also. Granted that consumers do not generally travel merely to buy, it seems likely that innovations in retailing, such as catalog, computer-based, and television sales, will displace shopping commutes, just as electronic funds transfer has tended to shorten or eliminate trips made for financial purposes. Thus, some of the impulsive use of cars could be displaced or combined in new ways.

*Toll Roads.* Toll roads are springing up here and there, and they could proliferate. Like the paths worn by students on campuses, they will no doubt arise where the need can be made manifest. Perhaps making a toll road is like performing bypass surgery on a blocked artery. While toll roads (or any system of pay-for-use) might seem to exacerbate a two-tiered social system, they might also be used to promote egalitarian practices. A system of electronic accounts that levied tolls depending upon time of day (such as has been proposed) also could be programmed easily to provide a sliding scale of charges depending upon ability to pay or other variables. Indeed, such thinking could easily be extended to user fees for our publicly owned streets and roadways, billing being done electronically by a system of automatic tag-readers. Such proposals raise moral and ethical issues such as we must face in making more general future choices about how our cities are to work and how things are to be paid for. It is not a good idea to suppress these issues; they should be dealt with openly. But we must not, in thinking about them, simply attribute to future versions of any idea or practice all the limitations and rigidities of its past versions.

*Auto-navigation schemes.* If the car could drive us to our destinations auto-matically, taking into account myriad variables that we cannot and avoiding both collisions and congestion, one of our age-old dreams—the magic carpet—might almost be realized. The technology is imminent, but the poli-tics and economics of conversion could remain prohibitive for some time. After all, as Edgardo Contini pointed out years ago, who wants to pay for an automated car unless the control infrastructure is in place and everyone else's car is appropriately equipped already? And what jurisdiction can put in place the expensive and complex control infrastructure unless prospective users are prepared to use it at once? Is this one of the opportunities for public-private collaboration and planning? As costs of technology drop, sooner or later such systems will become feasible, and pilot versions are being devel-oped.

### REPRISE

Ideas for change, such as the foregoing list, float around the surface of active dialogue all the time. Each idea generally contains a useful kernel together with some unworkable chaff. Nobody is smart enough to see just where we are going or ought to go nor in a position to bring about what's needed. Some argue that a one dollar–per-gallon gas tax would do more to change things than all the innovative proposals imaginable. I would argue that it is itself an innovative proposal whose virtues are questionable. Moreover, even if it were enacted, things would still need imaginative and able steering, preferably with rather broad, thoughtful, and informed participation in the process.

The dialogue deserves attention and needs enriching. Both public and private decisions are involved, and they must be made interactively. Thus, it is up to us to enliven the dialogue and not pretend that the last idea has been put forward or that whatever we are not already doing is foolish or infeasible.

The future is, in part, decidable and designable. Although some things are probable, we would be wrong to be too certain about which they are. Some are uncontrollable and will, no doubt, be partly surprising, helping us all to control the hubris with which our society seems to be afflicted right now. We know what we do want, but none of us knows just what we should want. We can work better at it together. And we should get on with it.

# NOTES

## Chapter 1

**1.** Robert M. Fogelson, *Fragmented Metropolis: Los Angeles, 1850–1930* (Cambridge, Mass.: Harvard University Press, 1967).

**2.** Scott L. Bottles, *Los Angeles and the Automobile* (Berkeley: University of California Press, 1987); Mark S. Foster, *From Streetcar to Superhighway: American City Planners and Urban Transportation, 1900–1940* (Philadelphia: Temple University Press, 1981).

**3.** Marc A. Weiss, *The Rise of the Community Builders: The American Real Estate Industry and Urban Land Planning* (New York: Columbia University Press, 1987), chaps. 4 and 5.

**4.** All statistics drawn from U.S. Bureau of the Census, *State and Metropolitan Data Book, 1986* (Washington, D.C.: Government Printing Office, 1986), Los Angeles–Anaheim-Riverside CMSA and Chicago-Gary-Lake county CMSA.

**5.** Mark Baldassare, *Trouble in Paradise: The Suburban Transformation of America* (New York: Columbia University Press, 1986), 97, 207.

**6.** Dolores Hayden, *Redesigning the American Dream: The Future of Housing, Work and Family Life* (New York: W. W. Norton, 1984).

**7.** George Sternlieb, *Patterns of Development* (New Brunswick, N.J.: Rutgers University Press, 1986), 10–19.

**8.** Professor Robert Cervero, Department of City and Regional Planning, University of California, Berkeley *Suburban Gridlock* (New Brunswick, N.J.: Center for Urban Policy Research, 1986) (Study of Santa Clara County commuting, the case of 258,000 jobs and 78,000 homes); Truman A. Hartshorn and Peter O. Muller, "Suburban Business Centers: Employment Implications" (Final report prepared for U.S. Department of Commerce, Economic Development Administration, Technical Assistance and Research Division, Project #RED-808-G-84–5 [approved November, 1986]).

**9.** Gerda R. Wekerle, "Women in the Urban Environment," *Signs: Journal of Women in Culture and Society* 5 (supp., 1980): 188–214; and *New York Times*, poll, "Women Still Aren't Out of the Kitchen," February 24, 1988, col. 10; Donald N. Rothblatt et al., *The Suburban Environment and Women* (New York: Praeger, 1979), 164–74.

**10.** Hayden, *Redesigning the American Dream*, 208.

## Chapter 3

**1.** For a recent, and particularly sensitive, explication of the romance theme, see Stephen Bayley, *Sex, Drink and Fast Cars* (New York: Pantheon Books, 1986).

**2.** James J. Flink comprehensively develops this perspective in his magisterial study, *The Automobile Age* (Cambridge, Mass.: MIT Press, 1988).

**3.** Cited in Ashleigh E. Brilliant, "Social Effects of the Automobile in Southern California during the 1920s" (Ph.D. diss., University of California, 1964). Scholars have paid relatively little attention to how people actually used cars. Two notable exceptions are: Norman T. Moline, *Mobility and the Small Town, 1900–1930*, Research paper no. 132, (Chicago: University of Chicago Department of Geography, 1971); and Michael Berger, *The Devil Wagon in God's Country: The Automobile and Social Change in Rural America, 1893–1929* (Hamden, Conn.: Archon Books, 1979).

**4.** J. B. Jackson, "Truck City," in this volume.

**5.** James J. Flink, *America Adopts the Automobile, 1895–1910* (Cambridge, Mass.: MIT Press, 1970); see also his 1988 study, *The Automobile Age.*

**6.** Jackson, "Truck City," in this volume.

**7.** Little has been written about these specialized vehicles, although the Buick experience seems typical. From 1929 through 1941, the company offered business coupes and, starting in 1941, a so-called Estate Wagon, deemed a cut above a mere station wagon. Terry B. Dunham and Lawrence R. Gustin, *The Buick; A Complete History* (n.p.: Automobile Quarterly, 1987, 3d ed.), 406–13. For station wagons, see also Paul C. Wilson, *Chrome Dreams: Automobile Styling Since 1893* (Radnor, Pa.: Chilton, 1976), 222–24.

**8.** Ruth Schwartz Cowan, *More Work for Mother: The Ironies of Household Technology from the Open Hearth to the Microwave* (New York: Basic Books, 1983), 83–85.

**9.** Twenty years of scholarship in the history of technology as measured by the articles published in the journal *Technology and Culture* produced no study focused on maintenance and repair. See John M. Staudenmaier, S. J., *Technology's Storytellers: Reweaving the Human Fabric* (Cambridge, Mass.: MIT Press, 1985). Staudenmaier himself, however, acknowledges the need for studying the "maintenance constituency" behind any successful technology, that is, the various people who are needed to keep it in existence during the "momentum phase" of its life cycle (between what he calls the "design phase" and "senility phase"). Although Staudenmaier does not explicitly mention mechanics, those persons who adjust, maintain, and repair a complex technology are crucial to his momentum phase and, in my view, worthy of study (195–96).

**10.** Although the monumental three-volume study of the Ford Motor Company by Allan Nevins and Frank Ernest Hill makes occasional mention of service, maintenance, and repair, the index does not refer to such topics. *Ford: The Times, the Man, the Company, 1865–1915* (New York: Scribner's, 1954); *Ford: Expansion and Challenge, 1915–1933* (1957); *Ford: Decline and Rebirth, 1933–62* (1962).

**11.** For a typical statement of the notion that successful operation of cars demanded mechanical knowledge and skill, see Morris A. Hall, *Care and Operation of Automobiles: A Handbook on Driving, Road Troubles, and Home Repairs* (Chicago: American School of Correspondence, 1912), intro., n.p.

**12.** Personal interview with John Goldsmith, 1987.

**13.** Many motorists temporarily stopped leaks with chewing gum, masticated rye bread, shellac, and other commonly available materials, and automobile manuals recommended such remedies. For an example, see Thomas H. Russell, *Questions and Answers for Automobile Students and Mechanics* (Chicago: Charles G. Thompson, 1911), 86, 105.

**14.** Statistics from National Automobile Chamber of Commerce, quoted in Joseph Hall, *Layouts and Equipment for Automobile School Shops*, U.S. Federal Board for Vocational Education, Bulletin no. 109 (Washington, D.C.: Government Printing Office, May, 1926), vii.

**15.** Chester H. Liebs, *Main Street to Miracle Mile: American Roadside Architecture* (Boston: Little, Brown, 1985), 95–115.

**16.** For a view that implicitly acknowledges the complexity of the origins of the automobile service occupation, see Flink, *America Adopts the Automobile*, 216–17.

**17.** For lament "that the servicing of Ford cars has become less attractive to the larger service stations, due to competition with 'shade tree' mechanics or small shops," see Fairlane Papers, Accession 235, box 37, no. 155, "Finance-FoMoCo. Mich," "Parts Discounts to Service Dealers and Garages," February 17, 1926, 1.

**18.** For a basic chronology of dealer service at Ford, but with little analysis, see Henry L. Dominguez, *The Ford Agency: A Pictorial History* (Osceola, Wis.: Motorbooks International, 1981).

**19.** I refer here to the Fairlane Papers, dealing with the life of Henry Ford and with the activities of the Ford Motor Company (FoMoCo) into the 1940s. These papers are held at the library of the Edison Institute, Henry Ford Museum and Greenfield Village in Dearborn, Michigan. From at least the mid-1910s, FoMoCo sought to force dealers to sell only genuine Ford parts, partly for business reasons but also because "spurious" parts often were inferior. See, for example, Fairlane Papers, Accession 235, boxes 37–39, "General Letters—Canceled," no. 155, "Discount on Repair Parts to Garages," May 3, 1916.

**20.** "General Letters—Canceled," no. 1536, "Garage Stock Unit," August 19, 1924.

**21.** Fairlane Papers, Accession 235, box 73, "General Letters, Service Department, Jan. 1933–Dec. 1934," "Uniforms for Mechanics and Neighborhood Service Station Attendants," March 1, 1934.

**22.** See, for example, Fairlane Papers, Accession, box 73, "General Letters, Service Department, Jan. 1933–Dec. 1934," "Running Board Repair Kit," January 2, 1934; and, for engine gasket sets, "Parts Sales," August 27, 1934.

**23.** In today's automotive repair industry, "the replacement of repairable parts or of whole rather than partial systems can be 'necessary,' although the waste involved is a source of consumer loss." Paul Michael Taylor and Michael J. Paolisso, "California's Auto Repair Industry: An Ethnographic Study of Consumer Loss" (Report presented to the Federal Trade Commission, Bureau of Consumer Protection, rev. version, December, 1983 [unpublished manuscripts in author's possession]), 29. Underlying this "necessity" are the twin factors of high wages for mechanics, which make it less expensive to replace a defective unit, say a generator, with a wholly rebuilt one, plus the desire of shops to guarantee the system repair they have done. It is doubtful, however, that similar conditions prevailed in the 1920s or 1930s.

### Chapter 4

**1.** U.S. Department of Transportation, Federal Highway Administration, *1983–84 Nationwide Personal Transportation Study: Summary of NPTS Trends* (Draft), April, 1986.

**2.** U.S. Bureau of the Census, *Women in the American Economy*, Current Population Reports, ser. P-23, no. 146, by Cynthia M. Tauber and Victor Valdisera (Washington, D.C.: Government Printing Office, 1986), 9; U.S. Bureau of the Census, *Statistical Portrait of Women in the U.S.* (Washington, D.C.: Government Printing Office, 1978) calculated from tables 6–5 and 6–6.

**3.** U.S. Bureau of the Census, *Household and Family Characteristics: March 1986*, Current Population Reports, Population Characteristics, ser. P-20, no. 419, calculated from table A2, U.S. Bureau of the Census, *Women in the American Economy*, 9.

**4.** Eno Foundation for Transportation, *Commuting in America: A National Report on Commuting Patterns and Trends*, prepared by Alan E. Pisarski (Westport, Conn.: Eno Foundation, 1987).

**5.** U.S. Department of Transportation, *1983–84 Nationwide Personal Transportation Study*.

**6.** U.S. Department of Transportation, *1983–84 Nationwide Personal Transportation Study*.

**7.** U.S. Bureau of the Census, *Women in the American Economy*, 9.

**8.** U.S. Bureau of the Census, *Women in the American Economy*, 9.

**9.** U.S. Bureau of the Census, *Women in the American Economy*, 9.

**10.** U.S. Bureau of the Census, *Household and Family Characteristics, March 1986*, 2.

**11.** U.S. Bureau of the Census, *Statistical Portrait of Women in the U.S., 1978*.

**12.** See Eno Foundation, *Commuting in America*, 27, table 2–3; and Robert Cervero, *Suburban Gridlock* (Rutgers, N.J.: State University of New Jersey, 1987).

**13.** Eno Foundation, *Commuting in America*, 48.

**14.** Cervero, *Suburban Gridlock*, 12–13.

**15.** Sandra Rosenbloom, *The Transportation Patterns and Needs of Salaried Mothers: A Comparative Assessment* (Final Report to the Gender Roles Program, Rockefeller Foundation, rev. ed., Spring 1988) 21–27.

**16.** While buses travel faster in the suburbs than these metropolitan averages would indicate, so do cars. In fact, the disparity in speed between the two modes is greatest in low-density areas because buses still must stop and start frequently while cars take advantage of freer traffic flows. Even in suburban operations, buses and streetcars rarely average over sixteen miles per hour.

**17.** Eno Foundation, *Commuting in America*, 48.

### Chapter 5

**1.** Flink, *America Adopts the Automobile*, 65.

**2.** Quoted in Frank Donovan, *Wheels for a Nation* (New York: Thomas Y. Crowell, 1965), 8.

**3.** In so doing, this essay draws upon some material first presented in Michael Berger, *The Devil Wagon in God's Country*, 55–74, 205–13.

**4.** President's Research Committee on Social Trends, *Recent Social Trends in the United States* (New York: McGraw-Hill, 1933), 177.

**5.** Robert S. Lynd and Helen Merrell Lynd, *Middletown: A Study in Modern American Culture* (New York: Harcourt, Brace and World, 1929), 153n.

**6.** Marsh K. Powers, "The Forgotten Fireside," *Outlook* (April 12, 1922): 608.

**7.** Blaine A. Brownell, "A Symbol of Modernity: Attitudes Toward the Automobile in Southern Cities in the 1920s," *American Quarterly* 24 (March, 1972): 39–40.

**8.** Quoted in Brownell, "A Symbol of Modernity," 40.

**9.** N. S. Hayner, "The Tourist Family," *Social Forces* 11 (October, 1932): 83.

**10.** Ernest R. Mowrer, *The Family* (Chicago: University of Chicago Press, 1932), 96.

**11.** Quoted in Kenneth T. Jackson, *Crabgrass Frontier: The Suburbanization of the United States* (New York: Oxford University Press, 1985), 182.

**12.** Lynd and Lynd, *Middletown*, 257.

**13.** See, for example, Theodore M. Shlechter and Paul V. Gump, "Car Availability and the Daily Life of the Teenage Male," *Adolescence* 18 (1983): 101–13.

**14.** Quoted in Brownell, "A Symbol of Modernity," 37.

**15.** Brownell, "A Symbol of Modernity," 38.

**16.** Quoted in Albert Blumenthal, *Small-Town Stuff* (Chicago: University of Chicago Press, 1932), 251.

**17.** Lynd and Lynd, *Middletown*, 137–38.

**18.** Blumenthal, *Small-Town Stuff*, 256.

**19.** Gretchen W. Sinon, "Changes During My Life," Ms., 1, personal files.

**20.** "Where Women Motorists Excel Mere Men," *Literary Digest* (December 4, 1920): 76.

**21.** Portions of the remainder of this section first appeared in a different format in Michael Berger, "Women Drivers! The Emergence of Folklore and Stereotypic Opinions Concerning Feminine Automotive Behavior," *Women's Studies International Forum* 9, no. 3 (1986): 257–63. Copyright © 1986. Pergamon Press plc. Reprinted with permission.

**22.** Mrs. A. Sherman Hitchcock, "Woman at the Motor Wheel," *American Homes and Gardens* 10 (April, 1913): supp. 6.

**23.** For instance, see George W. Sutton, Jr., "The Woman at the Wheel: The Help A Car Can Be in Home-Making," *Pictorial Review* 28 (November, 1926): 69.

**24.** Geraldine Sartain, "You and Your Car," *Independent Woman* 18 (May, 1939): 146.

**25.** See, for instance, Ian T. McDougall, "American Women as Drivers," *The Spectator* (July 27, 1926): 85–86; Priscilla Hovey Wright, "The Car Belongs to Mother," *Ladies' Home Journal* 56 (November, 1939): 82; Lewis Bergman, "Less Deadly than the Male," *New York Times Magazine* (July 14, 1940): 10.

**26.** "What Do the Women of America Think about Automobile Driving," *Ladies' Home Journal* 56 (December, 1939): 12.

**27.** M. F. Nimkoff, "What Do Modern Inventions Do to Family Life?" *Annals of the American Academy of Political and Social Science* 272 (November, 1950): 54.

**28.** President's Research Committee on Social Trends, *Recent Social Trends*, 177.

**29.** Jackson, *Crabgrass Frontier*, 172.

**30.** Jesse F. Steiner, "Recreation and Leisure Time Activities," in President's Research Committee on Social Trends, *Recent Social Trends*, 944.

**31.** Charles Sanford, "'Woman's Place' in American Car Culture," in *The Automobile and American Culture*, ed. David L. Lewis, special issue, *Michigan Quarterly Review* 19/20 (Fall 1980/Winter 1981): 534.

## Chapter 6

**1.** Joan W. Scott, "Gender: A Useful Category of Historical Analysis," *American Historical Review* 91, no. 5 (December, 1986): 1053–75.

**2.** Hayden, *Redesigning the American Dream;* Martin Wachs, "Separate Spheres, Mass Transit, and the Early Suburbs," (unpublished manuscript in author's possession); and Martin Wachs, "Men, Women, and Wheels: The Historical Basis of Gender Differences in Travel Patterns" (Paper presented to the Transportation Research Board, Washington, D.C., January, 1987). See also Gwendolyn Wright, *Building the Dream: A Social History of Housing in America* (New York: Pantheon, 1981).

**3.** Michael Berger, "Women Drivers: How a Stereotype Kept Distaff Drivers in Their Place," *Road and Track* 36, no. 9 (May, 1985): 55–60; and Michael Berger, "Women Drivers!," 257–63. See also Beth Kraig, "Driving toward the Future: Images of Women Drivers in Liberated America" (Paper presented to the Berkshire Conference on Women's History, Wellesley, Massachusetts, June, 1987).

**4.** For a particularly pointed discussion of the significance of gender in history and the politics of studying "gender" and "women," see Joan W. Scott, "On Language, Gender, and Working-Class History," *International Labor and Working-Class History* 31 (Spring 1987): 1–13; Bryan D. Palmer, "Response to Joan Scott," *International Labor and Working-Class History* 31 (Spring 1987): 14–23; Christine Stansell, "A Response to Joan Scott," *International Labor and Working-Class History* 31 (Spring 1987): 24–29; Joan W. Scott, "A Reply to Criticism," *International Labor and Working-Class History* 32 (Fall 1987): 39–45.

**5.** Phil M. Riley, "What an Electric Car Can Do," *Country Life in America* 23 (January, 1913): 23–26, 70–76. Victoria Bissell Brown, "Golden Girls: Female Socialization in Los Angeles, 1880–1910" (Ph.D. diss., University of California at San Diego, 1985), 93–153, richly documents the use of similar language to describe woman's nature and prescribe sex-role socialization in the United States during the Progressive Era.

**6.** C. H. Claudy, "The Electric as a Convenience and a Necessity," *Motor* (April, 1907): 47–48.

**7.** "Motoring in Society," *Motor* (April, 1904): 22–23.

**8.** Nevins and Hill, *Ford: The Times, the Man, the Company*, 373–74. Ford may have delayed buying his wife such a vehicle earlier out of pique at the Electric Vehicle Company, which had held sole rights to the celebrated Selden patent until 1903 and had joined with gasoline car manufacturers in 1903 to form Ford's nemesis, the Association of Licensed Automobile Manufacturers, in 1903. He may also have been scornful of such vehicles due to the fact that he had begun to develop his gasoline motor while working for Alexander Dow, president of the Detroit Edison Company, who had forced Ford's resignation by insisting that he confine his experimenting to electrical power. See Theodore F. McManus and Norman Beasley, *Men, Money, and Motors: The Drama of the Automobile* (New York: Harper and Brothers, 1930), 9. On the Selden patent fight, see Flink, *America Adopts the Automobile*, 318–28; also Nevins and Hill, *Ford: The Times, the Man, the Company*, 284; John B. Rae, *The American Automobile: A Brief History* (Chicago and London: University of Chicago Press, 1965), 11–13. The Electric Vehicle Company went bankrupt in 1907.

**9.** Joseph B. Baker, "The Care of the Electric Vehicle," *Motor* (May, 1910): 79–80: Claudy, "The Electric as a Convenience and a Necessity"; "The Lady and the Electric," *Country Life in America* 22 (July 15, 1912): 36, 44, 46, 48; "The Woman and Her Car," *Country Life in America* 23 (January, 1913): 41–42; "Establishing the Electric," *Motor* (October, 1915): 58–59, 132: Wilhelm Nassau, "The Number of Electrics in Use," *Motor* (July, 1908): 54: Phil M. Riley, "What an Electric Car Can Do." I have also surveyed advertising in all issues of *Motor* from 1903 through 1929.

**10.** *Motor* (December, 1910).

**11.** Claudy, "The Woman and Her Car," 41; Riley, "What an Electric Car Can Do," 23.

**12.** Claudy, "The Lady and the Electric," 36.

**13.** Claudy, "The Lady and the Electric," 36.

**14.** Though some historians have misunderstood the role of gender in the making of the car culture, auto manufacturers have been forthcoming. In 1973 Charlotte Fancett, staff correspondent for the *Automotive News*, a weekly newspaper of the auto industry, admitted that "manufacturers want to avoid stereotyping a car as a 'woman's car.'" See Bonnie Remsberg, "Women Behind the Wheel," *Redbook* (September, 1973), reprinted in the Motor Vehicle Manufacturers' Association, *News Review* (September 12, 1973): 1.

**15.** *Tucson Automobile Directory* (Tucson: J. A. Scott, 1914).

**16.** Rae, *The American Automobile*, 65–67.

**17.** Claudy, "The Lady and the Electric," 36.

**18.** Claudy, "The Lady and the Electric," 36, 44.

**19.** Flink, *America Adopts the Automobile*, 238–42, 305–6; James J. Flink, *The Car Culture* (Cambridge: MIT Press, 1975), 45; Nevins and Hill, *Ford: The Times, the Man, the Company*, 197–8; and Rae, *The American Automobile*, 8, 12–13.

**20.** Flink, *America Adopts the Automobile*, 238.

**21.** Clay McShane, "American Cities and the Coming of the Automobile, 1890–1915" (Ph.D. diss., University of Wisconsin, 1975), has drawn attention to the importance of ideology in shaping the accep tance of automotive technology. Looking carefully at the popular rejection of steam-powered vehicles (though saying nothing about electric cars), McShane concluded that "the key question in the innovation of the auto, then, is what attitudes changed in American society during the late nineteenth century that brought not only tolerance but even a hearty welcome for vehicles differing only in their motive power from these previously banned machines" (ii). For a landmark study of the ways in which ideology has structured the emergence of the modern market, see William M. Reddy, *The Rise of Market Culture: The Textile Trade and French Society, 1750–1900* (New York: Cambridge University Press, 1984).

**22.** Alice Huyler Ramsey, *Veil, Duster, and Tire Iron* (Covina, Calif.: Castle Press, 1961), 1.

**23.** *Motor* (December, 1909): 11.

**24.** *Motor* (December, 1909) 11.

**25.** Flink, *America Adopts the Automobile*, 238. Interestingly, Flink illustrates this contention with a picture of a 1906 Woods Electric "Surrey," a model that did not reflect the trend in electric vehicles toward boxiness and enclosed design apparent to contemporary observers as early as 1910. One magazine writer reported that "gasoline cars set the style, in open cars, although they have borrowed many of the closed car ideas from the electric town car." See "Trend in Electric Car Construction," *Motor* (December, 1910): 101. I have discussed the relationship between gender ideology and the trend toward closed vehicles in my dissertation, "Reinventing the Wheel: American Women and the Automobile in the Early Car Culture" (Ph.D. diss., University of Arizona, 1987), 177–225.

**26.** Rae, *The American Automobile*, 47.

**27.** Donovan, *Wheels for a Nation*, 138.

**28.** Herbert G. Gutman, *Work, Culture, and Society in Industrializing America* (New York: Vintage Books, 1977), has explored the struggle between industrial workers and managers over work discipline, cultural life, and personal habits. C. Wright Mills's *White Collar: The American Middle Classes* (London: Oxford University Press, 1971) is a classic study of the emergence of corporate bureaucracies and the behavior such institutions elicit.

**29.** Rae, *The American Automobile*, 48.

**30.** Rae, *The American Automobile*, 47–48.

**31.** M. M. Musselman (*Get a Horse! The Story of the Automobile in America* [Philadelphia: J. B. Lippincott, 1950], 243) recalled his mother's determination to crank and drive the family car, despite the danger, which, in one cranking mishap, earned her a badly bruised face. Women who drove ambulances and trucks in World War I not only routinely cranked their vehicles but generally maintained them as well. See Scharff, "Reinventing the Wheel," 151–77.

**32.** Donovan, *Wheels for a Nation*, 138.

**33.** McManus and Beasley, *Men, Money, and Motors*, 126–27.

**34.** McManus and Beasley, *Men, Money, and Motors*, 126–28.

**35.** Rae, *The American Automobile*, 48.

**36.** Nevins and Hill, *Ford: The Times, the Man, the Company*, 481.

**37.** *Motor* (December, 1913).

### Chapter 7

**1.** U.S. Department of Transportation, *Personal Travel in the U.S.: Nationwide Personal Transportation Study*, vol. 2, November, 1986, table E-11.

**2.** Genevieve Giuliano, "Public Transportation and the Travel Needs of Women," *Traffic Quarterly* 33:4 (October, 1979): 607–16.

**3.** Susan Hanson and Ibopo Johnston, "Gender Differences in Work-Trip Length: Explanations and Implications," *Urban Geography* 6, no. 3 (1985): 193–219.

**4.** U.S. Department of Transportation, Federal Highway Administration, Office of Highway Information Management, *1983–84 Nationwide Personal Transportation Study: Survey Data Tabulations*, November, 1985.

**5.** Sandra Rosenbloom, *The Transportation Patterns and Needs of Salaried Mothers.*

**6.** George Rogers Taylor, "The Beginnings of Mass Transportation in Urban America," *Smithsonian Journal of History* 1, no. 1 and no. 2 (Summer and Fall 1966).

**7.** Carl N. Degler, *At Odds: Women and Family in America from the Revolution to the Present* (New York: Oxford University Press, 1980).

**8.** Charles Horton Cooley II, "The Theory of Transportation," *Publications of the American Economic Association* 9, no. 3 (May, 1894): 298.

**9.** Theodore Hershberg, Dale Light, Jr., Harold E. Cox, and Richard R. Greenfield, "The Journey To Work: An Empirical Investigation of Work, Residence, and Transportation, Philadelphia, 1850 and 1880," in *Philadelphia: Work, Space, and Group Experience in the Nineteenth Century*, ed. Theodore Hershberg (New York: Oxford University Press, 1981): 128–73.

**10.** Peter Derrick, "Catalyst for Development: Rapid Transit in New York," *New York Affairs* 9, no. 4 (Fall 1986).

**11.** Mrs. V. G. Simkhovitch (Address to the First National Conference on City Planning, May 22, 1909, published in Senate doc. no. 422, 61st Congress, 2d sess. [Washington: Government Printing Office, 1910]), 101–5.

**12.** Lloyd Morris, *Postscript to Yesterday: America, The Last Fifty Years* (New York: Random House, 1947): 27–28.

**13.** Emily Post, *By Motor to the Golden Gate* (New York: D. Appleton, 1916).

**14.** Mark Smith and Naomi Black, *America on Wheels: Tales and Trivia of the Automobile* (New York: Morrow, 1986): 72–73.

**15.** Hilda Ward, *The Girl and the Motor* (Cincinnati: Gas Engine Publishing Company, 1908).

**16.** Rose Wilder Lane and Helen Dore Boylston, *Travels With Zenobia: Paris to Albania by Model T Ford* (Columbia: University of Missouri Press, 1983), 102.

**17.** Virginia Scharff, "The Ideology of Separate Spheres and Automotive Technology, 1898–1919" (Unpublished manuscript, 1986).

**18.** Committee on Recent Economic Changes of the President's Conference on Unemployment, *Recent Economic Changes in the United States* (New York: McGraw-Hill, 1929), 59.

**19.** Evans Clark, "The Worker and His Gains," *The Survey* 62, no. 5 (June 1, 1929), 283.

**20.** Beulah Amidon, "Why Prosperity Keeps Up," *The Survey* 62, no. 5 (June 1, 1929), 279–80.

**21.** Ruth Schwartz Cowan, "The Industrial Revolution in the Home: Household Technology and Social Change in the Twentieth Century," *Technology and Culture* 17, no. 1 (January, 1976), 1–23.

**22.** Barbara Peterson, "The Emergence of the Modern Woman," in *The Evolution of Mass Culture in America: 1877 to the Present*, ed. Gerald R. Baydo (St. Louis, Mo.: Forum Press, 1982), 81–99.

**23.** General Motors advertisement, *American Magazine* (June, 1929): 115.

**24.** Chevrolet advertisement, *Literary Digest* (October 6, 1923): 41.

**25.** Chevrolet advertisement, *Literary Digest* (July 28, 1923).

**26.** Chevrolet advertisements, *Literary Digest* (January and March, 1923).

**27.** Harlan Paul Douglass, *The Suburban Trend* (New York: Century, 1925), 194–95.

**28.** H. C. Wendt, "Meeting Woman's Taste in Body Style," *Automobile Topics* 78 (June 20, 1925): 531–33.

**29.** Walter B. Pitkin, *The Consumer: His Nature and His Changing Habits* (New York: McGraw-Hill, 1932), 282.

**30.** Michael A. Berger, "Women Drivers: The Origins of a Twentieth Century Stereotype" (Paper delivered at the Detroit Historical Society's Conference on the Automobile and American Culture, October 1, 1982).

**31.** Pitkin, *The Consumer*, 282.

**32.** Hayden, *Redesigning the American Dream.*

**33.** Susan Saegert, "Masculine Cities and Feminine Suburbs: Polarized Ideas, Contradictory Realities," *Signs: Journal of Women in Culture and Society* 5, no. 3, (supp. Spring 1980): S96–S111.

**34.** Hanson and Johnston, "Gender Difference in Work-Trip Length," 193–219.

**35.** Saegert, "Masculine Cities and Feminine Suburbs," S96–S111.

### Chapter 8

**1.** *American Architect: Garages, Country and Suburban* (New York: American Architect, 1911).

**2.** *American Architect: Garages*, 1.

**3.** J. B. Jackson, "The Domestication of the Garage," *Landscape* 20, no. 2 (Winter 1976): 10–19.

**4.** Typical of these early discussions were: Horace Wells Sellers, "The Home of the Motor Car; How the Garage Should Be Planned With a View to Attractiveness and Practical Use," *Indoors and Out* 4 (April, 1907): 101–10; C. M. Winslow, "The Garage for the Country or Suburban Home," *House and Garden* 17 (1910): 92–94; William Phillips Comstock, *Garages and Motor Boat Houses* (New York: Comstock, 1911).

**5.** Charles E. White, Jr., "Housing the Automobile," *House Beautiful* 30 (August, 1911): 84–87.

**6.** Tyler Stewart Rogers, "The Automobile and the Private Estate," *Architectural Forum* 32 (March–June, 1920): 113–16, 171–74, 253–54; 33 (July–August, 1920): 23–25, 69–72. P. M. Riley, "Housing Your Car For Convenience," *Garden Magazine* 41 (March, 1925): 39–42; J. C. Campbell, "Garages, Sites and Entrance Drives," *House and Garden* 40 (November, 1921): 46–47.

**7.** A. Lawrence Kocher and Albert Frey, "Planning the House Garage," *Architectural Record* 69 (January, 1931): 52–57; R. C. David, "Garages without Regrets: Architects Have Turned the Front Yard Garage into a Decorative Asset," *House and Garden* 19 (December, 1940): 18–19.

**8.** "Car Ports Make Sense," *Sunset* 113 (October, 1954): 4; "Garages Have Become the Front Entrance," *House and Garden* 101 (February, 1952): 92–95.

**9.** White, "Housing the Automobile," 84.

**10.** White, "Housing the Automobile," 84.

**11.** David Gebhard, *The Architecture of Purcell and Elmslie* (Chicago: Prairie School Press, 1965), 87.

**12.** White, "Housing the Automobile," 84–85.

**13.** *American Architect: Garages,* pl. 51.

**14.** John Taylor Boyd, Jr., "The Garage in the House," *Country Life* 33 (May, 1917): 56.

**15.** Boyd, "The Garage in the House," 56; also, "Keeping the Car in the House," *Ladies Home Journal* 33 (March, 1916): 5.

**16.** Boyd, "The Garage in the House," 58.

**17.** *American Architect: Garages,* pls. 62 and 63.

**18.** "Town and Community Planning: Walter Burley Griffin," *The Western Architect* 19 (August, 1913): no pl. nos.

**19.** "Town and Community Planning."

**20.** Royal Cortissoz, *Monograph of the Work of Charles Platt* (New York: Architectural Book Publishing, 1913), 19, 49.

**21.** *American Architect: Garages,* pl. 38.

**22.** White, "Housing the Automobile," 85.

**23.** White, "Housing the Automobile," 84.

**24.** A. Raymond Ellis, *Making a Garage* (New York: McBride, Nast, 1915), 40–60.

**25.** Ellis, *Making a Garage* 46–50.

**26.** Dorothy Olney and Julian Olney, *The American Home Book of Garages* (Garden City: Doubleday, Doran, 1931), 64–97.

**27.** "'El Fureidis' at Montecito, California: The Villa of James Waldron Gillespie, Esq.," *House and Garden* 6 (September, 1903): 97–103.

**28.** Sears Roebuck Company, *Modern Homes* (Chicago: Sears Roebuck Company, 1919); *Aladdin Homes: Built in a Day,* catalog no. 22 (Bay City, Mich.: Aladdin Homes, 1919); *Pacific's Book of Homes* (Los Angeles: Pacific Ready-Cut Homes, 1925), 132–33.

**29.** Lillian Ferguson, "What is Home without a Garage?" *Sunset* 37 (September, 1916): 48.

**30.** "Picturesque Entrances to California Garages," *Touchstone* 8 (January, 1921): 312.

**31.** Ferguson, "What is Home?" 48–49.

**32.** Theodore Baer, "The Attached Garage," *House Beautiful* 52 (September, 1922): 189.

**33.** Henry W. Rowe, "The Garage Comes into Its Own," *Garden and Home Builder* 45 (June, 1927): 369.

**34.** Burton Ashford Bugbee, "The Garage's Place is in the Home," *House Beautiful* 71 (February, 1932): 134.

**35.** The Roy Hilton Company, *Spanish Homes of California* (Long Beach, Calif.: Roy Hilton, 1925), 24, 37.

**36.** Angeles House-Plan Service Company, *300 Distinctive Homes* (Los Angeles: Angeles House-Plan Service, 1928), 37, 43.

**37.** Marc Goodnow, "The Garage Incorporated in House or Grounds," *Arts and Decoration* 28 (April, 1928): 124.

**38.** Kocher and Frey, "Planning the House Garage," 56.

**39.** Gerald K. Geerlings, "Courtyards and Garages," *House and Garden* 69 (January, 1936): 54.

**40.** "A Modern Ranch House," *Good Housekeeping* 100 (March, 1935): 72.

**41.** "Car Ports Make Sense," 4–5; "Garage Becomes Car Port," *Sunset* 114 (February, 1955): 67; "Carport Makes a Fine Front Entrance," *House and Garden* 114 (October, 1958): 183.

**42.** "New Things in 1955: The Drive-In House," *House Beautiful* 97 (February, 1955): 70.

**43.** "Not Just any Port in a Storm: Carports," *Better Homes and Gardens* 31 (June, 1953): 36.

**44.** "Life with the Auto," *Sunset* 116 (June, 1956): 73–89.

**45.** "Life with the Auto," 73.

**46.** Cliff May, *Sunset Western Ranch Houses* (San Francisco: Lane, 1946); Paul R. Williams, *New Homes for Today* (Hollywood, Calif.: Murray and Gee, 1946).

**47.** O. G. Soderstrom, "Dad Goes to the Garage, But Not for the Car!" *American Home* 29 (May, 1943): 20.

**48.** Eloise Roberts, "Picturesque Entrances to California Garages," *Touchstone* 8 (January, 1921): 311.

### Chapter 9

**1.** Jackson, "Domestication of the Garage," 10–19.

**2.** Marius C. Krarup, "The Domestication of the Automobile: A Financial and Architectural Movement," *Harper's Weekly* 20 (November, 1907): 1599–1600.

**3.** Henry Way, "Finding a Place for Your Garage: A Few Ways of Solving Problems Arising When There is Little or No Land Available," *House Beautiful* (January, 1919): 86–87. The fire hazards of the early garage were not exaggerated; many garages had both furnaces (to make engines start easier) and gasoline storage tanks in close proximity. An attached garage meant a 10 percent increase of fire insurance premiums for the entire house. See "Garage Hazards," *Scientific American* (supp., August 1, 1914): 18.

**4.** White, "Housing the Automobile," 84.

**5.** Katherine Verdery, "Beauty in the Back Yard," *Craftsman* 22 (September, 1912): 682–83. Verdery notes that the monotony of the common asphalt backyard was relieved only on wash day when "perhaps pink or blue pajamas may lend a note of gaiety to the scene."

**6.** Mary Rankin Cranston, "Converting Back Yards into Gardens: The Happiness and Economy Found in Cultivating Plants and Vegetables," *Craftsman* 16 (April, 1909): 79; Walter A. Dyer, "The

Humble Annals of a Backyard," *Craftsman* 24 (June, 1913): 308; see also George Lundberg, Mira Komarovsky, and Mary Alice McIrney, *Leisure: A Suburban Study* (New York: Columbia University Press, 1934), 61.

**7.** Lillian Hart Tryon, "Reflections of a Housewife: Piazza Conversation," *House Beautiful* (August, 1915): 74.

**8.** Esther Johnson, "Back Yard versus Front Porch," *House Beautiful* (June, 1922): 604–06.

**9.** Flink, *The Car Culture*, 158.

**10.** John Ihdler, "The Obsolete Backyard," in *Proceedings of the Tenth National Conference on Housing*, Philadelphia, January 28–30, 1929, by the National Housing Association (New York: National Housing Association, 1929), 145.

**11.** Johnson, "Back Yard," 604; Sinclair Lewis, *Babbit* (New York: Harcourt, Brace and World, 1922), 38.

**12.** Henry L. Wilson, *The Bungalow Book* (Chicago: Henry L. Wilson, 1910).

**13.** Flink, *The Car Culture*, 142.

**14.** Advertisement, *Los Angeles Times*, August 18, 1918, 4; advertisement, *Los Angeles Herald*, May 7, 1927; Hilton Company, *Spanish Homes of California*.

**15.** John Taylor Boyd, Jr., "The House That Will Keep a Car," *Country Life* (May, 1920): 67; Boyd, "The Garage in the House," 56.

**16.** Henry Way, "Finding a Place for Your Garage," 86.

**17.** "Garages," *Architectural Record* 65 (February, 1929): 196.

**18.** Louis Brownlow, "Some Problems in New Planning," in *Planning Problems of Town City and Region: Papers and Discussions at the Twenty-First National Conference on City Planning*, May 20–23, 1929 (Philadelphia: Wm. F. Fell, 1929), 5–6; see also Daniel Schaffer, *Garden Cities for America: The Radburn Experience* (Philadelphia: Temple University Press, 1982), 156.

**19.** "Garages," 196.

**20.** Kocher and Frey, "Planning the House Garage," 52–55.

**21.** Theodore A. Koetzli, "Diversified Use Seen in Garage," *Los Angeles Times*, May 12, 1929, pt. 4, 6.

**22.** Quoted in Flink, *The Car Culture*, 157; Allan Ruoff, "House Site Factors Shown," *Los Angeles Times*, June 12, 1927.

**23.** Quoted in Flink, *The Car Culture*, 154–55. Although the setting for the Middletown study was a small town rather than a suburb, the influence of the automobile was similar in both settings.

**24.** Folke T. Kihlstedt, "The Automobile and the Transformation of the American House, 1910 1935," *Michigan Quarterly Review* (Fall 1980): 557.

**25.** Quoted in Flink, *The Car Culture*, 157.

**26.** Perry M. Duncan, "When Entered from the Street," *Woman's Home Companion* (November, 1934): 36; "FHA's Low-Cost Housing Studies," *American Architect* 148 (May, 1936): 50; "Plans without Pictures," *American Architect* 148 (May, 1936): 28–34.

**27.** Franklin M. Reck, *A Car Traveling People: How the Automobile Has Changed the Life of Americans—A Study of Social Effects* (Detroit: Automobile Manufactures' Association, 1945), 26; John P. Dean and Simon Breines, *The Book of Houses* (New York: Crown, 1946), 60; Robert Culshaw, "Here is How to Handle a Useless Porch," *Better Homes and Gardens* (March, 1952): 232–33.

**28.** "A Pleasant Center for 20 Housekeeping Activities," *Better Homes and Gardens* (May, 1945): 16–19.

**29.** Reck, *Car Traveling People*, 29, 27.

**30.** Glenn H. Beyer, Thomas W. Mackesey, and James E. Montgomery, *Houses are for People: A Study of Home Buyer Motivations* (Ithaca, N.Y.: Cornell University Housing Research Center, 1955), 25–39.

**31.** Jackson, *Crabgrass Frontier*, 272, 278–79.

## Chapter 10

**1.** "The Perils of a Parkless Town," *Los Angeles Times*, February 29, 1920, 2–1; "No-Parking Law Proves Motor Cars Absolutely Essential," *Los Angeles Times*, April 25, 1920, 6–1, 6. For background, see Scott L. Bottles, *Los Angeles and the Automobile: The Making of the Modern City* (Berkeley, Los Angeles, and London: University of California Press, 1987), 63–91.

**2.** "Automobile is Now a Necessity," *Los Angeles Times*, March 20, 1921, 3–3; "Traffic Proves City's Noose," *Los Angeles Times*, June 12, 1938, 2–1, Bottles, *Los Angeles*, 92–94.

**3.** Robert M. Fogelson, *The Fragmented Metropolis: Los Angeles, 1850–1930* (Cambridge, Mass.: Harvard University Press, 1967), 146; Bottles, *Los Angeles*, 187, 189.

**4.** Concerning the Motor Inn, see "Hotel Chain for Autoists," *Los Angeles Times*, July 31, 1921, 6–2; and *Los Angeles Times*, May 21, 1922, 6–4. The Vernon branch of the Security First National Bank was not the first such facility in which a drive-up teller window was installed, but it is the earliest known example designed with such an amenity as well as other conveniences for the motorist. The project received widespread coverage; see, for example: "Auto into Bank—That's the Idea," *Los Angeles Times*, February 14, 1937, 5–3; "A New 'Drive-In' Bank," *Bankers Monthly* 54 (April, 1937): 234; "Increased Mobility Alters Building Design," *Architectural Record* 82 (July, 1937): 31; "Banking by Automobile," *Scientific American* 157 (September, 1937): 151; and "'Drive-In' Bank Opens New Field," *American Builder and Building Age* 60 (February, 1938): 52–53.

**5.** Useful accounts of the region's drive-in restaurants include: C. A. Patterson, "Glimpses of California Specialty Shops," *American Restaurant* 12 (May, 1929): 46–49, 100; Madeline O'Talk, "Carpenter's Catering Choices," *Pacific Coast Record* 23 (January, 1933): 12–13; "Tam O'Shanter," *Pacific Coast Record* 30 (September, 1939): 14–16; S. A. Lewis, "Drive-In for Profits," *Restaurant Management* 47 (July, 1940): 19–23, 36, 38, 50, 42, 44; "From Stand to Stand-Out," *Pacific Coast Record* 32 (January, 1942): 18–19; and "Los Angeles," *The Diner* 3 (September, 1946): 8–9. For background, see Liebs, *Main Street to Miracle Mile*, 204–12; Alan Hess, *Googie: Fifties Coffee Shop Architecture* (San Francisco: Chronicle Books, 1985), 19–29; and Philip Langdon, *Orange Roofs, Golden Arches: The Architecture of*

*American Chain Restaurants* (New York: Alfred A. Knopf, 1986), 57–64. Concerning the drive-in laundry, see *Hollywood Daily Citizen*, December 5, 1930, Moderncraft Laundry sec.; Elmer L. Marks, "Drive In and Save," *Laundry Age* 19 (February, 1939): 6–8; J. Edward Tufft, "Drive-In Service Deluxe," *Laundry Age* 19 (October, 1939): 74–75; and "Magic Service Given Drive-In Customers," *Pacific Laundry and Cleaning Journal* 35 (October, 1939): 12, 36.

**6.** Among the most detailed period accounts of the type are four articles by Willard D. Morgan: "California Drive-In Markets Serve Motorists on the Go," *Chain Store Review* 1 (September 1928): 29–31; "'Drive-Ins' Drive On While Stores Sleep," *Chain Store Review* 2 (May, 1929): 15–16, 30–32; "At Last—A Place to Park!" *American Builder* 47 (July, 1929): 58–61; and "The Super Drive-In Emerges from Competitive Whirl," *Chain Store Review* 3 (October, 1930): 10–12, 40. See also Walter Van de Kamp, "An Innovation in Retail Selling," *Magazine of Business* 56 (July, 1929): 42–43; Marc N. Goodnow, "Drive In and Shop," *Forbes* 25 (February 1, 1930): 16–17; Albert Frey, "Amerikanische Notizen," *Werk* 20 (October, 1933): 314; and M. J. Rowoldt, "We Study a California Market for You," *Progressive Grocer* 15 (October, 1936): 34–35, 99.

**7.** For a sampling of contemporary accounts see "Now Comes the Service Town, Going the Service Station One Better," *Filling Station* 1 (December, 1921): 51, 53; B. V. Ellzey, "Experimenting with 'Super-Service' on the West Coast," *Filling Station* 2 (March, 1923): 21, 23, 25, 27; William V. Gross, "'Super-Service' in California Means Everything for the Automobile," *Filling Station* 6 (September 10, 1925): 31–33; James V. Murray, "This Super-Service Station Idea—Will It Spread East?" *Filling Station* 8 (June 10, 1926): 26–28; James V. Murray, "Super-Service Station Caters to Stars in Hollywood," *Filling Station* 9 (January 10, 1927): 24–25; William E. Green, "Super Service Stations Thrive Best Operated by Individual Owner," *National Petroleum News* 20 (July 25, 1928): 83, 86; and Brad Mills, "Mullers' Complete Service," *Petroleum Marketer* 12 (June, 1929): 23.

**8.** There were a few notable exceptions, such as the very large Chapman Park Market in the mid-Wilshire district; see Olive Gray, "New Market Unusual One," *Los Angeles Times*, June 20, 1929, 2–2; and Frank H. Williams, "495 Autos Can Park in this New Drive-In Market," *Progressive Grocer* 8 (October, 1929): 30–31, 130.

**9.** Concerning the former, see "Clock Market to Open on Saturday," *Beverly Hills Citizen*, May 9, 1929, 8; the latter, see *Hollywood Daily Citizen*, March 23, 1929, Mandarin Market sec.; and "Picturesque Charms of Mandarin Market," *Saturday Night* 10 (March 8, 1930): 17.

**10.** Concerning the project, see "Modern Marketplace Celebrates Opening . . . ," *Hollywood Daily Citizen*, December 19, 1930: 8; and "Corrugated Galvanized Iron . . . ," *American Architect* 90 (March, 1932): 22–23.

**11.** Willard Morgan covered Richard Neutra's ideas on the subject in several of his articles, see "California Drive-In Markets," 31; "At Last," 59–61; and "Super Drive-In," 11–12. See also Thomas S. Hines, "Designing for the Motor Age: Richard Neutra and the Automobile," *Oppositions* 21 (Summer 1980): 44–46. Concerning the Mesa-Vernon Market, see Morgan, "'Drive-Ins' Drive On," 15–16, 30–31 and "At Last," 60.

**12.** Wright gave a detailed account of this aspect of the Broadacres scheme in his *When Democracy Builds* (Chicago: University of Chicago Press, 1945), 93–95.

**13.** "New Stores Opened Unique in Capital," *Washington Post*, December 7, 1930, 3–2; "Park and Shop," *American City* 52 (October, 1937): 71–72; F. Wallace Stoever, "Park-and-Shop Projects for Neighborhood Improvement," *Real Estate Record* 141 (February 5, 1938): 30–31.

**14.** Useful sources for on the company include: Harriet Burdsal, "Ralphs Building and Methods Reflect Age," *Hollywood Daily Citizen*, June 8, 1928, 11; "Story of Ralphs Store Growth is Like Fiction," *Santa Monica Evening Outlook*, November 20, 1929, 18; J. Gordon Wright, "Sharing Economies with Public Ralphs' Policy," *Super Market Merchandising* 2 (September, 1937): 6, 8; *Los Angeles Times*, April 28, 1939, Ralphs Grocery sec.; and "Ralphs Opens 28th Super Unit," *Super Market Merchandising* 5 (March, 1940): 14–15.

**15.** See, for example: A. E. Holden, "Super-Markets on Coast Set Modernization Pace," *Chain Store Age*, Grocery ed. 11 (May, 1935): 20–21, 58, 60; J. Gordon Wright, "Food and Functionalism," *California Arts and Architecture* 54 (October, 1938): 28, 36; Walter H. Leimert, "The Super Markets of Los Angeles," *Freehold* 4 (March 15, 1939): 198–203; M. M. Zimmerman, "A Cross Country Impression," *Super Market Merchandising* 5 (April, 1940): 37, 40–41, 53; Ben H. O'Connor, "Planning the Supermarket," *Architect and Engineer* 146 (September, 1941): 14–19; "Super Markets: The Office of Stiles Clements, Architect," *Architectural Record* 89 (October, 1941): 72–73; and Lucius S. Flint, "The Los Angeles Super," *Chain Store Age*, Grocery ed. 26 (June, 1950): J34–J35.

**16.** Wilshire Boulevard has been the subject of an informative popular account, by Ralph Hancock (*Fabulous Boulevard* [New York: Funk and Wagnalls, 1949]); and an insightful forthcoming scholarly essay by Thomas S. Hines, "The Linear City: Wilshire Boulevard, Los Angeles, 1895–1945." The general importance of such thoroughfares to the region is addressed in Douglas R. Suisman, *Los Angeles Boulevard: Eight X-rays of the Body Public* (Princeton, N.J.: Princeton Architectural Press, 1990).

**17.** Contemporary accounts on the subject are meager; see, for example: Charles Gormack, "Enter New Locality and Develop It, Says Operator," *Super Market Merchandising* 3 (May, 1938): 6–7; J. Gordon Wright, "75,000 Help Celebrate Vons New Opening," *Super Market Merchandising* 4 (November, 1939): 12, 38–39; and "Shopping Centers: An Analysis," *Urban Land Institute Technical Bulletin* 11 (July, 1949): 9–11. Interviews with several people who were involved in design, retail management, and real estate development and brokerage during the period yielded much additional information. Those individuals include the late S. Charles Lee (Beverly Hills, Calif., June 26, 1987), Philip Lyon (Los Angeles, April 7, 1988), William McAdam (Newport Beach, Calif., April 8, 1988), Eaton Ballard (Pasadena, Calif., November 14, 1989), and Fred Marlow (Los Angeles, November 16, 1989).

**18.** For background, see "Work Started on Large Shopping Center to Serve Lakewood Park," *Southwest Builder and Contractor* 116 (October 27, 1950): 30–31; and "Accent on Shopping and Parking Convenience in New Lakewood Center," *Women's Wear Daily*, January 2, 1952, 34–35. The first section of Lakewood opened in 1952. To my knowledge the only regional malls in operation prior to that time were Northgate in Seattle (1947–50) and Shopper's World in Framingham, Mass. (1948–51). Stonestown in San Francisco is more or less contemporaneous with Lakewood. Two valuable scholarly accounts on the early development of the type are: Meredith L. Clausen, "Northgate Regional Shopping Center—Paradigm from the Provinces," *Journal of the Society of Architectural Historians* 43 (May, 1984): 144–61; and Howard Gillette, Jr., "The Evolution of the Planned Shopping Center in Suburb and City," *Journal of the American Planning Association* 51 (Autumn, 1985): 449–60.

**19.** According to Albert C. Martin, Jr., principal architect of Lakewood Center, the internal layout of department stores provided the underlying conceptual springboard for the scheme with the pedestrian mall functioning in a manner roughly analogous to a department store aisle (interview, Los Angeles, November 7, 1989).

**20.** For background, see James Rainey and Nancy Yoshihara, "Mini-Malls: Life in the Fast Aisle," *Los Angeles Times*, September 7, 1984, I, 1, 22; James Rainey, "Explosion if Mini-Malls Spurs a Maxi-Dispute," *Los Angeles Times*, September 23, 1985, II, 1, 6; "Podmalls: Getting a Corner on the Market," *Convenience Store Merchandiser* 12 (November, 1985): 48, 50, 52, 54; Greg Critser, "King of the Mini-malls," *Los Angeles* 31 (October, 1986): 165–70; Judy Pasternak, "The Men of La Mancha" *Los Angeles Times Magazine*, September 28, 1986: 23–27. Additional insights were provided by Samuel Bachner, president of La Mancha Development Company (interview, Los Angeles, March 12, 1990).

### Chapter 11

**1.** Richard Burns Carson, *The Olympian Cars: The Great American Luxury Automobiles of the Twenties and Thirties* (New York: Alfred A. Knopf, 1976).

**2.** Paul Brennan, "The Golden Age of the Luxury Car," *Automobile Quarterly* 20 (Spring 1982): 207.

**3.** Flink, *America Adopts the Automobile.*

**4.** Lynwood Bryant, "The Beginnings of the Internal-Combustion Engine," in *Technology in Western Civilization*, ed., Melvin Kranzberg and Carroll W. Pursell, Jr. (New York and London: Oxford University Press, 1967), vol. 1, 661.

**5.** Flink, "Entrepreneurship in the Early Automobile Industry" (Paper presented at the annual meeting of the Society for the History of Technology, Pittsburgh, Pa., October 25, 1986).

**6.** Carson, *The Olympian Cars*, 7.

**7.** Carson, *The Olympian Cars*, 7.

**8.** Brennan, "The Golden Age of the Luxury Car," 213.

**9.** Hugo Pfau, *The Custom Body Era* (Cranbury, N.J.: A. S. Barnes, 1970), 133, 135.

**10.** Carson, *The Olympian Cars*, 10.

**11.** Carson, *The Olympian Cars*, 10.

**12.** Hugo Pfau, "Hall of Fame: A Listing of American Coachbuilders," in *Automobile Quarterly: The American Car since 1776* (New York: Automobile Quarterly, 1971), 148–54.

**13.** David H. Ross, "Notes on American Coachbuilders," *Automobile Quarterly* 6 (Fall 1967): 166.

**14.** Carson, *The Olympian Cars*, 54–55.

**15.** Pfau, *The Custom Body Era*, 215, 218.

16. Herman C. Brunn, "Brunn," *Classic Car* 6 (Summer 1958): 4.

17. Strother MacMinn, "Walter M. Murphy, Coach Builders: Daring Elegance of the Classic Era," *Automobile Quarterly* 24 (Winter, 1985): 369.

18. MacMinn, "Walter M. Murphy," 352.

19. Alfred P. Sloan, Jr., *My Years with General Motors*, (Garden City, N.Y.: Doubleday, 1964), 276.

20. Sloan, *My Years with General Motors*, 276.

21. Quoted in Sloan, *My Years with General Motors*, 274.

22. Carson, *The Olympian Cars*, 48–52.

23. William J. Abernathy, *The Productivity Dilemma: Roadblock to Innovation in the Automobile Industry* (Baltimore: Johns Hopkins University Press, 1978), 183.

24. Abernathy, *Productivity Dilemma*, 185.

25. Hugo Pfau, "The Master Craftsmen: The Golden Age of the Coachbuilder in America," in *Automobile Quarterly: The American Car since 1776* (New York: Automobile Quarterly, 1971), 146.

26. Carson, *The Olympian Cars*, 41, 45, 98.

## Chapter 12

1. Aldous Huxley, *After Many a Summer*, 1939.

2. General Motors Styling Staff, "Styling: The Look of Things" (1955), Detroit: General Motors Corporation, 14.

3. Kathryn B. Hiesinger and George H. Marcus, eds., *Design since 1945* (Philadelphia Museum of Art, 1983).

4. Edgar Kaufmann, Jr., "Good Design '51 as Seen by Its Director and by Its Designer," *Interiors* 110 (March, 1951): 100.

## Chapter 13

1. Arthur M. Schlesinger, "The City in American History," *Mississippi Valley Historical Review* 27 (June, 1940): 43–66; Eric E. Lampard, "American Historians and the Study of Urbanization," *American Historical Review* 67 (October, 1961): 50, 60; George Mowry, *The Urban Nation, 1920–1960* (New York: Hill and Wang, 1965); Blake McKelvey, *The Urbanization of American, 1865–1915* (New Brunswick, N.J.: Rutgers University Press, 1963); Roy Lubove, "The Urbanization Process: An Approach to Historical Research," *Journal of the American Institute of Planners* 33 (January, 1967): 33–39.

2. Michael H. Ebner, "Urban History: Retrospect and Prospect," *Journal of American History* 68 (June, 1981): 84.

3. Sam Bass Warner, Jr., *Streetcar Suburbs: The Process of Growth in Boston, 1870–1900* (Cambridge, Mass.: Harvard University Press, 1962); George R. Taylor, "The Beginnings of Mass Transportation in Urban America," pts. 1 and 2, *Smithsonian Journal of History* 1, no. 2 and 1, no.3 (1966): 35–50 and 31–54, respectively; George Smerk, "The Streetcar: The Shaper of American Cities," *Traffic Quar-*

*terly* 21 (October, 1967): 569–84; Joel A. Tarr, *Transportation and Changing Spatial Patterns in Pittsburgh, 1850–1934* (Pittsburgh: Public Works Historical Society, 1978).

**4.** Rae, *The American Automobile;* and *The Road and Car in American Life* (Cambridge, Mass.: MIT Press, 1971); Flink, *America Adopts the Automobile;* and Flink, *The Car Culture.*

**5.** Sam Bass Warner, Jr., *The Urban Wilderness* (New York: Random House, 1972); Paul Barrett, *The Automobile and Urban Transit; The Formation of Public Policy in Chicago, 1900–1930* (Philadelphia: Temple University Press, 1983); Blaine A. Brownell, "A Symbol of Modernity: Attitudes toward the Automobile in Southern Cities in the 1920s," *American Quarterly* 24 (March, 1972): 20–44; Glen E. Holt, "The Changing Perception of Urban Pathology: An Essay on the Development of Mass Transit in the United States," in *Cities in American History*, ed. Kenneth T. Jackson and Stanley K. Schultz (New York: Alfred A. Knopf, 1972), 324–43; Howard L. Preston, *Automobile Age Atlanta; The Making of a Southern Metropolis, 1900–1935* (Athens: University of Georgia Press, 1979).

**6.** Spencer Crump, *Ride the Big Red Cars*, 5th ed. (Corona Del Mar, Calif.: Trans-Anglo Books, 1970); Robert M. Fogelson, *The Fragmented Metropolis: Los Angeles, 1850–1930* (Cambridge, Mass.: Harvard University Press, 1967); Marc A. Weiss, *The Rise of the Community Builders: The American Real Estate Industry and Urban Land Planning* (New York: Columbia University Press, 1987); Mark S. Foster, "The Model-T, the 'Hard Sell,' and Los Angeles's Urban Growth: The Decentralization of Los Angeles During the 1920s," *Pacific Historical Review* 44 (November, 1975): 459–84; Martin Wachs, "Autos, Transit, and the Sprawl of Los Angeles: The 1920s," *Journal of the American Planning Association* 50 (Summer 1984): 297–310.

**7.** Bottles, *Los Angeles*, 253–54.

**8.** Kevin Starr, *Inventing the Dream: California through the Progressive Era* (New York: Oxford University Press, 1985).

**9.** Starr, *Inventing the Dream*, 294.

**10.** Gerald D. Nash, *The American West in the Twentieth Century: A Short History of a Cultural Oasis* (Englewood Cliffs, N.J.: Prentice-Hall, 1973).

**11.** David H. Fisher, *Historians' Fallacies: Toward a Logic of Historical Thought* (New York: Harper and Row, 1970), 95–100; Gordon Whitnall, *Bulletin of the Municipal League of Los Angeles* 5 (November 30, 1927): 3–6; Reyner Banham, *Los Angeles: The Architecture of Four Ecologies* (New York: Harper and Row, 1971), 24.

**12.** Muller, *Contemporary Suburban America* (Englewood Cliffs, N.J.: Prentice-Hall, 1981).

**13.** John W. Reps, *Cities of the American West: A History of Frontier Urban Planning* (Princeton: Princeton University Press, 1979).

**14.** Foster, *From Streetcar to Superhighway: American City Planners and Urban Transportation, 1900–1940* (Philadelphia: Temple University Press, 1981).

**15.** Foster, *From Streetcar to Superhighway*, 80–86, 165, 174.

**16.** Automobile Club of Southern California, *Traffic Survey: Los Angeles Metropolitan Area, 1937* (Los Angeles: Automobile Club of Southern California, 1937).

## Chapter 14

**1.** U.S. Congress, Senate Committee on the Judiciary, "The Industrial Reorganization Act: Hearings before a Subcommittee on S. 1167," 93d Cong., 2d sess., 1974. Part 4a contains Snell's "American Ground Transportation."

**2.** One of Snell's more egregious claims was that General Motors aided the Nazi war effort during World War II. Snell also repeatedly mistook the Pacific Electric for LARY. Despite these and other serious problems in Snell's analysis, many subsequent authors cite Snell as proof of a conspiracy. See, for instance, Glenn Yago, "Urban Transportation in the Eighties," *Democracy* 3 (Winter 1983): 45–47; and *The Decline of Transit: Urban Transportation in German and U.S. Cities* (Cambridge: Cambridge University Press, 1984), 56–58, 245; Robert B. Carson, *Whatever Happened to the Trolleys?* (Washington, D.C.: University Press of America, 1978), 92–95; and James V. Cornehls and Delbert A. Taebel, *The Political Economy of Urban Transportation* (Port Washington, N.Y.: Kennikat Press, 1977), 23.

**3.** For information on LARY and the Pacific Electric, see Robert Fogelson, *The Fragmented Metropolis* (Cambridge, Mass.: Harvard University Press, 1967), 85–86, 92, 104, 165; and Spencer Crump, *Ride the Big Red Cars* (Corona del Mar: Trans-Anglo Books, 1970), 72–75, 91–92, 109–10. The connection between railway building and real estate promotion is explored in Paul Barrett, *The Automobile and Urban Transit: The Formation of Public Policy in Chicago, 1900–1930* (Philadelphia: Temple University Press, 1983), 12; Kenneth T. Jackson, *Crabgrass Frontier* (New York: Oxford University Press, 1985), 120–24; and Glen E. Holt, "The Changing Perception of Urban Pathology: An Essay on the Development of Mass Transportation in the United States," in *Cities in American History*, ed., Kenneth T. Jackson and Stanley K. Schultz (New York: Alfred A. Knopf, 1972), 328–29.

**4.** *California Outlook* 11 (August 26, 1911): 3–4.

**5.** See, for instance, *Los Angeles Times*, January 27, 1907; *Los Angeles Herald*, March 16, 1910; *Los Angeles Examiner*, November 21, 1912, and November 11, 1913.

**6.** *Los Angeles Record*, December 10, 1912.

**7.** Los Angeles Board of Public Utilities, *Second Annual Report: 1910–1911*, 120.

**8.** Quoted in Los Angeles Board of Public Utilities, *Ninth Annual Report: 1917–1918*, 54.

**9.** Los Angeles Board of Public Utilities and California Railroad Commission Engineering Departments, "Report on Service, Operating and Financial Conditions of the Los Angeles Railway Corporation, 1919" (Unpublished report in the Los Angeles City archives).

**10.** *Los Angeles Times*, December 23 and 24, 1919.

**11.** *Los Angeles Times*, December 21, 23, 24, and 26, 1919.

**12.** *Los Angeles Record*, January 13, 1920; *Los Angeles Times*, December 24, 25, 26, 1919.

**13.** *Los Angeles Times*, April 20, 1920.

**14.** *Los Angeles Times*, April 25, 1920.

**15.** *Los Angeles Times*, January 1, 1925. See also April 13 and December 29, 1924.

**16.** E. E. East, "Streets," in *A Preface to a Master Plan*, ed., George W. Robbins and L. Deming Tilton (Los Angeles: Pacific Southwest Academy, 1941), 97.

**17.** I am indebted to Sam Bass Warner, Jr., for this insight.

**18.** Los Angeles Board of City Planning Commissioners, *Conference on the Rapid Transit Question* (Los Angeles: City Planning Commission, 1930), 8, 19, 21.

**19.** Los Angeles Board of City Planning Commissioners, *Second Conference on Mass Transportation* (Los Angeles: City Planning Commission, 1930), 5–18.

**20.** James Weinstein, *The Corporate Ideal in the Liberal State, 1900–1910* (Boston: Beacon Press, 1968); Gabriel Kolko, *The Triumph of Conservatism: A Reinterpretation of American History, 1900–1916* (New York: Free Press, 1963).

### Chapter 15

**1.** Rebecca Morales, "The Los Angeles Automobile Industry in Historical Perspective," *Society and Space* 4 (September, 1986): 289–303.

**2.** Flink, *America Adopts the Automobile.*

**3.** Cornehls and Taebel, *The Political Economy of Urban Transportation.*

**4.** William J. Abernathy, *The Productivity Dilemma: Roadblock to Innovation in the Automobile Industry* (Baltimore: Johns Hopkins University Press, 1978).

**5.** David Friedman, "Beyond the Age of Ford: The Strategic Basis of the Japanese Success in Automobiles," in *American Industry in International Competition: Government Policies and Corporate Strategies*, ed. John Zysman and Laura Tyson (Ithaca: Cornell University Press, 1983), 350–90.

**6.** Clifford M. Zierer, ed., *California and the Southwest* (New York: Wiley, 1956).

**7.** David Fisher, "Why Chrysler Closed L.A. Plant," *Ward's Auto World* 7, no. 8; 30–31.

**8.** Heinz C. Prechter, "Niche Vehicle Marketing: A Look at the Future" (Presentation delivered to the International Motor Vehicle Association, New York City, October 22, 1987).

**9.** Martin Anderson, "Shake-out in Detroit: New Technology, New Problems," *Technology Review* 85, no. 6 (1982): 56–70.

**10.** Michael A. Cusumano, *The Japanese Automobile Industry: Technology and Management at Nissan and Toyota* (Cambridge, Mass.: Harvard University Press, 1985).

**11.** Kuniko Fujita and Richard Child Hill, "Toyota's City: Corporation and Community in Japan" (Department of Sociology, Michigan State University, East Lansing, 1987).

### Chapter 16

**1.** Reyner Banham, *Los Angeles: The Architecture of Four Ecologies* (New York: Harper and Row, 1971).

**2.** Charles Moore and Gerald Allen, "You Have to Pay for the Public Life," *Dimensions* (New York: Architectural Record Books, 1976).

**3.** John Chase, "Unvernacular Vernacular," *Design Quarterly* 131 (1986): 25.

**4.** Chase's article, "Unvernacular Vernacular," offers a provocative discussion of this type of architecture. I am indebted to many of his insights.

5. Chase's, "Unvernacular Vernacular," 24.

6. Edward Relph, *The Modern Urban Landscape* (Baltimore: Johns Hopkins University Press, 1987), 188.

7. "Next Stop Wolfgangland," *Los Angeles Times*, Calendar sec., September 20, 1987.

8. Jean Baudrillard, *Simulations* (New York: Semiotexte, 1983).

9. Umberto Eco has explored the permutations of the hyper-real in the American tourist environment in *Travels in Hyper-Reality* (New York: Harcourt Brace Jovanovich, 1976).

10. Marc Treib, "Dissolution of Place: The Drift of Roadside Architecture" (Paper presented at "The Car and the City" symposium, University of California, Los Angeles, April 9, 1988).

11. Jean Baudrillard, *Amerique* (Paris: Bernard Grasset, 1986).

12. Marc Treib and Philip Langdon, "Burgers! Shakes!" *Atlantic Monthly* (December, 1985): 75–89.

13. Stephen Kiernan, "Theory and Design in a Marketing Age," *Harvard Architecture Review* 6 (1987): 102–113.

## Chapter 17

1. Christopher Hibbert, *Rome: The Biography of a City* (Middlesex: Penguin Books, 1985).

2. Norbert Schmidt-Relenberg, "On the Sociology of Car Traffic in Towns," in *Transport Sociology*, ed. Enne deBoer (Oxford: Pergamon Press, 1986): 121–32.

3. In another writing (in press), I have developed a typology of roadway aggression forms, differentiating six different types: (1) roadway shootings/throwings, (2) assault with the vehicle, (3) sniper/robber attacks, (4) drive-by shootings, (5) suicide/murder crashes, and (6) roadside confrontations. These various forms were also arrayed in that typology with regard to six contextual factors, which were target location, aggressor location, target identity, temporal interval, intentional quality, and traffic relevance. A thorough review of the literature pertaining to roadway aggression was also undertaken in that work, and the disinhibition of aggression concept was articulated with a discussion of violence contagions. Raymond W. Novaco, "Aggression on Roadways," in *Targets of Violence and Aggression*, ed. Ronald Baenninger (Amsterdam: Elsevier Science Publishers, 1991): 253–326.

4. Personal communication with Commander Susan Cowen-Scott, August, 1989, California Highway Patrol Headquarters, Sacramento.

5. W. A. Tillman and G. E. Hobbs, "The Accident Prone Automobile Driver," *American Journal of Psychiatry* 106 (1949): 321–31. Cf. T. S. Skillman, *Road Safety* (London: Reappraisal Society, 1965); Meyer H. Parry, *Aggression on the Road* (London: Tavistock, 1968); Francis Anthony Whitlock, *Death on the Road: A Study in Social Violence* (London: Tavistock, 1971); and John MacMillan, *Deviant Drivers* (Westmead, U.K.: Saxon House, D. C. Heath, 1975), along with a variety of studies in the psychiatric and behavioral literature.

6. Albert Bandura, *Aggression: A Social Learning Analysis* (Englewood Cliffs, N.J.: Prentice-Hall, 1973).

7. Michael Stone, "Incident at Exit 20," *New York* (October 5, 1987): 50–56.

8. Stone, "Incident at Exit 20."

---

**9.** Cf. Raymond W. Novaco, Daniel S. Stokols, Joan Campbell, and Jeannette Stokols, "Transportation, Stress and Community Psychology," *American Journal of Community Psychology* 7 (1979): 361–80, and Daniel S. Stokols, Raymond W. Novaco, Jeannette Stokols, and Joan Campbell, "Traffic Congestion, Type-A Behavior, and Stress," *Journal of Applied Psychology* 63 (1978): 467–80. See also Daniel S. Stokols and Raymond W. Novaco, "Transportation and Well-Being," in *Transportation and Behavior*, ed. Irwin Altman, Joachim F. Wohlwill, and Peter B. Everett (New York: Plenum Press, 1981).

**10.** Raymond W. Novaco, Daniel S. Stokols, and Louis Milanesi, "Objective and Subjective Dimensions of Travel Impedance as Determinants of Commuting Stress," *American Journal of Community Psychology* 18 (1990): 231–57.

**11.** Raymond J. Michalowski, "Violence in the Road: The Crime of Vehicular Homicide," *Journal of Research in Crime and Delinquency* 12 (1975): 30–43; J. R. Spencer, "Motor Vehicles as Weapons of Offense," *Criminal Law Review* (January, 1985): 29–41.

**12.** The naturalistic observations of Konrad Lorenz (1966) are among the most well-known academic works in this regard, and the writings of Robert Ardrey (1966) are prominent in the popular literature. As noted by Roger Johnson (1972) in his review of scientific literature, territorial conflict is widespread among animal species, but it is not universal; in fact, most primates do not defend territories. Ardrey himself notes that baboons, who are highly aggressive, are not territorial. Observations about territoriality among animal species, however, have been extrapolated into arguments for an aggressive instinct.

**13.** Francis Anthony Whitlock, *Death on the Road: A Study in Social Violence* (London: Tavistock, 1971).

**14.** Joel Richman, "The Motor Car and the Territorial Aggression Thesis: Some Aspects of the Sociology of the Street," *Sociological Review* 20 (1972): 5–25.

**15.** Peter E. Marsh and Peter Collett, *Driving Passion: The Psychology of the Car* (London: Jonathan Cape, 1986).

**16.** John Dollard, Leonard W. Doob, Neil E. Miller, O. Hobart Mowrer, and Robert R. Sears, *Frustration and Aggression* (New Haven, Conn.: Yale University Press, 1939).

**17.** Leonard Berkowitz, *Aggression: A Social Psychological Analysis* (New York: McGraw-Hill, 1962).

**18.** Albert Bandura, *Aggression*.

**19.** Novaco, Stokols, and Milanesi, 1990.

**20.** Mark Baldassare, *Orange County Annual Survey: 1987 Final Report* (Irvine: University of California: Public Policy Research Organization, 1987); and Mark Baldassare and Cheryl Katz, *Orange County Annual Survey: 1988 Final Report* (Irvine: University of California: Public Policy Research Organization, 1988).

**21.** Leonard Berkowitz, *Aggression*.

**22.** Cf. Leonard Berkowitz, "Some Determinants of Impulsive Aggression: Role of Medicated Associations with Reinforcements for Aggression," *Psychology Review* 81 (1974): 165–176; and Leonard Berkowitz, "The Experience of Anger as a Parallel Process in the Display of Impulsive 'Angry' Aggression," in *Aggression: Theoretical and Empirical Reviews*, ed. Russell G. Geen and Edward I. Donnerstein (New York: Academic Press, 1983); 103–33.

**23.** Anthony Doob and Alan E. Gross, "Status of Frustrator as an Inhibitor of Horn-Honking Responses," *Journal of Social Psychology* 76 (1968): 213–18; Charles Turner, John F. Layton, and Lynn S. Simons, "Naturalistic Studies of Aggressive Behavior: Aggressive Stimuli, Victim Visibility, and Horn-Honking," *Journal of Personality and Social Psychology* 31 (1975): 1098–1107.

**24.** Meyer Parry, *Aggression on the Road*.

**25.** Turner et al., "Naturalistic Studies of Aggressive Behavior," M. Parry, *Aggression on the Road*.

**26.** Marsh and Collett, *Driving Passion*.

**27.** Leonard Berkowitz and Anthony LePage, "Weapons as Aggression-Eliciting Stimuli," *Journal of Personality and Social Psychology* 7 (1967): 202–7.

**28.** Frank Clifford, "Traffic or No, We Love Our Autos," *Los Angeles Times*, October 4, 1989, 1–3.

### Chapter 18

**1.** The design strategies that Vacant Lottery advocates are: (1) alternatives to building only high-rise structures in the central city core: the use of low-rise infill development strategies; (2) alternatives to the bulldozer: preservation and reuse of existing buildings; (3) alternatives to buildings as isolated objects: connected, additive buildings; (4) alternatives to erasing of historical traces: combinations of old and new buildings; (5) alternatives to residual, useless open spaces: creation of identifiable urban spaces—streets, courtyards, squares, and "galleria" streets; (6) alternatives to universal International Style modern architecture: a reinterpretation of regional buildings elements and materials; (7) alternatives to introversion of retail frontage: retail shops that address and support public spaces; (8) alternatives to single-use zoning districts: mixed use districts and neighborhoods; (9) alternatives to singular, specialized housing types: development of a range of medium-density urban housing prototypes; and (10) alternatives to the "tower in a park" or "tower in a plaza" idea: development of tower bases that have a positive, formative relationship to streets, squares, and blocks.

**2.** It is probably safe to say that a whole series of ideas and circumstances gave rise to North America's nearly uniform acceptance of the unicentered, nuclear city. Among these are a lingering nineteenth-century distrust of big cities; the poetic power of the "garden city" concepts of Ebeneezer Howard, reinterpreted by early modernists, including Le Corbusier, into tower in the park concepts for inner core development; the automobile; cheap energy, land, and servicing; and the extraordinary marketability of the single, detached suburban house as the North American dream.

**3.** Barton Myers Associates with ELS Design Group and BOOR/A, (Broome, Orinigdulph, O'Toole, Rudolf, Boles & Associates) 1987.

**4.** The Intermediate Theater is now the home of the Oregon Shakespeare Festival Company; see *Time* magazine, December 12, 1988.

**5.** Barton Myers Associates.

**6.** Barton Myers Associates with Edgardo Contini, Gehry and Krueger, Lawrence Halprin, Hardy

Holzman Pfeiffer Associates, KDG Architecture, Legorretta Arquitectos, Charles Moore, Cesar Pelli and Associates, Harvey Perloff, and Urban Innovations Group, 1980.

**7.** Barton Myers Associates, 1985–86.

### Chapter 20

**1.** See Christopher B. Leinberger and Charles Lockwood, "L.A. Comes of Age," *Atlantic*, January 1988; Frank E. Hotchkiss, "Galaxy for the Future: The Emerging World City of Southern California." Address delivered May 21, 1987, at Congreso de la Asociación Mundial de Grandes Metropolis, Mexico City. See also City of Los Angeles Planning Department, Concept Los Angeles, Los Angeles, 1974. City of Los Angeles Planning Department, Centers Definition Report. Centers Implementation Project Volume I, Section II. See esp. footnote (1), p. 3, "Concept Los Angeles, with its emphasis on developing urban centers, was adopted by the Mayor and City Council in 1974 to provide overall long-range guidance to the development of Los Angeles. This plan was chosen as the most desirable of four possible future development options to maintain the unique lifestyle that people find so attractive in Los Angeles. It is through the concept that centers "with high intensity of varied urban activities . . . have become a fundamental part of the City's General Plan."

# CONTRIBUTORS

## MARVIN ADELSON

is professor of architecture at the University of California, Los Angeles.

## MICHAEL L. BERGER

is professor and head of the Division of Human Development at St. Mary's College of Maryland.

## SCOTT L. BOTTLES

is vice-president and manager of the Real Estate Finance Group at Wells Fargo Bank in Los Angeles.

## DRUMMOND BUCKLEY

is an urban planner with the City of Santa Monica, California.

## JOSEPH J. CORN

is a senior lecturer in the Department of History at Stanford University.

## MARGARET CRAWFORD

is chair of the History and Theory of Architecture Program at the Southern California Institute of Architecture.

## JAMES J. FLINK

is professor of comparative culture at the University of California, Irvine.

## MARK S. FOSTER

is professor of history at the University of Colorado at Denver.

---

**DAVID GEBHARD**

is professor of art history at the University of California,
Santa Barbara.

**ALAN HESS**

is architecture critic for the *San Jose Mercury News* and
teaches at the Southern California Institute of
Architecture.

**JOHN B. JACKSON**

is the founder of *Landscapes* magazine and a writer on
architectural and urban history; he lives in
Santa Fe, New Mexico.

**RICHARD LONGSTRETH**

is associate professor of architectural history and director
of the Graduate Program in Historic Preservation at
George Washington University in Washington, D.C.

**REBECCA MORALES**

is a visiting research fellow at the U.S.-Mexican Studies
Center, University of California, San Diego.

**BARTON MYERS**

is professor of architecture at the University of California,
Los Angeles, and principal of Barton Myers Associates in
Los Angeles.

**RAYMOND W. NOVACO**

is associate professor of social ecology at the University of
California, Irvine.

**TAINA MARJATTA RIKALA**

is a Ph.D. student at the Graduate School of Architecture
and Urban Planning at the University of California,
Los Angeles.

**SANDRA ROSENBLOOM**

is director of the Roy P. Drachman Institute for Land and
Regional Development Studies at the University
of Arizona.

**VIRGINIA SCHARFF**

is assistant professor of history at the University
of New Mexico.

**MARTIN WACHS**

is professor of urban planning at the University of
California, Los Angeles.

**SAM BASS WARNER, JR.,**

is Jack Meyerhoff Professor of Environmental Studies at
Brandeis University.

**MELVIN M. WEBBER**

is professor emeritus of city and regional planning and
director of the University of California Transportation
Center at the University of California, Berkeley.

**SUSAN MARIE WIRKA**

is a Ph.D. student in urban planning at the Graduate
School of Architecture and Urban Planning at the
University of California, Los Angeles.

*Contributors*